The Don

Rob Robertson, a former Scotland Young Journalist of the Year, is an award-winning sports writer with *The Scottish Daily Mail*. In a varied career he has been on assignments in Bosnia, during the Balkans crisis; Northern Ireland, during the Troubles; and Russia, as Boris Yelstin came to power. He collaborated with Willie Miller for five years on his column for *The Herald* and has remained in touch ever since. Rob has previously written books on the rise of Scottish tennis star Andy Murray and the inside story of how Vladimir Romanov took control of Heart of Midlothian football club.

The Don

BY WILLIE MILLER
WITH ROB ROBERTSON

BIRLINN

This edition first published in Great Britain in 2008 by
Birlinn Ltd
West Newington House
10 Newington Road
Edinburgh
EH9 1QS

www.birlinn.co.uk

ISBN 13: 978 1 84158 723 3
ISBN 10: 1 84158 723 0

British Library Cataloguing-in-Publication Data
A catalogue record for this book is available on request from the British Library

Typeset by Iolaire Typesetting, Newtonmore
Printed and bound in Britain by CPI Cox & Wyman, Reading RG1 8EX

CONTENTS

ACKNOWLEDGEMENTS

This book is dedicated to the people who have supported me so much during my life, especially Claire, Victoria and Mark, all of my immediate family and some very close friends. It is also dedicated to every Aberdeen and Scotland supporter the world over.

I would like to thank my collaborator Rob Robertson: I have known him for more than 10 years, and he is a respected sportswriter on the *Scottish Daily Mail*. We first worked together over five years on my column for *The Herald* newspaper, and that working relationship made putting this book together an enjoyable experience. In turn, Rob would like to thank his partner Claire for all her support and encouragement throughout the writing process and to Kirsten and Clare for making them smile.

We thank the team at Birlinn Ltd, including Neville Moir, Peter Burns, Jan Rutherford, Kenny Redpath and our editor Duggie Middleton. A very special thanks to Kevin Stirling, the Aberdeen club historian, who checked the manuscript from top to bottom, and whose knowledge of the club is second to none.

I am grateful for all the support in print given to me earlier in my career by that great north-east of Scotland football journalist Alastair Macdonald, who was chief football correspondent of the *Aberdeen Press and Journal*. I also thank broadcaster Richard Gordon, an Aberdeen fan through and through, who helped me a lot when I joined the BBC Scotland sports broadcasting team.

I also wish to take this opportunity to thank everyone who has influenced my playing career, including Ian Stevenson, Jimmy Carswell, Bobby Calder, George Murray, Teddy Scott, Archie Knox, Dick Donald and most importantly, Sir Alex Ferguson. There are many references to Sir Alex in the book: he is a man that I believe to be the greatest British football manager of all time.

I won more than 50 Scotland caps under the late, great Jock Stein, who was another huge influence on my career, as were the other managers I played for.

I would like to thank all the great players I took the field with, and who helped to jog my memory when it came to compiling this book. I shared great experiences with them through the years, especially my team-mates in the European Cup-Winners' Cup success. It was on May 11, 1983 that I proudly held aloft the European Cup-Winners' Cup after our famous victory over Real Madrid. It was the proudest moment of my football career, and one that I will remember for ever, as will tens of thousands of Aberdeen fans.

Can I say to you all, fans and players alike: thanks for the memories!

Willie Miller
Aberdeen, 2007

FOREWORD BY SIR ALEX FERGUSON

Willie Miller is the best penalty-box defender I have ever seen. On the pitch he had that glazed, incredibly-focused look that I have only ever seen in the eyes of Bryan Robson and Roy Keane. Willie had marvellous concentration linked with an unerring instinct to make the right tackle at just the right time. He was a major force as captain of Aberdeen Football Club when I was manager, and had a personal drive that exceeded most other players I have ever come in contact with. He had a steely determination and a real will to win, and was a man who never gave up.

Yes, Willie had some shortcomings as a player, like everybody else, but he was still head and shoulders above most defenders in the game. In his case he did not have great pace, had no great height for a central defender and was not a great passer of the ball, although he was adequate in that department. For all of that, nobody, but nobody, could get past him!

As he developed his captaincy skills, he took on the stature and authority of figures such as John Greig and Billy McNeill who, with their tremendous presence, could influence everyone on the field. Considering the inbuilt advantage in this respect that Greig and McNeill had as captains of the Old Firm teams, it was an even greater achievement for an Aberdeen skipper to be able to dominate a game in this way.

In the summer of 1984, Gordon Strachan, Mark McGhee and Doug Rougvie all left Aberdeen Football Club. All three were great players and vital to my plans, but I felt they were replace-able. I brought in Frank McDougall to replace McGhee, and believe Frank went on to become the best striker to ever play for Aberdeen. I had signed Billy Stark to replace Strachan, and Billy scored more goals than he did, while Tommy McQueen proved an able replacement for Rougvie.

Although I could cope with such big players leaving, I was adamant that the one player I couldn't do without was Willie Miller. I remember speaking to the chairman Dick Donald about Strachan, McGhee and Rougvie all leaving at the same time, and told him I could cope with that, but asked him to pray Willie Miller didn't decide to leave as well! Willie was that important to me, and I knew that his leadership, his drive, his defensive skills and his influence would be impossible to replace. I was proved right in my assumption that we could cope without Strachan, McGhee and Rougvie, as with McDougall, Stark and McQueen in the side and with Willie once again as captain, we went on to win the 1984-85 Scottish League title.

Throughout his career, Willie brought self-belief to the other players, and helped me knock into the minds of the Aberdeen team that they could go to Parkhead and Ibrox and beat Celtic and Rangers on a regular basis. His partnership with Alex McLeish, in the centre of the Aberdeen defence, was the rock on which much of our success was built. Willie was the head of a great dressing-room where humour was a big part of our success. Most of the players I had at Aberdeen had come through the ranks together, and there was a real family atmosphere at the club. There were strong personalities in the dressing-room like Willie, and great humour from many others like our full-back Stuart Kennedy, whose acid assessments could suss out a person in ten seconds flat. However, the wind-ups and the banter were done without malice, and they all played and worked for each other, which was a vital part of our success.

The departure of Willie from Aberdeen Football Club, whenever it happens, and hopefully it won't be for a very long time, will mark the close of a chapter in the club's history, remarkable not only for the length of Willie's association with the one club, but for the fact that it is almost certainly something that will never be duplicated in the future anywhere else.

With the Bosman ruling and the increasing financial hunger of players' agents, there are a lot of disturbing points for me about modern football. However, I am thankful to have had such loyalty from players like Willie at Aberdeen, and others like Gary Neville, Paul Scholes and Ryan Giggs, who have been with me from the start at Manchester United.

The circumstances in present-day professional football are such that players are moving around more frequently, and a 20-year stay in a playing capacity at any one club, which happened with Willie at Aberdeen, is now an unheard-of occurrence. To head towards 30 years at Aberdeen, when you take in time as manager and director of football, is a remarkable achievement. In a personal message to Willie, I want to thank him for the role he played as captain at Aberdeen when I was manager and for everything he has done for the football club he has served so well, and for so long.

Good luck Willie, I wish you all the best for the future.

Sir Alex Ferguson

1.

INSPIRED BY WORLD CUP WILLIE

'Observing such violence close-up was one of the reasons I did not support either Old Firm team'

Glasgow is one of the world's football-mad cities. Mention Celtic and Rangers anywhere on the planet, and you are likely to gain instant recognition from sports fans. Though it may be hard to believe, as a little boy growing up in a football hot-spot I had no real interest in the game or in the fortunes of either Old Firm club. The fact that I lived in Bridgeton, a Rangers stronghold situated near Celtic Park, makes it even more difficult for people to accept that, throughout my Glasgow childhood, I was one of the few kids who did not inevitably take an interest in football. Indeed, when my pals and their dads were heading off to matches, I would be mucking about in the street and would always refuse offers to join them. Sure, I sometimes took part in kick-abouts with friends, but I did so reluctantly. I was more interested in my school work, and up to the age of 11 the game held little appeal. An uncle did run the bingo nights at Dennistoun Waverley football team's social club, and that was where my association with the game started, and ended, in those days. I suppose you could say that I came from a tough area, and certainly in the late 1950s and early 1960s the city of my birth was much different to the flourishing Glasgow of today. Then, it was blighted by gang violence, sectarianism and bad housing, and football and a good education were looked upon as escape routes. Now, I am proud to say that things are dramatically different, and whenever I return I am struck by the vibrancy of the city and by the great strides that are being made to end the religious bigotry.

I was born William Ferguson Miller in the maternity unit of Glasgow Royal Infirmary, Duke Street, on May 2, 1955, to mum Jean, who worked as a cleaner, and dad Bill, a toolmaker with Rolls-Royce. My middle name of Ferguson ran in the family, and little did I realize in my early years how much influence a man also bearing that name would wield upon my career. I had two younger brothers, Graham and Brian, a younger sister Jean and half-sister Mary, who was destined to captain the Scotland netball team. My brothers were worthwhile footballers, but did not perform at senior level.

I reckon it took some guts *not* to support a football team when you grew up in Bridgeton, an area that was home territory to some of the most fanatical Rangers supporters anywhere. The community would come alive after victories over Celtic. Flags would be flown from tenement windows, car horns would be sounded and naturally the pubs would be packed to overflowing. The proximity to the Parkhead stadium of such a Rangers stronghold led to some ugly scenes involving Old Firm supporters on match days. I would witness the fights between rival fans from my bedroom window, and these were certainly not spectacles that earned any credit for my home area. In fact, observing such violence close-up was one of the reasons that I did not support either Old Firm team: I just could not understand why the fans were kicking lumps out of each other. It had nothing to do with football and everything to do with bigotry, and I did not wish to be part of that scenario. Because I was not indoctrinated into supporting a football team, I didn't really care who won matches between Celtic and Rangers, though obviously most of my Rangers-loving neighbours held rather stronger views. I did have some Old Firm favourites from that era, however, among them John Greig, Willie Henderson, Jimmy Johnstone and Billy McNeill. Each was superb, and each deserves his place in the annals of Scottish football.

Despite the negative points about Bridgeton, I always felt that it reflected a great sense of community. The area still tends to get a bad press, and at times some criticism is justified, but I associated with some good people there. I was brought up in Bernard Street, in a flat within a three-storey tenement which featured gas lights, a tin bath placed modestly behind a curtain and an outside toilet. The family were crammed together in just one room with a kitchen off it, and a bed built into the wall folded down when it was required at night-time. As the oldest child, it was just mum and dad and me to begin with, but when my brothers and sisters came along, the flat proved to be too small. In 1959, when I was four, we moved to Marquis Street and to a tenement flat that boasted two bedrooms. Sheer bloody luxury! We still had to make use of an outside toilet and a tin bath, and sometimes I took a trip to the 'steamie' to keep myself clean. Most people of a certain vintage will remember the Glasgow 'steamie' as a place for washing clothes, but you could take a bath there too, and I nipped down regularly. I may have grown up in cramped conditions and without the benefits of an inside toilet, but I recall my childhood as a sequence of happy days.

Though I was more interested in classroom studies, there was no lack of encouragement from staff at Dalmarnock Primary School to become involved in football. The people who spotted that I had potential were my teachers, Mr Taylor and Mr Wright, who had me down as a goalkeeper, but only in my final year at primary school did football start to take a hold. If asked what flicked my switch and turned me on, I would point to the 1966 World Cup competition that was contested at various venues in England. Let me make clear that I have always been a proud and patriotic Scot, who would always wish my country to win at any sporting activity – and I know that we were not involved in the final stages in 1966 – but the euphoria surrounding the event whetted my appetite for football. I did not have a television in the house, so I viewed highlights from every game that I could at my aunt's home or listened to the radio commentaries. And I devoured newspaper coverage to find out all about the players. What also drew me in was the fact that the tournament mascot was a lion called World Cup Willie. Not named after me, of course, but as a youngster I was intrigued to share my name with the World Cup mascot. I ran around Bridgeton proudly sporting a World Cup Willie tracksuit, blissfully unaware that I would be scampering past some Scots who would gladly have seen England knocked out of the competition. I was oblivious to that, and didn't even mind when England won the trophy, but I was young! Eusebio, the Portuguese wizard, Franz Beckenbauer of West Germany and England's Bobby Charlton and Bobby Moore were my favourite players in the tournament, and who could forget the heroics of Gordon Banks in the England goals? Certainly not a young, would-be goalkeeper, like me. My favourite match from 1966 was not the Wembley final involving England and the West Germans, but the quarter-final between Portugal and North Korea at Goodison Park. Eusebio was magnificent that day. He hauled Portugal back into the game after they had gone 3-0 down, and thanks to him they won 5-3.

I found the World Cup to be such an inspiring experience that I decided there and then that I wanted to be a footballer. I told my mum of my new found ambition, and she gave me a little smile. I was completely hooked. I played at every opportunity, morning, noon and night, in the street or elsewhere, and sometimes on those dreaded red-blaes pitches which burned and scuffed your skin whenever you fell. I did not wish to be a goalkeeper despite the fact that my form between the goalposts was developing pretty well, but unfortunately my teachers were reluctant to play me anywhere else. Indeed, the only times that I played outfield was with my pals in bounce games at the back of the tenement flats in Bridgeton. Our pitch was the square area where the rubbish bins were kept in big concrete sheds, and I played long into the gathering dusk until my mum shouted me in for bed.

Despite my desire to operate elsewhere in the team line-up, I was asked to trial for goalkeeper for the Glasgow primary schools' select, and if I was finally selected I would be heading off on an American tour. I had not been out of Scotland in my 11 years of existence, so the thought of crossing the Atlantic was pretty daunting for a lad. The trial match was staged on a pitch across from Ibrox, and the fact that we were beaten by 10 goals to one rather convinced me that I had no chance of making the squad. But then maybe the selectors thought my performance prevented a score of 20-1; whatever, I was the most surprised laddie in Glasgow when I received a letter confirming that I had been selected as one of three goalkeepers in the party. I was delighted, although still a bit apprehensive about travelling all that way without my parents. Flying from Glasgow to New York in 1966 so soon after the World Cup was an incredible journey, a big adventure. I didn't know anybody in the Glasgow primaries' select, but I became friendly with a young midfielder at the airport and we sat together on the outward flight. He went by the name of Jimmy Calderwood, and though we were pals on the ensuing tour, we lost touch after we returned home. I could not have predicted that the tousle-haired 11-year-old with whom I got on so well with in the USA would one day be my choice as the manager of Aberdeen Football Club.

I realize that football, or soccer as it known in North America, has come on leaps and bounds in recent years, but when I travelled there for the first time they had no proper grip on the rules. During a match in Trenton, New Jersey, the referee stopped the clock every time the ball went out of play, and re-started it when the ball was thrown back in, as in American football. That meant our game lasted for about 110 minutes, and all the outfield players were knackered at the end. It was the only time that I was pleased to be playing in goal. The family who looked after me in Trenton took a shine to the lad frae Bonnie Scotland. I don't know what background they thought I had emerged from, but they seemed to consider that I was some sort of deprived little boy, which was nonsense. They even went so far as to write to my mother asking if they could adopt me, as they already had a little girl and thought that I would be the perfect brother for her. By the time the adoption request had been delivered from New Jersey, I was safely back in Scotland. Just as well, for if the letter had arrived while I was still on tour, I could have guaranteed that my mum would have been on the first available flight to the USA to bring me back to Glasgow – just in case the American hosts were of a mind to kidnap me. After I returned from the USA, I found that I had passed my 11-plus tests and would progress to John Street Senior Secondary School, and a major aim when I got there was to convince the teachers who ran the school team that I should play *out* of goals. I had made progress as an outfield player, but it was a struggle to convince others. I had been pigeon-holed because I had made the Glasgow primaries' squad, and good goalies were hard to find.

SEEING RED OVER BLAES

Now it occurs to me that Willie Miller playing in goal at any stage of his football career may seem faintly ridiculous, but I would argue that it made me tough. Any Glaswegian youngster who featured in goal in the 1960s was a brave young man because of the dreadful surfaces on which we were forced to compete. I played most of my schoolboy football on Glasgow Green, with its collection of red-blaes pitches, and for those lucky enough to have avoided performing on such grim and gritty surfaces, let me assure you that you missed nothing, except excruciating pain.

The red blaes – an evil concoction of ash and gravel spread on a firm, concrete base – made for dreadful experiences, and after my first match in goals on the blaes, I returned home with my legs covered in sores and bleeding because of the damage done by diving about to stop the ball. Indeed, on some occasions when I got back to the house, the wear and tear on my legs and arms was so painful that I had to try to sleep on one side, because rolling over on to my back would be too fretful. And if I did manage to get some rest while on my back, my lacerated legs would stick to the sheets, and I had to get peeled off the bedclothes come the morning.

There is absolutely nothing that I can offer in defence of red-blaes pitches. They were vicious, and still are, and they did nothing to develop individual skills, though in retrospect I suppose they did enhance my ability to balance. Good schoolboy footballers would endure playing anywhere, anytime just to get a game, but when I was growing up in the west of Scotland, I was obliged to risk serious injury for the dubious privilege of pursuing the sport that I had grown to love. Moreover, when I think back, I have to wonder how many promising performers stopped playing football because they were sickened by such bad surfaces.

Nowadays, the new generation of all-weather pitches allows youngsters to enjoy the game come rain or shine, but there is a long way to go before all young people in Scotland, particularly in urban areas, are given the chance to play on grass or all-weather facilities all year round. I am pleased that the Scottish Football Association and Scottish Executive are addressing the problem, and have invested £31 million in recent years towards improving facilities at the grass roots. The campaign must be kept up to offer good pitches and changing facilities, and red-blaes pitches must go, once and for all!

○ ○ ○

While I'm on the vital subject of facilities, or the lack of them, playing in the street was not a pastime that deserves the romanticizing punted by some folk with selective memories. Yes, at times it was good fun, but it was a sad indictment of the times that I had to depend so much on street games to improve my skills, and it was downright dangerous in a busy place like Glasgow, as I can confirm from first-hand experience. One day I was playing with my mates when a car, which had been stolen, came speeding round the corner. I had my eye on the ball, and was warned by shouts from my pals only at the last moment. The side of the car struck me, and though I was lucky to avoid the full impact, the bruising certainly hurt like hell, and the mental shock of the incident meant that I did not play football in the street much after that. One exception was when my pals and I spotted Harry Hood, the well-known Celtic player, in the neighbourhood as he was on his way to meet a girlfriend at her dad's pub, Tony's Bar, on the corner of Bernard Street. Anyway, all the kids joined in an impromptu game with Harry, though he didn't stay with us that long. This was Bridgeton and Rangers territory, after all.

It took a lot of moaning and groaning and a few notable performances playing outfield for my school team before I finally got my wish to leave goalkeeping forever. But don't think for a minute that I settled into the role of a central defender straight away, for like every budding footballer with ambitions to be a star, I wanted to score lots of goals. I dreamed of becoming a top-class centre-forward, perhaps a mix of Bobby Charlton and Eusebio. I made the transition from goalkeeper to striker pretty well, to the extent that I was picked for the Glasgow secondary schools' select in that position in my first year at the 'big' school. I remained in the team throughout my high-school years, operating through the middle or wide left. It was as a striker that I first caught the eye of the scouts from professional clubs, who were starting to keep a close eye on my progress. I had undergone a transformation from decent goalkeeper to decent striker, and from a youngster who had not bothered too much about football to one who was fanatical about it. I played for John Street Secondary School every Saturday morning, for Annfield Boys' Club, who were based in the Gallowgate area of Glasgow, on Saturday afternoons, and for Morton Boys' Club on Sunday afternoons. All three teams were pretty good, and in the age group above me at Morton Boys' Club was Tommy Burns, who went on to enjoy a successful playing career with Celtic. John Street Secondary was one of the smallest schools in Glasgow, but we had some fine players and won the Glasgow under-14 cup, which was a fantastic achievement. I thought that lots of the players would progress to careers in the game, but apart from me, only Tommy Brannigan, who played for Leeds United, and John

Docherty, who signed for Bury, took such a course. That statistic confirms how difficult it is to make the transition from promising schoolboy player to a top professional.

It is worth noting here the positive role played by the boys' club movement in inspiring youngsters to develop their football, for industrial action by Scottish teachers during the 1970s undermined the input of the schools. Many teachers no longer supervised teams because of the dispute, and many kids missed out on football training in school. The boys' clubs did a good job – and still do – instanced by the fact that I turned out for two of their teams at the weekend, but lack of provision in schools was bound to have a long-term negative effect on the national game. Tragedy is not too strong a word.

Around my 14th birthday, scouts from Aberdeen and from other clubs, Celtic included, started talking about signing me up. Aberdeen's legendary scout, Bobby Calder, was first to get in touch with my parents, and Jimmy Carswell, who went on to become chief scout at Aberdeen, also helped to convince me that my future lay at Pittodrie. Bobby and Jimmy were a real double act: Jimmy did the ground-work by watching me play, highlighting my good and bad points and checking out my temperament, and Bobby, who invariably sported a trilby hat, was a great public-relations man, who could charm the birds from the tree. My mum was concerned that I was set to sign for a team based in faraway Aberdeen, but Bobby sweet-talked her superbly. It was interesting to note that my mum's first and only concern was for her son's wellbeing, and she did not inquire about how much money I would earn. I'm sure that nowadays the first priority of parents would still be their offspring's welfare, but I'm certain too that they would ask about the financial deal on offer, such is the huge amount of money swilling about in the professional game.

I was delighted to sign schoolboy forms for Aberdeen because Eddie Turnbull was in charge, and the first team were doing well. During the 1950s, Eddie had been was one of the Famous Five, the inspirational Hibernian forward line, along with

Gordon Smith, Bobby Johnstone, Lawrie Reilly and Willie Ormond, and he was a legend of Scottish football. I was signed in late 1969, four years into Eddie's time as manager and the year before he led Aberdeen to a famous Scottish Cup win over Celtic. I knew I was joining a club on the up. Bury and Bristol City had been interested in taking me south of the Border, but my mind was made up to head to the north-east of Scotland. The first time that I visited Aberdeen for any length of time, I was a 15-year-old, and I trained with the other schoolboy signings. I was put up at the Brentwood Hotel in Crown Street, which I enjoyed, and I was obviously excited at the prospect of becoming a real football player.

All the practice that I was putting into my football was paying dividends, and a number of amateur clubs came to watch me perform for my school team and for the Glasgow secondary schools' select. I was most impressed by the guys who ran Eastercraigs, and when I joined them they were starting to build an excellent reputation. Discipline, which is not an easy quality to instill in teenage Glaswegian footballers, was a vital part of their doctrine. They made us wear club blazers to matches, which took some doing as most of the squad did not wear such garments to school. If I did not train or turn up properly dressed, I did not play. These were important rules which helped to discipline me, and I have never forgotten the lessons that I learned. Ian Stevenson and Tommy Rowlands at Eastercraigs taught me the good habits, and encouraged me to be the best that I could. I trained at Shettleston with the team on two evenings each week. The training pitches were awkward to reach, as my family did not possess a car, and I was obliged to catch a bus from Bridgeton – dressed in my club blazer. Not many blazer-clad kids in Bridgeton travelled by bus, and at first I was a bit self-conscious. After a while, though, I was simply proud to wear the Eastercraigs blazer and to carry my kit.

On March 3, 1971, when I was still just 15, I played for Glasgow Boys against London Boys at White Hart Lane, the home of Tottenham Hotspur – a glamour tie that I will never forget. For someone so young to play at such a venue was quite fantastic, and I lined up just behind the strikers with orders to get forward as much as I could. Ian Hair, who was at Duncanrigg Secondary and who would join me at Aberdeen, was in the team, as was Jimmy Calderwood. I hadn't seen Jimmy, who attended Grange Secondary, since we had visited the USA with Glasgow primary schools, and we were reunited to play against the English. It is interesting, though, to note how few made the grade from that game. Jimmy and me apart, no-one on either side remained in the game as professionals, and our team included useful youngsters such as Jim Scotland from Cranhill Secondary, Paul Feenan of Bellarmine High School and Fred Wright from Govan Secondary.

As football took a hold on my life, I let the academic side drift. At secondary I passed five of six O-Grades that I attempted, and felt that I could have done well if I had proceeded to take Highers. I enjoyed school and was extremely lucky eventually to make it in the world of football, but a career can be ended with one bad tackle, so I would advise any youngsters to take advantage of a sound education. The riches available to modern footballers are huge, but it is important to make plans in case your dreams don't come true. Not everyone can earn on the scale of a Beckham or a Ronaldo, and salaries at the bottom end of the game are not brilliant. It is hard to get youngsters to listen when I stress the importance of a good education. I'm certainly not trying to suggest that players should not take the risk and give their all to make it in the game. However, I do think it is important that young footballers have some sort of profession or qualification to which they can tap into if things go awry.

In saying that I was lucky enough to make it in football, although my career at Pittodrie nearly did not happen because of an oversight with my registration. Aberdeen sat on my documents, and they were not processed properly for nearly two years. I thought that I had signed, coaches Bobby Calder and Jimmy Carswell were under the impression that they had signed me up, but someone left my forms in a drawer at Pittodrie, and they were not sent on to the SFA, as required. Apparently, I wasn't the first or last youngster signed on a schoolboy form who found that his registration had not been officially recognised. It seems that clubs would collect players on S-forms rather like stamps, and sometimes they ended up with more than they were allowed by the SFA, thus the surplus youngsters could not be registered. That's what happened to me, and Aberdeen's indecision nearly saw me turn my back on the club and sign for Celtic instead. I was 16, and playing striker for the Glasgow secondary schools, when a Celtic scout approached me. This came two years after I thought I had signed up for Aberdeen, and he asked if I wanted to train at Parkhead with a view to possibly becoming an apprentice. I must say that I was tempted, and obviously my mum was keen on such a move, as the stadium was just up the road from our house rather than away up north. Tempted yes, but the persuasive double act of Bobby Calder and Jimmy Carswell had done such a great job in selling Aberdeen to me that I just couldn't let them down.

The other reason that I did not sign for Celtic was the fact that I had made up my mind that I wanted to get away from Glasgow because of the religious bigotry which affected the city at that time. As I have related previously, I did not support either side of the Old Firm and attended few games. I went to Ibrox and Parkhead perhaps once or twice before the age of 16, and I played at both grounds as a professional far more often than I attended as a spectator. Much of what was going on in Glasgow at that time, it must be said, I just did not like, the gang fights and sectarianism bothered me, and I wanted out. Aberdeen suited me, and if any doubts lurked in my mind about my destination, they were swept away when I saw a picture in a newspaper of a chap who had attended my school – and he was brandishing an open razor at a police officer during an Orange Walk. More positively, there was something special about Aberdeen and its environs that I could not put my finger on. I had gone on a school trip to Rosehearty, Aberdeenshire, and I loved the place. Even back then before my football life was mapped out, I felt an affinity with the north-east. Some sort of force was driving me there, and I really did feel it was my destiny to sign for Aberdeen Football Club. On a long bus journey from Glasgow to Aberdeen, I promised myself that I would work as hard as I could, and make it into the first team. When my dream became a reality, it happened in a way that I could not have predicted.

2

DRINKING ON DUTY: A DAFT IDEA

'I wanted to play beside Joe Harper in the first team, rather than just shine his boots'

My Aberdeen career started officially in the summer of 1971. I arrived at Pittodrie bearing my packed suitcase and with £60 of the £250 apprentice's signing-on fee in my pocket. My bed and board would cost £5 a week, with another £5 sent back to my mum in Glasgow. I wasn't rich, but I was being paid to do a job that I loved. I was 16 years old, and though confident that I could make the grade as a striker, I possessed all the insecurities of a teenager who had been dispatched to live away from home for the first time. I had to settle down in an unfamiliar city, and the only people that I knew were a few individuals at the football club. On my first day as an apprentice at Pittodrie, Eddie Turnbull, the manager who had sanctioned my signing, welcomed me into his office, but any thoughts that I harboured of a glamorous life as a teenage footballer were quickly dispelled: I was asked to clean the boots and sweep the terraces. Thus, I realised straight away that, although I was part of a big club, it was up to me to get noticed and to force my way into the first team. I would receive expert coaching, but it was up to me to make my mark at Aberdeen Football Club. I liked the fact that my destiny was in my own hands.

I was put up at first in the Brentwood Hotel, where schoolboy signings were accommodated when they trained at Pittodrie during the summer holidays. I had done that a few times, but I was obliged to stay behind on this occasion when the rest of the lads left for home, and just as I was settling into my new life, there came a bolt from the blue. I wandered into the dressing-room on a morning three weeks into my career to be greeted with the disturbing news that Eddie Turnbull had handed in his resignation to take over at his old club Hibernian. I took it badly, for Eddie had signed me. What would the new manager think of me? Who would he be? To make things worse, on the day that Eddie departed I was wound up by the rest of the apprentices, who joked that it was all my fault that he had left, as he realised it was a huge mistake to bring me to the club.

I heard lots of stories about Eddie and how hard a man he was. Everybody rated him highly as a manager, and he was a very strong character. It did not matter if you were an apprentice or a first- team player: if you stepped out of line, he would be down on you like a ton of bricks. The day of Eddie's departure, reserve team coach Teddy Scott revealed to me that the manager had been obliged to lay down the law at Aberdeen to deal with some strong characters present in the dressing-room during his time in charge. Teddy said that during one Christmas period, Derek Mackay, Ernie McGarr and Joe Harper couldn't find a taxi after a night-out because all the cabs had been booked in the wintry weather. As they started to walk home, they noticed a road-gritting lorry with the keys in the ignition, so they 'borrowed' the vehicle in an attempt to get home. Police stopped them – grit was cascading from the back of the lorry – and duly took them to the station to help with their inquiries. Joe phoned Eddie seeking help. The manager blew his top, telling Joe and the rest that they had got themselves into trouble, and it was up to them to get themselves out of it. He would see them in his office first thing on Monday morning.

Obviously, I would have preferred Eddie to have stayed longer, as he was the man who had signed me. The club decided to promote from within, and Eddie's assistant, Jimmy Bonthrone, took over. I would have to prove myself to Jimmy, but then I was so far down the pecking order at that stage that it took a while for him to turn his attention to evaluating the potential of the young players. By the time that he did so, I was

more confident and had played a few games for the reserves, and
felt that Jimmy was keen to keep me on. Eddie and Jimmy were
like chalk and cheese, Eddie had been very animated at training
sessions, while Jimmy was much more reserved and quiet.

After a few months in harness, I was given the responsibility of
cleaning the boots of Joe Harper and other first-team players.
However, growing confidence dictated that I wanted to play
beside Joe in the first team, rather than just shine his boots. I
moved from the Brentwood Hotel into digs close to Pittodrie.
Bess and George Sharp had looked after hundreds of young
Aberdeen football players through the years, and they warmly
welcomed me into their home. I shared a room with another
young player, Ian Hair, and we became close friends. After
spending much of my childhood squeezed into a two-bedroom
flat with two brothers and two sisters, it was great to be sharing a
room with just one person, even if it had to be Ian Hair, who had
played for Glasgow boys with me in that memorable visit to
White Hart Lane. I felt as if I had all the space in the world, and
Mr and Mrs Sharp acted like surrogate parents, always ensuring
that I was safe in my room by ten o'clock at night. The club
obviously wanted their young players to avoid any trouble and to
stick to the straight and narrow, and if the regime seems rather
restrictive, remember that I was still a wee bit wet behind the
ears, and in need of a few helping hands while settling in
Aberdeen. The club trusted my landlady and her husband
implicitly, and there was no need for a club representative to
come round to check on us. What made living in digs even better
was the fact I had to drag myself only a few hundred yards to
Pittodrie, which meant that I seldom arrived late for training –
and enjoyed a longer sleep than many of my colleagues.

When not involved in training, I was expected to undertake
all sorts of errands for first-team players, and was sent here, there
and everywhere. It amounted to a heartless task, especially when
things went wrong, for instance forgetting to pack George
Murray's boots for a match against Dundee. He went mad.
Quite understandably. Still, I trained with the reserves under

Teddy Scott, a huge influence on me and one of the most significant figures to be associated with Aberdeen Football Club. A great coach and a great man, he is a Pittodrie legend who devoted his working life to the club, and he richly deserves thanks and praise from every Dons fan. When I started in the reserves under Teddy, training facilities were dire, and invariably I found myself on a mini-bus with the rest of the apprentices trying to find a decent pitch on which to train or play. Sometimes we used grass pitches near a local golf course, and other times we had access to university playing fields.

Though I was full of the impetuosity of youth and had faith in my footballing abilities, I did realize that I would struggle to make the breakthrough into the first team at such a young age, and it was clear that I needed more tough matches under my belt to help my overall game. A few weeks after I turned 16, Jimmy Bonthrone called me into his office to offer me full-time professional terms. He felt that I had potential, but emphasized that I needed to play on a regular basis, and he wanted to send me on loan to Peterhead Football Club for season 1971-72. I accepted Jimmy's thoughts on my progression. Aberdeen fielded a reserve team, but they did not play that many games, so it made sense to embrace regular football away from the club. Another young player, John McMaster, who would carve out a great career at Pittodrie, was assigned to Peterhead a year later. Although I had signed professional forms, my money did not improve much. I was getting £5 a week in my hand and £5 was still going back to my mum, and the only change was that I would get an extra £5 a week for going on loan to Peterhead. Jimmy considered that the change would help my game through my experiencing the rough and tumble of the Highland League, and he wasn't kidding. From my first encounter to the last in that field of conflict, no prisoners were taken.

Aye, playing centre-forward in the Highland League was not for the faint-hearted. I was a tough teenager, and my years playing on those dreadful red-blaes pitches and in the street made me physically strong enough for anything that Highland League players could throw at me. And aim at me they certainly did. They kicked me, elbowed me, swore at me and made it clear they would give no quarter, especially to some upstart from Glasgow who thought he was a bit of a player. I was given a hard time, and opposition players did not flinch from any challenge. They certainly didn't stand on ceremony, and I learned a lot from my season there. I also scored a lot of goals, which did me a power of good. In one match I came up against John 'Tubby' Ogston, who had played for Aberdeen and was a thoroughly-experienced goalkeeper. He knew every trick of the trade, and here was a raw 17-year-old trying to get the better of him. I wasn't scared of him, and at every corner-kick I positioned myself as close to his goals as possible, so that I could challenge him and his defenders for the ball. Clearly, Tubby had had enough of my presence, and thought that I was a bit of an irritation and needed to be taught a lesson. Midway through the match, we went up for the ball from a corner-kick together, and once again I didn't flinch in the challenge. As we both hit the ground, the experienced professional punched me in the ribs when the referee was looking the other way. It hurt, I stayed down and needed treatment, and I struggled for the rest of the game. Suffice to say, the ref saw nothing, and Tubby got off with his off-the-ball punch. It was his way of saying: 'Stay out of my way, young man', and if I learned anything from that incident, it was to make sure that if I ever did lose my temper, I would make sure it happened when the referee was not looking in my direction. Getting away with off-the-ball incidents like that is well-nigh impossible these days, particularly in big matches, because of all the cameras present. But back then, as I painfully recall, off-the-ball punches or kicks were seldom spotted by the officials.

The other significant lesson that I learned from my time with Peterhead was not to drink before a game. I did it once, but never again. It was Hogmanay 1972 and I was in Aberdeen with none of my family around me on a snow-covered evening, with revellers about to go out to the pubs to celebrate the New Year.

Football games in many parts of the country had been called off because of bad weather, and I felt there was no chance of our match against Buckie, which was scheduled for the next day, going ahead. So I went out and got very, very drunk. But my assumption that I would not be playing was *wrong*. I was roused in the morning by Mrs Sharp, who knocked on the door of my room to tell me that I had a phone-call. On the line was a member of the Peterhead committee, and he confirmed that the game was on. I was horrified and wondered whether I could tell him that I did not feel well, but I was not thinking quickly or clearly enough, stunned as I was that the match against Buckie would go ahead. He probably would have seen through such an excuse, anyway. I dragged myself to the shower in the hope that cold water would bring me round. Not a chance. I put on my tracksuit, and went outside to find Aberdeen covered in snow. How could the game be on?

Five men from Aberdeen had to drive the 30-odd miles to Peterhead, and guess what? The other four, who had spent a quiet Hogmanay, were bright-eyed and bushy-tailed but I felt sick for the entire journey. We had to negotiate snowdrifts, and I was slumped in the back of the car hoping against hope that the game would be called off. Actually, I was praying, but when we arrived, the Peterhead officials said that the game was still on. I transferred to the team bus heading for Buckie, and another slog by road, this time of around 50 miles. Snow lay everywhere, but when we arrived in Buckie, a coastal fishing port like Peterhead, it looked as if a bad-weather exclusion zone had been set up round the burgh. The pitch was in decent condition and playable. I wanted to die.

By this stage, the committee-men had concluded that I was under the weather, though I had not admitted as much. Despite my feeble condition, they decided to play me from the start because I was scoring so many goals for Peterhead, though I might as well have remained on the bus for all that I contributed on the pitch. I could hardly run, my chest hurt, and every time I headed the ball I thought my brain was about to explode. I felt

like an old man rather than a young striker, and we were beaten.
I felt dreadful after one of my worst football experiences. It was
also a good lesson: drinking alcohol on the night before a match
is a bad idea and I did not make the same mistake again.

That, as you may have gathered, was the low point in what
proved to be of a very productive season for me at Peterhead. I
performed so well over the piece, netting 24 times, and remain
very proud of that. During my stint at the club, we won the
Aberdeenshire Cup by beating Huntly 2-1 in the final, and we
had a good side. I made some great friends in the Blue Toon, and
played with some fine players, including Johnny Anderson,
Adrian Conell, Ally Christie and Louis Duncan. The success
that I enjoyed with the Recreation Park outfit also brought a
boost to my bank balance. I was still being paid an extra £5 by
Aberdeen for being on loan, but I gained win-bonuses from the
Peterhead committee. I must admit that I was meant to receive a
£2 win-bonus when appropriate, and to collect the sum from
one of three committee-men allotted to the task. Confusion
often reigned over who had paid what and to whom, and I
sometimes ended up with a total of £6. I was not the only player
who benefited from such miscalculations, but when I pocketed
£6 rather than £2 after a victory, I laughed it off, justifying the
extra money to myself as a reward for scoring so many goals!

After my success in Peterhead's campaigns, I honestly thought
that I would make a go of performing as a centre-forward with
Aberdeen when I returned to Pittodrie for the start of the 1972-
73 season. I proudly took up my position in the reserve team, and
thought that I could easily maintain my goal-scoring exploits.
How wrong I was. I scored five times in my first 13 appearances
for the reserve side, which was hardly a grand record for a centre-
forward.

I shrugged it off as a blip in my scoring spree, and the first team
had Joe Harper banging in the goals, so I had no complaints
about being made to bide my time in the reserves. I kept
plodding along upfront, but goals just did not materialize, and
I started to drift out of the reserve team. This was simply

disappointing at first, then very worrying. I found myself on the bench for the reserve team on several occasions, and that was not a place that I was willing to occupy. In all, concern mounted that my football career might be over before I had even played a first-team game, and I had visions of heading back to Glasgow with my tail between my legs, and of pursuing a career away from football. I was still confident in my ability as a player, but in retrospect the hard fact was that I was not sufficiently mobile to play upfront in a standard of football above that of the Highland League. The physical side of my play had gone down well at Peterhead, but I lacked the refined touches necessary to be a successful striker at Pittodrie. My fortunes had fallen back so much that by mid-December I was sometimes not even making the bench.

Just as I was nearing rock-bottom, fortunes took a turn for the better. Sometimes in life there comes a pivotal moment, an occasion you look back upon that changed your life. For me it happened in a match between Aberdeen and Rangers reserves at Pittodrie on December 16, 1972. A couple of hours before kick-off, reserve team coach Teddy Scott received a phone-call telling him that my pal Ian Hair, one of his central defenders, had gone down with a 'flu bug. Tommy Wilson, another young central defender, had been promoted to the first team, which left Teddy with a selection headache. He decided to move right-back Billy Williamson to the middle of defence and to bring me, the out-of-favour centre-forward who was struggling even to make the bench, into central defence! It was a move that I could not have predicted, but one that I welcomed, for there was no point in getting precious about being played out of position. Now I needed to grasp any chance to make an impression, so I swallowed my pride and pulled on my jersey and got on with the job, temporarily forgetting about my dreams of being a centre-forward. My new role in defence was just temporary, of course. Or so I thought.

As kick-off time approached, I was really looking forward to playing after spending so much time on the sidelines. I didn't get much advice from Teddy about playing in defence, but I do remember him telling me not to do anything fancy. It was my first game as a defender, and I was not planning to do anything too clever, anyway. He did tell me to mark my man tightly, to win the ball early in the tackle and pass it forward. All good basic stuff. I stuck to the game plan, though initially I felt a bit uncomfortable playing at the back, and wanted to run forward to try to score. I managed to curb the temptation to move up for corners, however, and settled into my defensive role pretty well. As the game progressed, I started to shout instructions to other defenders, and my confidence was boosted. I actually quite enjoyed myself, and the fact that we beat Rangers reserves by 2-0 boosted my morale. Back in the dressing-room, Teddy Scott praised my performance, and gave me the impression that he was thinking of playing me in the centre of defence in the next reserve match. I wasn't sure how I felt about that, as I had been signed as a striker, and in my view I had not become a bad player in that position overnight.

In the next match, I was duly handed the Number 6 jersey. I played alongside Billy Williamson in the centre of defence, and when Billy was promoted to the first team later on, I was joined by Ian Hair, whose injury had led to me playing in defence in the first place. I was wearing my Aberdeen shirt with pride, regardless of position, but still felt this basic need to score goals. I had started the 1972-73 campaign with ambitions of becoming the next Aberdeen star centre-forward, but on the other hand the reserve side were fielding excellent players, many of whom would go on to play for the first team, and we were so effective that we won the Reserve League title and the Reserve League Cup. In the Scottish Second XI Cup, we lost to Hearts in the semi-final in a replay. Our outstanding team included Andy Geoghegan in goal, Billy Williamson, Chic McLelland, me and Ian Hair in defence, with Joe Smith, John Craig and Jimmy Miller in the middle of the park. Upfront – an indication of why I couldn't get a game as a striker – we had Bertie Miller, Duncan Davidson, Bobby Street, Ian Purdie and Ian Taylor vying for places.

It was clear that my switch of position to defender and the success of the reserve team had got me noticed at the club. If I had been told that I would be knocking on the first-team door as a defender rather than a centre-forward, I would not have believed such a daft notion. The problem I faced now, though, was that the first team had some tremendous central defenders on the books. They included Willie Young, who went on to play for Tottenham Hotspur, and other established stars in George Murray, Tommy Wilson and Henning Boel. It would not be easy to break into a side that could call upon players such as those, but on the other hand one factor acting in my favour was that Martin Buchan, who had signed for Manchester United in February 1972, had not been adequately replaced as sweeper. I was a long way from filling Martin's boots, but I was beginning to think that I at least had a chance of making the Number 6 jersey my very own.

When I started out as a defender, I did not look upon myself as a centre-half and did not enjoy being described as such. Alex McLeish was a centre-half, but I was a sweeper, the last man, and when Aberdeen played a four at the back, as we usually did, I was the final defender. I liked to think of myself as a thinker and a communicator on the park, and I took control when necessary. That came naturally, and though I am sometimes quiet off the field, I would be barking orders for the 90 minutes of every game. When the reserve campaign concluded, George Murray, who became an Aberdeen coach, suggested that I should train with the first team for their last few games of the 1972-73 season. He was one who saw me as a potential long-term replacement for Martin Buchan, and I am grateful for his support to this day. I thought being moved to the first-team squad was merely to extend my experience, and I did not contemplate making my debut by the end of the season, as only five games were left on the fixture list. Wrong again. Though the position I filled when my first-team opportunity arose came as another surprise.

3.

THE TOUR TO MAYHEM

*'As we kicked off, I could hear shooting coming from the
mountains'*

Making my Aberdeen first-team debut was an achievement I will
remember with pride until my dying day. What made it even
more special was the fact that my first game was significant for us,
and not a meaningless friendly. My big moment came on April
28 in the last league game of the 1972-73 season against Morton
at Cappielow. I had travelled with the first team on a few
occasions, but was not even called upon as a substitute. Two
days before the Morton game, however, Jimmy Bonthrone
invited me into his office and said that he had been pleased
with my attitude, and so he was putting me on the bench. To say
that I was elated was an under-statement, though I didn't think I
had much chance of playing. Because I thought I was on the
bench only to make up the numbers, I slept soundly on the
Friday night without a care in the world. Another reason I did
not consider that I would feature was because the encounter with
Morton was so vital to Aberdeen's fortunes. We were a point
behind Dundee in the battle to secure the final UEFA Cup spot,
which fourth place in the league would bring. We had to win
and hope that Dundee failed to overcome Hearts at Tynecastle.
Could we squeeze into Europe? Nerves were jangling in the
dressing-room before kick-off.

I watched from the bench as Morton went in at half-time 1-0
up, and we heard that Dundee were drawing with Hearts. We
were up against it, and our hopes of playing in the UEFA Cup the
following season seemed to be slipping away. During the break I

went through my paces out on the pitch with the rest of the Aberdeen substitutes, still thinking I would not get on after play resumed. In the second half we were struggling to break Morton down, and with 53 minutes gone the manager motioned to someone on the bench to get stripped, and I had to look around for a bit before realising that he meant me. I was excited but taken aback, and my heart sank slightly when he confirmed that I was to replace Arthur Graham. Now Arthur was one of the fastest players at the club, a pacey winger who left defenders standing, which was not one of the qualities that I possessed. I was extremely nervous as I stood on the touchline watching Arthur come off the pitch. The conundrum was that I now fulfilled the role of first-choice reserve-team defender, who had all but given up the notion of playing as a striker, and now that role was about to be reversed with me filling in up front. And not just up front, but in a wide position. Gulp! Not an easy situation for a young player to cope with on his debut in the top team. On the other hand, the chance to perform for Aberdeen was a great honour, and I was determined to make a real go of it, even if I was replacing one of the quickest and finest forwards in Scotland. I entered the fray with chest puffed out to play upfront with Barry Mitchell, and I felt that I put in a satisfactory shift for 37 minutes in what proved to be a successful conclusion for the team. I ran all over the place and chased every ball, and I like to think that I created space to allow Willie Young to equalise on the hour-mark, and that I contributed to the effective link-up play from which Drew Jarvie clinched the winner a few minutes later. Dundee drawing 2-2 with Hearts meant that we finished fourth in the league, ahead of the Dens Park club on goal difference. Aberdeen would play UEFA Cup football in the 1973-74 season.

ZOLTAN: A LEGENDARY FIGURE?

Though I was unaware of the fact at the time, my debut coincided with Zoltan Varga's last game for Aberdeen. Zoltan has taken on a legendary status among some followers, but I must admit that for the life of me, I don't know why. I had watched him in training since he had joined us from Hertha Berlin in September 1972, and he was a skilful player without doubt, but I think the adulation that he received was way over the top.

He came to Aberdeen only after he was banned from German football following a bribes scandal, and he did not stay long. In my book, to be described as a great player for a club, you must show ability over a longer period than the 13 months that Zoltan served. I accept that he had great talent, and at training he could nutmeg an opponent at will, and perform all sorts of fancy tricks.

○ ○ ○

After the success at Morton, I asked Jimmy Bonthrone why he had played me up front, and he explained that he had agreed with George Murray, the coach who had been pressing my case for first-team inclusion that I had great potential. But the manager thought I was a bit too young and inexperienced to operate in defence, once I got my chance. He judged that the further up the park I was placed on my debut the better, as there would be less responsibility to deal with. When he realised that Arthur Graham was having an off-day, he took a risk and put me on as a striker. He had been delighted with my performance. I learned a salutary lesson from those last few games of the season until I ran on at Cappielow – I hated being stuck on the bench. Thereafter, I told every manager I played under not to put me there. I would rather not be at a game or in a squad if I was destined to languish on the bench. Not my scene. Before I departed for a summer break in 1973, Jimmy urged me to work hard so that I would have a chance of developing into a first-team regular the following season. The question in my mind was: would it be as a striker or a defender? In truth, I now felt more comfortable playing in defence, and I resolved to work hard on my defensive skills and to try to make the Number 6 jersey my own, casting aside my schoolboy dreams of becoming a star striker. I studied closely the skills of Willie Young, who was an out-and-out ball-winning centre-half, particularly the way he marked defenders, and the drills he undertook during training, although he was a very different player to me. Henning Boel also played centre-back at times, and I learned a lot from him. He reflected a smoother approach than Willie, and I liked his style.

At the start of season 1973-74, Willie and Henning formed the first-choice central defensive partnership, but I realised that Henning was prone to injuries, and that the door would open up for me at some stage if I kept training hard. I was disappointed not to be included in the line-up to play Motherwell in the opening game in the Scottish League Cup on August 11, 1973. I didn't have to wait long to get my chance, though, as Henning picked up a knee injury in that game, and I moved into the side in his absence. Our League Cup section included Motherwell, Dundee United and East Fife, and my first game, versus United at Tannadice, ended 0-0. The section match that I recall vividly was away to East Fife on Saturday August 25, 1973. We had been playing well and were two goals up, when I gave away a penalty. It was the first penalty that I had surrendered in my professional career, and it was a telling experience. I was adjudged to have fouled Kevin Hegarty in the box, and Billy McPhee stepped up to take the penalty-kick. My heart was in my mouth, but Bobby Clark pulled off a tremendous save. I started to run towards the goalkeeper in celebration, but realised that a young player should keep his composure. I expressed my relief and gratitude by giving Bobby a pat on the back as we went up the tunnel at the end, and by standing him a drink later.

We progressed in the League Cup, and played Stirling Albion in the second round, beating them by margins of 3-0 home and away to set up a quarter-final against Celtic. We lost an exciting tie 3-2 at Parkhead, and drew the second leg 0-0 at Pittodrie, to go out of the tournament. We had played ten games just to get to that stage. The second leg proved to be slightly unusual because we had to play in the afternoon, as use of Pittodrie's floodlights to illuminate matches was not permitted for a spell. A stand-off between the Government and trade unions had led to power

shortages and a three-day working week. A good run of form in
the League Cup ties meant that I kept my place when the league
season started on September 1, 1973. I played alongside Willie
Young against Motherwell at Fir Park in a no-scoring draw. Of
the early games, the stand-out was the one away to St Johnstone,
which we won 2-1, my enjoyment heightened by close friend
Ian Hair scoring the winner to record what proved to be his only
goal of the season. I must say that Willie Young coaxed and
cajoled me through that opening sequence of games, and as the
season progressed I felt at home in the Aberdeen first team. I did
have lots to learn, and I recall with embarrassment gifting a goal
to Alan Gordon of Hibs at Pittodrie in the fifth game of the
season; thankfully, Drew Jarvie saved some of my blushes by
scoring an equaliser. In the next match, as if to express my thanks
to Drew, I put in an accurate cross which eluded the Dumbarton
goalkeeper, and allowed him to head into goal after 61 minutes
to give us a 1-0 victory away from home. Obviously, I was not
the only novice starting to make his way in the football world in
'73-74. We were controlling matters against Dundee United on
October 27, 1973, when a young man named Andy Gray came
on for United, and he proved to be a handful. We may have
claimed the spoils by 3-1, but Andy scored the United goal and
had a great game. He was fearless and showed outstanding talent
in the air, and was particularly adept at diving in to head balls that
other strikers would not go near. I was not at all surprised that he
went on to become a star performer with Dundee United,
Everton, Aston Villa, Rangers and Scotland, then gravitated
to feature as a star TV pundit on Sky Sport.

An intriguing, if rather confusing, aside to the season came
with the surfeit of Millers who were devoted to grinding out
results as members of Aberdeen's first-team squad: Bertie, Jimmy
and me. I started against Falkirk on November 10, 1973, Jimmy
came on in the second half, and Bertie was an unused substitute.
I scored my first first-team goal, which I reckon was one of the
best of my career, against Hearts at Pittodrie on November 17.
The score was 1-1 and I was around 20 yards from goal and, if I

say so myself, I hit a screamer into the top corner of the net. Kenny Garland in Hearts' goal had no chance of saving my shot, and we went on to win 3-1. When centre-half Henning Boel returned after knee surgery around New Year '74, he played at full-back because I was performing so well in the centre of defence. Jimmy Bonthrone showed his faith in me by moving Henning, and that convinced me that a regular place in the centre of defence was mine for the taking. I was in possession of the Number 6 jersey, and determined to keep a firm hold of it. I soon learned, however, that a league season resembles a long and winding road, and many things can go wrong along the way. For whatever reason, and I still can't put my finger on it to this day, Aberdeen started to lose form at an alarming rate from mid-season, which coincided with a dip in my performances, and the fans obviously noted that we were not doing well. This was reflected in only 4,000 spectators bothering to turn up to watch us confront Dumbarton on February 9, 1974. We may have won 3-0, but it was a bad day for poor Bobby Street, who broke his leg after just five minutes' play. Bobby and I had signed for Aberdeen around the same time, and to witness him suffering such bad luck made me realise how lucky I had been in not picking up any bad injuries during my early playing years. In the end, we could not come close to a magnificent Celtic team, who won the club's ninth league championship in a row with 53 points. With Danny McGrain, Davie Hay, Billy McNeill, Jimmy Johnstone and Kenny Dalglish in their ranks, it was easy to see why they were such a great side. We finished fourth, 11 points behind the champions, but then few could live with the Celtic team of that era.

Our Scottish Cup campaign was short and hardly sweet, as it saw us beaten 2-0 by Dundee at Pittodrie on January 27, 1974 in our first tie, which came in the third round of the tournament proper. It happened to be the first official game held on a Sunday in Scotland, and 23,574 turned up to watch. I was substituted after receiving a knock, and I can but apologise on behalf of the Aberdeen team for spoiling our fans' enjoyment of their Sabbath.

The tournament that I did enjoy that season was the UEFA Cup. I had made my debut in the last game of the previous season against Morton, when we had qualified for Europe, so I felt that I had contributed to our achievement. Who would we be drawn against in the first round for my first appearance on the European stage – perhaps a big team from West Germany, France or Italy? It turned out to be Finn Harps of the Republic of Ireland, the fickle luck of the draw failing to set up the glamour tie or exciting foreign trip that I had anticipated. But we won 4-1 at Pittodrie and should have scored a lot more, and we took the second leg by 3-1 at Finn Park, Ballybofey, for a hefty 7-2 aggregate. Next up was a glamour tie, against Tottenham Hotspur, who had won the UEFA Cup in the past and could boast an aristocratic football pedigree. They were struggling a bit in the English League, but they could tap into a pool of talented players, and I was truly excited to have the chance of facing outstanding Scottish striker Alan Gilzean and English internationalists Steve Perryman, Martin Peters and Martin Chivers. As a budding schoolboy striker, I had watched a lot of Chivers, and liked his style, and what impressed me most about Spurs was that they seemed to be giants compared to us. They looked as if they were from a different planet and Chivers, in particular, was huge and did his best to noise me up in the return match at White Hart Lane, having missed the first leg at Pittodrie because of injury. He was a good player, and I have met him since at charity golf outings, and he has but a vague recollection of our confrontation. The game obviously meant a lot more to me. A crowd of 30,000 packed Pittodrie for the first match, which was closely fought. Spurs took the lead when Ralph Coates scored after 15 minutes, but after that I felt we pegged them back. We got our just reward with three minutes left when Jim Hermiston scored from the penalty-spot after our substitute, Bertie Miller, had been brought down. A 1-1 home draw wasn't great, but it gave us a chance to progress, and I went to White Hart Lane feeling pretty confident, but any hopes of victory were banished pretty quickly. After 13 minutes Martin Peters scored, then Jimmy Neighbour, and two goals from Chris McGrath put them out of sight. Drew Jarvie claimed a consolation goal in a 4-1 defeat.

I played 45 games in 1973-74, made up of 31 league appearances, nine League Cup ties, four in the UEFA Cup and one in the Scottish Cup. I felt that it was my breakthrough season, though odd happenings in which I was engulfed during the summer of 1974 had to be experienced to be believed. Scotland had qualified for the World Cup in West Germany, and the nation's thoughts were with Willie Ormond and the team, but for reasons that were not clear to me then or now, Aberdeen decided to embark on a *world tour*. For a month. To far-flung outposts. Clearly the club must have thought that they would make money from the trip, but the choice of some destinations was bizarre. Playing in Australia and New Zealand was okay, but we also fulfilled fixtures in Iran and New Caledonia, a small island in the remote south-west Pacific. It was as if we were heading off on a cricket tour rather than a series of football friendlies. Arthur Graham, Doug Rougvie, Walker McCall, Jim Hermiston, Drew Jarvie and Duncan Davidson were among the individuals involved on the month-long expedition along with Eddie Thomson, who had been bought from Hearts for £65,000 to play in defence. It was Eddie's first time away with his new club, and he must have been baffled by what transpired. He had been signed to vie with me for a position in defence, but I saw him off and he ended up employed in midfield.

This was, at least, a tour to remember, and one of the craziest adventures of my life, for mayhem was likely to take hold at any time. You had to feel sorry for Jimmy Bonthrone, who was like a headmaster trying to control a bunch of unruly schoolboys. Even the straight-laced Bobby Clark, one of the nicest men in the game, let his hair down, and I knew we were in for moments of madness when Doug Rougvie turned up at Aberdeen Airport with the biggest suitcase I had seen, stuffed with cornflakes, rashers of bacon and tomato sauce. It was if he was being exiled to Siberia for a month, with no prospect of encountering decent food. We flew from Aberdeen to London then to Iran, and our

first match was arranged for May 7 against a team called
Persepolis in Teheran. It was a crazy venue for a crazy match,
and as we kicked off, I could hear shooting coming from the
mountains which surrounded the stadium in the Iranian capital.
The explosive noises got louder as the game progressed, and it
wasn't easy to concentrate on football. It was also sweltering hot,
and I could hardly breathe, let alone run. We were beaten 2-0,
and I was never so thankful to get off a pitch. We had intended to
stay the night in Teheran, but the Iranian Government told us
that they could not guarantee our safety. We were bundled out
to the airport in taxis and grabbed the next available flight, which
was heading for Bangkok, an unscheduled destination, but we
were not about to complain. Thailand offered a most entertaining stop-over – the colourful night life was something that most
of us had not experienced previously – and though we spent only
one night there, we made the most of it and hit quite a few bars.
From there we flew to Singapore, a city that impressed me
greatly. I swam in a hotel pool while rain splashed into the water,
and felt wonderfully refreshed despite the humid conditions. We
also enjoyed a stop-over in Hong Kong, which I remember for
the fact that all the taxis I saw there were Mercedes models. Here
was Willie Miller, who did not own a car and was still catching
the Number 11 bus to Pittodrie from his flat in Hartington
Road, hiring Mercedes carriages at will, for the equivalent of
twelve-and-a half-pence. Well worth the fare in any currency.

   By the time we caught the flight from Hong Kong to
Australia, we were jet-lagged and things were starting to get
out of hand, in a way that would not be tolerated for a moment
in these security-conscious days. Indeed, the plane was in danger
of being turned back as the drink flowed and we fooled about
during the flight, with some players chucking beer around. The
airline crew were mighty relieved to see the back of us when we
eventually made Perth, Western Australia. As an indication of the
in-flight shenanigans, Arthur Graham's club suit, the only one
that he had to wear for the duration of the trip, was sticky with
alcohol, so he decided to wash it in the laundry when we reached

our hotel. When he removed the suit from the washing machine, it was beautifully creased and wrinkled, and had shrunk by a factor of about six inches. He had to wear the sorry garments at official functions for a month or so thereafter. A single-vent blazer was the main item of uniform, and some of the boys decided that Arthur was giving them too much cheek, so they split the jacket up the back. He spent the rest of the tour parading in a club blazer with a big rip in its rear section, and in unpressed trousers which were six inches too short.

In our first game Down Under, we beat Western Australia 5-3 in Perth, then set off on a comprehensive tour of the Australian states, drawing 2-2 with South Australia in Adelaide, losing 2-1 to Queensland in Brisbane and beating Northern New South Wales 4-1 in Newcastle before finishing off with a 2-1 win over New South Wales in Sydney. I had enjoyed the most fun in Perth, as I met my Auntie Molly Whitelaw and her son John and visited their home, and admired at first hand why so many Scots had decided to move to Oz to start new lives. The weather was magnificent, as were the houses.

During our final night in Australia, we stayed in a top-class hotel and, surprise, surprise, had a bit too much to drink. Eddie Thomson was adept at winding people up, despite the fact that he had just joined Aberdeen, and he dared Bobby Clark to go skinny-dipping in the pool. Bobby, ever the gentleman, took up the challenge, stripped off and dived in. Unfortunately for Clarky, an elderly man of the cloth and his wife were also guests in the hotel, and they complained to the management about the naked man cavorting in the swimming pool. Jimmy Bonthrone was called to reception to be given a stern warning about the behaviour of his players: one of his football missionaries had shocked an Australian minister and his good lady. Jimmy was a strict disciplinarian, but he shrugged when Clarky got into trouble. He remarked memorably that if he could not control Bobby Clark, then he might as well pack up and go home – and pack it all in. We travelled on to New Caledonia in the south Pacific to play a team named Noumea in a double-header. We won the first match 3-0, lost the second 2-1, and took advantage of the tropical surroundings to swim off a sun-kissed beach fringed by palm-trees and decorated by beautiful girls. While we were plunging in the sea, Andy Geoghegan let out a yell and claimed that he had been bitten. We laughed and laughed and offered scant sympathy as he limped out of the water in agony, calling for a doctor. The poor man was writhing around on the sand, and had to be taken to hospital, where he was informed that he had been bitten by a conger eel. The unfortunate marine attack was unlikely to be replicated on the beach at Aberdeen, but the stricken Andy was confined to a wheelchair for the rest of his time on the island, and the sight of him being wheeled into the airport at New Caledonia with his foot bandaged up was too much for the rest of us. As he passed us in his wheelchair, we started to dance the conga (geddit?) behind him – all the way through check-in and customs and pranced on to the foot of the aircraft steps. Da-ra-ra-ra. Da-ra-ra-ra.

Even when we arrived back in London at the end of a gruelling month, the fun continued. While in Hong Kong, we had been attracted by the cheap imitation watches. I had bought two and Bobby Clark and Drew Jarvie had also made modest purchases, but Willie Young had invested in a dozen of the glittering timepieces and packed them securely in his luggage. Unfortunately for Willie, he was stopped by customs at Heathrow, and all his bags were opened. Out popped a selection of 'Rolex' watches which, because they were top-quality fakes, looked better than was the reality. The customs officers suspected that he was trying to smuggle them into Britain to avoid paying the duty, which I just could not believe of my trusted colleague.

Various crises behind us, it was a relief to return to the relative normality of life in Aberdeen after our adventures across the globe, for I was worn out after our month of madness. Because Scotland had contested the 1974 World Cup finals, few observers had noticed that we had been out of the country, let alone to such far-flung corners of the globe. And when I mentioned to friends the antics of a nude Bobby Clark, an attack on a mate by an evil conger eel, an impromptu airport conga and a consignment of fake 'Rolex' watches, they thought I was making it up . . .

As I had been promoted to a first pick on Jimmy Bonthrone's team-sheet, I felt that I could make a big impression in 1974-75. The Scottish League was to be reconstituted for the following season into a top division of ten, and it was vital for Aberdeen Football Club to ensure that we finished in that top-ten group before reorganisation. Our first match of the league campaign is one that I will always remember as it was at home to Hibs, who had signed a former Pittodrie favourite, Joe Harper, whose boots I had been ordered to polish when a novice. Joe is one of the all-time great goal-scorers for Aberdeen, and unfortunately for us, he had taken that talent with him to enhance our Edinburgh opponents' attacking options. He had a fine game, and though we were 2-1 up with 13 minutes left, Joe must have realised that the script had been written specially for him. He hit an un-stoppable free-kick past Bobby Clark to make it 2-2, then in the last minute cracked a shot which Willie Young did well to block. Unfortunately for Aberdeen, Alex Cropley was lurking in the six-yard box, and scored to give Hibs victory by 3-2. The period towards Christmas was marked by inconsistency, and on De-cember 7, 1974 we played Rangers at Pittodrie. Unfortunately, Rangers fans charged across the pitch towards the King Street End before kick-off. Police told us what had happened and kept us in the dressing-room, and order was restored only after Willie Waddell and Jock Wallace from Rangers had appealed for calm. Derek Johnstone put Rangers ahead after half-an-hour, my mate Ian Hair equalised, but then Tommy McLean clinched the winner for the visitors with three minutes left to end a dismal day for me, for Aberdeen and for the reputation of Scottish football, which was tarnished by the wild antics of some so-called supporters of the game.

O O O

THE VIEW FROM THE PARK

I must say that as a player I was more or less oblivious to crowd trouble. I was obviously aware of the phenomenon, which affects the game of football at times wherever it is played, but my mind was so focused on the run of play during matches that what was happening in spectator areas tended not to bother me. Aberdeen did have a group of fans who were known as Casuals, who followed the club, particularly inspired by successes. They gathered with the sole purpose of causing trouble, stirring an undercurrent of violence, and while sometimes the atmosphere at games could be construed as intimidating to onlookers, players were intent on blanking out such distractions.

By March 1975, Aberdeen were fifth in the league on 29 points, and we had no chance of catching Rangers, who were top with 44 points, or Celtic, who lay second on 40. The positive aspect was that we were certain to make the top ten, thus ensuring our status within the reconstituted Scottish Premier League, and we also had a chance of making the UEFA Cup competition once more. However, we let ourselves down by allowing things to slip as the season drew to a close, and we finished in fifth position, four points behind Dundee United, who took the UEFA Cup spot, and 15 points adrift of Rangers, who won the last of the old-style championships. Our League Cup and Scottish Cup campaigns were equally inconsistent. In our League Cup section, we did not get close to qualification, finishing third behind leaders Hearts and Dunfermline and just above the bottom club, Morton. In the Scottish Cup, we started superbly, and I played a big part in a third-round tie, our first of the tournament, against Rangers at Pittodrie on January 25, 1975. The Ibrox club had taken the lead through Ally Scott with 23 minutes left, and it looked as though the tie was drifting away from us. With three minutes left, Stewart Kennedy, a tall and gangly Rangers goalkeeper, came off his line just a shade, and I thought it worth attempting to lob him. I caught the ball perfectly, and it soared over Kennedy and into the net to set off frantic scenes of celebration around Pittodrie. What was perhaps overlooked in the euphoria was that the job was not completed: we had to take on Rangers in a replay in Glasgow, never an easy proposition. We met on February 10 with Rangers, unusually, kitted out in an all-white strip. We got off to a stirring start when Arthur Graham scored after two minutes, but on the half-hour they got back into the game thanks to a Bobby McKean strike. We managed to take the game into extra-time when substitute Joe Smith headed a cross from Arthur Graham on to the post, and Duncan Davidson was there to score from close-in to give us a 2-1 victory.

I definitely thought that I had luck on my side in the Scottish Cup that season, and that this could help Aberdeen to win the trophy. In the fourth round against Dundee United, Drew Jarvie scored after 14 minutes, and I felt that I managed to keep Andy Gray and the rest of the United strikers under control. With five minutes left, I went up for a ball and was adjudged to have handled in the penalty-box. I had visions of all the good work unravelling with me to blame, then I remembered that Bobby Clark had saved a penalty against East Fife earlier in the season, after I had given away a foul. I ran up to Bobby before the penalty-kick and whispered that it was destiny that, every time I gave away a penalty, he would bring off a save. Nonsense, perhaps, but Bobby and I need not have worried, for Frank Kopel stepped up and blasted the ball wide of the goal. His miss meant that we had made it through to the quarter-finals against Motherwell, a match to be played at Pittodrie on Saturday, March 8, 1975. Because we had home advantage, I fancied our chances. I had performed well versus Dundee United and scored against Rangers; I had been part of the team that had beaten them in the replay at Ibrox, and my luck remained intact after Kopel had missed a penalty award, for which I had been deemed responsible. Though favourites against Motherwell, we did not get going at all. Bobby Graham gave them a lead just before half-time, and they held on for victory. It was a most disappointing day, as I truly believed that we could have gone all the way to the Scottish Cup final.

I had played 34 league games, six League Cup matches and four Scottish Cup ties in 1974-75, and I felt that we had under-performed and should have done better, particularly in the Scottish Cup. I was learning more and more about the game, but considered that as a team we should be doing much better. I knew that something would have to change in the 1975-76 season to take the club up to another level, and better players would have to be brought in. Unfortunately few fresh faces came to the club in the close season, and my fears that we would not do well were proved correct. As it happened, Aberdeen started the season badly, and failed to recover. The traditional curtain-raiser was the Scottish League Cup, and we were thrust into a difficult section including Celtic, Hearts and Dumbarton, with only one team qualifying for the later stages. Whatever the challenges, there was no excuse for our rather dismal perfor-mances. On August 9, 1975 we were beaten by Celtic at Parkhead with Kenny Dalglish getting the winner, three days later we beat Dumbarton 2-0 at home, but in our match against Hearts at Pittodrie we lost 2-1. It was a rotten game contested in weather to match. Heavy rain had even diluted the whitewash, and sawdust had to be sprinkled in abundance to pick out the lines on the park. We defeated Dumbarton 1-0 away, but Hearts beat us 1-0 at Tynecastle, a result that put an end to our qualification hopes. In our final game, Celtic were 2-0 winners at Pittodrie, hence we again finished a lowly third in the League Cup group, behind Celtic and Hearts.

Our league campaign started badly, too. We lost away to Dundee on the first day of the season, and could manage only a 2-2 draw with Motherwell at Pittodrie. If a game shaped a season, it was the unfortunate encounter with Dundee United at Pittodrie on Saturday, September 13, 1975. Paul Sturrock put United into the lead and Jocky Scott equalised, but the Tannadice men went ahead again on the stroke of half-time through Paul Hegarty. We then had Joe Smith sent off after a

confrontation with Hegarty, and matters went from bad to
worse. Jimmy Bonthrone sought a solution, and with 20 minutes
left on the clock he decided to take off Willie Young and to
replace him with Billy Pirie. Now Big Willie, never the most shy
and retiring man in our dressing-room, took the substitution
badly, and you could detect his anger rising as he made to leave
the field. The incident culminated on the touchline with Willie
removing his Aberdeen jersey and throwing it into the dugout. It
was an act of insubordination, and Willie should not have vented
his frustration in such an open fashion. It was now up to Jimmy
Bonthrone to take action. I felt sorry for the manager, as I knew
that Willie could be difficult to work with, could be disruptive
on the training field when the notion took him, and that Jimmy
found him awkward to control day by day. But then I knew that
Willie's attention was distracted, as Arsenal and Tottenham
Hotspur were said to be interested in taking him south. Newspapers on the morning of the game had suggested that a deal with
a top English club had all but been concluded, and I remarked to
the gaffer: 'Just get him off, because he is not focused on this
game.' When he stormed off the park and discarded his team top
before storming out of Pittodrie for the last time, I was not at all
surprised.

Jimmy would never have accepted such behaviour from one
of his players, and Willie was put on the transfer list the following
day, and had signed for Spurs by the end of the week. To be fair
to Willie, his public outburst must be put in context. Seven days
earlier, he had been one of five players from the Scotland Under-
23 team who were banned from future international selection for
bad behaviour, and he was clearly feeling under pressure from
various quarters when the Dundee United game came along. His
transfer split the dressing-room, as some players felt that tearing
his jersey off was an act to ensure that he achieved his lucrative
move to an English club. Others thought he was hard done by,
and that he should have been forced to stay at Pittodrie come
what may, as we were trying to build a team, not to dismantle
one. While on Teeside, three days after the Dundee United

game to take on Middlesbrough in an Anglo–Scottish Cup tie, Aberdeen players became involved an argument over whether Willie had been badly treated or not. Whatever, Jimmy was most unhappy about Willie's tantrum, and he felt the division in the dressing-room caused by his decision to transfer the player placed him in an invidious position as manager. We lost the Anglo–Scottish Cup tie in Middlesbrough by 2-0, and the atmosphere was bad on the coach returning to Aberdeen.

The Willie Young incident clearly had an affect on us, as our league form was dreadful after his departure. We descended close to the foot of the new Premier League, and with pressure growing on Jimmy Bonthrone as manager, we had to improve, and quickly. We did manage a draw against Hearts at Tynecastle, then beat Ayr United at home 3-1, with the latter game being notable because John Hather came on as a substitute for his only appearance that season. His father was Jack Hather, one of the great Aberdeen players of the 1950s, and a son following his dad into the same professional football team occurs only occasionally. We took on Celtic at Pittodrie on October 11, 1975 in a game that I want to forget. Paul Wilson had been sent off for throwing the ball in Eddie Thomson's face, and with the man advantage I felt that Aberdeen could secure a victory. However, I executed a dreadful back-pass to Bobby Clark, which Kenny Dalglish pounced upon to score. Jocky Scott equalised on the hour-mark, but I still considered that we could run out as easy winners against only 10 men. As it turned out, Celtic rallied for Dixie Deans to make the final score 2-1, which left us second bottom of the 10-strong division, a better goal difference placing us just above St Johnstone, who had also managed to gather only four points after seven games. The players knew that the Aberdeen board would not put up with the club being in such a precarious position, as relegation from the Scottish Premier League would have a devastating affect on finances. Gates would decline and depress income, which would make it harder to entice top players. Aberdeen's directors did not wish to risk such an outcome.

We recognised, too, that Jimmy Bonthrone was a man of honour who was all too aware of the implications of relegation, and it was no big shock when he resigned a few days after our home defeat to Celtic. His decision to step down was a personal disappointment, as he had demonstrated great faith in me and had helped me to develop into a first-team regular. He had given me my Aberdeen debut, albeit as a striker, and had nurtured my career. I will not forget all the advice that I gleaned from him, and without his support I might well not have been so successful at Pittodrie: I had played under him from April 28, 1973 to October 11, 1975 and learned a lot. George Murray, a member of the backroom staff who was also much admired by me, took temporary charge, and our first match with him occupying the hot seat was against St. Johnstone, which we won 2-0 thanks to a double from Billy Pirie. We had three more matches with George as caretaker until the Aberdeen board got the man that they wanted to take charge on a permanent basis. This personality turned out to be eccentric and incredibly enthusiastic, and he accorded me the greatest honour of my fledgling football career, by making me captain of Aberdeen Football Club.

4

ALLY MACLEOD'S CUP OVERFLOWED WITH ENTHUSIASM

'I'm going to make you captain of Aberdeen as my wedding present to you'

It was a cold November morning in 1975 when Ally MacLeod was introduced to me. I had been told that he was a larger-than-life character, and that turned out to be absolutely true. He almost shook my hand off when we met, and he was so full of nervous energy that he couldn't stop talking. He was like a wee boy, excited to be manager of Aberdeen Football Club, and yet it was gratifying to see a grown man who was so pleased to be at his work. Apart from his family, football was all that Ally really cared about. He was a true enthusiast who brought some razzmatazz to Pittodrie, and his positive attitude fitted perfectly with the mood of north-east Scotland at the time, as the area was enjoying the benefits of the North Sea oil boom and was on a high. I had been warned by players who had worked with him at his previous club, Ayr United, that he was an eccentric and a bit over the top. How true. Sometimes I wondered if he was inhabiting this planet. I had not experienced anything like having Ally in charge, nor have I since. Curious indeed.

From the start he said that he wanted us to play attacking football, and that ethos was welcomed by all the players and supporters. He wasn't just talk, as he had built up an excellent managerial pedigree, and a study of his CV confirmed that the Aberdeen board had done well to secure his services. He had started his coaching career in 1966, when he took charge of Ayr

United and gained promotion to the top division, maintaining their status in the top flight. He took them to a League Cup semi-final, and he was considered a true local hero to the extent that he was named Ayr's Citizen of the Year in 1973. He had served Ayr United for nine years before he decided to move to Aberdeen. He had galvanised the Ayrshire club on limited resources, and clearly he felt that he could do even better at Pittodrie with the benefits of a more generous budget. Ally's self-belief from day one was there for all to see. He lifted everybody with his infectious enthusiasm, and he thought that he could make us title challengers. It was certainly never dull when he was around, and you just did not know what might happen next. The only factor that bothered me when he took over was that Dick Donald, the club chairman, had told him that the squad he had inherited was mediocre, and he would get £100,000 to spend on new players. When that information leaked out, no player felt that his place was guaranteed.

I did not think that we were a bad a team, and I considered it a slap in the face for the departed Jimmy Bonthrone for Dick Donald to suggest to Ally that we were. We were a team in transition, and many of the men that Ally inherited were top quality, but perhaps nearing the end of their careers. Nevertheless, Ally was impressed with the overall set-up at Pittodrie. He thought that the club was very professionally run, which it was, but then he had come from part-time Ayr United, and he was not comparing like with like. However, we still had to jump into a mini-bus in the morning to drive to a decent training pitch, as we did not have one of our own. I didn't always see eye to eye with him at training, and I found his coaching methods to be a bit daft. The regimented, disciplined Bonthrone regime had been replaced by the madcap training-field antics of Ally MacLeod, and the new man took a long time to get used to. In fact, he got on my nerves quite a bit during training in his first week, because he kept telling me to keep it simple, to win tackles and simply roll the ball to Joe Smith. Joe was Ally's blue-eyed boy, and the manager intended to play him in a defensive midfield role in his first game in charge against Motherwell. Joe was a fine player who could ping passes all over the pitch, but I was damned if I would act as a fetcher and carrier for anyone. I felt there was more to my talents than simply winning tackles and playing it a few yards to Joe Smith. In training I tried the tactic of passing to Joe, and I found it most frustrating and all a bit pointless, and told Ally so. To be fair to him, he took my views on board, and he was wise enough to realise that he was wrong on this occasion. His decision to change his tactics helped my relationship with him, as I knew that he would listen to my opinion in future.

It was galling that Dick Donald's suggestion that the new manager had inherited a bad team was lent some credence in Ally's first match against Motherwell, for we were thumped 3-0 at Fir Park on November 8, 1975. Ally had spent the first half evaluating the team from the stand, but we went 2-0 down, and he decided to observe from the dugout for the second half. He was very animated on the touchline and clearly frustrated at our performance, and after the match he told us that we would have to buck up our ideas. We certainly took his advice, and in our next match we beat Dundee United 2-1 away, which was a tremendous result. As he started to settle in, Ally became more and more confident, but increasingly manic. He was a superb showman, and used the newspapers to stir up interest among Aberdeen's fans. Sometimes, though, it didn't go according to plan. After our 2-1 win at Tannadice, he held a press conference to urge Dons fans to turn up in droves for our next home match against Hearts, and he promised fast and fluent football. He boasted that Aberdeen would show how great a force they were under his management, and they would trounce Hearts. The hype did bring out the supporters. In our last home game before he had taken over – a 1-0 win over Dundee on November 1, 1975 – the crowd numbered 6,300. With Ally banging the drum, 11,400 turned up for Hearts' visit on November 22. And what happened? We played really badly, the game was awful, and we were lucky to escape with a 0-0 draw. The football just did not match up to Ally's rhetoric, and the occasion was a let-down for everybody.

Was the man embarrassed or downhearted by the rotten fare on offer? Not a bit of it. He shrugged it off and told the fans that it had just been a bad day, and that things would be better next time they came to Pittodrie. Things certainly did not improve in the next game, coincidentally against Ayr United at Somerset Park. We were beaten 1-0, and I witnessed another side to Ally MacLeod that day. He was furious at having to bear the indignity of defeat by his former club, and embarked on an extended dressing-room rant, slagging off the lot of us. Our next match up was Rangers at home, a stiff test considering our poor showing at Ayr and Ally's resultant fury. On the Tuesday before Rangers' visit, he called me into his office and I was prepared for the worst, fearing that I would be dropped in the wake of the Ayr United defeat. I was wrong. He sat me down and asked me when I was due to get married; I responded, and he went quiet for a moment. He told me that he had a very special wedding present for me, and I thanked him for the kind thought, wondering what he would be buying. 'I'm going to make you captain of Aberdeen as my wedding present to you, Willie,' he declared. I was puzzled and let out a nervous laugh. I thought he was joking. I was waiting for him to give me the reasons for making me captain; maybe he liked my leadership qualities or style of play. 'No, it isn't for any of these reasons,' he added vaguely. 'It's just a wedding present,' An acceptable gift it was, too, if rather unusual.

I was delighted at being appointed captain, but was conscious that I would be taking the armband from Bobby Clark, who was out of the team because of injury. Andy Geoghegan, survivor of the conger-eel attack on New Caledonia, had taken his place in goal, and I assumed that Bobby would be reinstated as skipper when he returned. Ally told me that would not be the case. Clarky was a true professional, but it was common knowledge that he did not always see eye to eye with Ally, and didn't feel comfortable with his style of coaching. Whether that clash of personalities led to me being handed the captaincy, I'm not sure, but it probably was a factor. The official reason for the change that Ally presented to newspaper and broadcast journalists was that he wanted an outfield player to don the captain's armband. It was a fair argument, but that was not what he had said to me. If he had couched it in these terms in his office rather than putting it down as a wedding gift, perhaps I would have been more excited, but then my first match as captain, a baptism of fire against Rangers at Pittodrie, certainly did not lack excitement. I had resolved to ease myself into the job rather than try to impose my will on team-mates immediately, which was easier said than done. Within 10 minutes of kick-off, I was barking out orders and urging the team on, and like every game in which I appeared against the Ibrox club, it was a feisty affair. Tempers were frayed, and midway through the second half Ally received a ticking-off from the referee for protesting over one too many decisions. I had thought that was my job! It looked as if the tense proceedings would finish 0-0, but with eight minutes left John McMaster put in a great ball for Drew Jarvie, who scored the winner. It was a vital victory, as our bad start to the season before Ally arrived meant that we were hovering in the relegation zone. The win over Rangers put us third bottom, just ahead of Dundee United and St Johnstone. I retained the captain's armband for the match against Celtic in Glasgow on December 13, and concluded that Ally was true to his word that I would retain the appointment until further notice. Celtic were the league leaders and no-one gave us a prayer, and yet first-half goals from Drew Jarvie and Arthur Graham gave us a 2-0 win. Successive successes over the Old Firm in my first two matches as Aberdeen skipper made it a very happy Christmas.

Despite being capable of defeating the top teams on our day, we had retained our inconsistent streak. Ally believed that the more supporters who turned up, the better we played, and that was why he kept appealing to fans to flock to Pittodrie in big numbers. He decided to usher in the New Year by using his public-relations bent to entice the fans, and in the days leading up to the home game against Motherwell, he encouraged them to come along to see the 'New Dons for 1976'. They were swayed by his tempting message, and when we walked on to the pitch carrying placards proclaiming 'Happy New Year', 16,000 people were in the ground, full of expectation. And what happened? We drew 0-0 in a dreadful game, and fans departed full of disappointment. Ally, though, could always pinpoint some reason for bad performances. He was the sort of character who could blame defeat on anything, other than the fact that the opposition were superior . . . The grass wasn't short enough, the half-time snacks in the dressing-room were not satisfactory, the sun got in our eyes. Take your pick. In truth, at times he seemed to inhabit a football dream-world, and by the end of January 1976 we were sitting fifth in the league, a familiar position, with nine games left to play. Dundee United, in ninth spot and prime candidates for relegation, lay a massive 11 points behind us. We thought that we were well clear of the drop zone, and maybe felt that because we were ensconsed in mid-table, we could simply glide along comfortably to the end of the season. That proved not to be the case. We developed a tailspin, and a 1-0 defeat against Dundee United at Tannadice on March 27 sucked us back into the relegation dogfight. With five games of the season remaining, we were battling against relegation with Ayr United, Dundee and Dundee United. St. Johnstone were already well adrift at the bottom of the table and destined for the first division, but the other relegation place was still in the balance.

I did not help our cause against Celtic at Parkhead on April 17, 1976 by being sent off at a crucial stage in a vital match. Kenny Dalglish had put Celtic ahead, but Johannes Edvaldsson gave away an own-goal to put us back in the hunt. I really fancied our chances in the second half, but after only 10 minutes I mistimed a tackle on Roy Aitken, putting him up in the air and on to the pitch-side track. Propelling big Roy skywards would do no-one a favour at Celtic Park, and I was red-carded immediately after the challenge. I protested, but did not have much of a case for my defence. I thought I had blown it for my team, but Bobby Clark, who had returned after injury, played a blinder in goals, and we held on for a point. In our second-last game of the season, we lost to St. Johnstone, who had already been relegated, and to make matters worse, Dundee United beat Rangers at Ibrox to put more pressure on us. Therefore, we were required to overcome Hibs at Pittodrie in the last game of the season to stay in the Scottish Premier League. This was not the conclusion to his first season that Ally MacLeod had envisaged, but an alarming drop in form had led us to crisis point. It was a nervy match, and our escape plan was not helped by Dave Robb missing a penalty. Thankfully, Drew Jarvie opened the scoring after half-an-hour, and Joe Smith and Dave Robb, much to his relief, secured our status in the second half. It had proved an easy victory, but it was vital because when we came off the park, we found out that we had stayed up merely on goal difference. Dundee, who were relegated with St. Johnstone, had finished on 32 points, the same total as Aberdeen and Dundee United. We stayed up because we had conceded fewer goals than Dundee, who had let in 62 that season compared to our tally of 50. Dundee United had conceded 48 goals.

At the end of a fretful season, the manager decided on a clear-out, and Ian Hair was among those who departed, which was a disappointment as he was a close friend who had come through the ranks with me after sharing a room in Mr and Mrs Sharp's cosy abode. But one of the new draft was Stuart Kennedy, who was destined to achieve legendary status at Aberdeen Football Club, and who proved to be the manager's best buy by any measure. He cost us £26,000 on a transfer from Falkirk, and was worth every penny. The manager's prize schoolboy signing was a Glasgow teenager, Alex McLeish. Ally clearly saw the inherent talent, and he pulled out all the stops to bring the boy to Pittodrie. Big Eck revealed that Ally, Aberdeen's chief scout Bobby Calder and his assistants, Jimmy Carswell and John McNab, had turned up at his door en masse to convince him to sign. Now Alex had brains in his heid as well as in his feet, and

Ally made it possible for him to work part-time in an accountants' office and to pursue evening classes on three days each week to ensure that he had a sound education, just in case he did not make it in the game. After taking account of his play in the reserves, I was convinced that he was destined to be a footballer rather than a number-cruncher.

The longer Ally was at the club, the more time I had to adjust to his eccentric ways. He was a stickler for discipline and, in keeping with his singular personality, punishments meted out for breaking the rules were rather strange. Willie Garner and a few of the fringe players misbehaved at one training session, and Ally told them to turn up that evening at Pittodrie. Nobody was sure what would happen, and the lads were quite relieved when they were told that they would only have to do a bit of extra training. They changed and ran on to the pitch, but the floodlights were not switched on, and there was no sign of Ally. Then they heard a voice in the darkness which was Ally ordering them to run round the pitch in the dark until he told them to stop. Whenever they thought they had finished their punishment laps, a voice in the distance would insist that they kept going, and it was only after they were absolutely knackered that he allowed them back into the changing-room. He didn't follow them in or say anything, merely departed Pittodrie. He had got his message across, and he was satisfied that Willie and the rest would not step out of line again.

His training regime was quirky, too, confirmed by the fact that you would have needed a degree in mathematics to calculate the score in practice matches using the impenetrable MacLeod formula. I wanted to know the real score in these games, as inevitably I wanted to be on the winning side, but Ally would be itching to join the action, and he could not be bothered to keep a proper note of who was in front. In one of the first games that he organized, I received a knock and went behind the goal to recover. No-one paid any attention to me until Ally came across to see how I was, and it was apparent that he hoped I would not be able to continue, so that he could take my place in the game.

You would think that keeping the score in a simple bounce game between grown men at training would be easy, but then under Ally's protocol each goal was allotted a distinctive value: if you scored with your right foot that was worth one goal, a strike with your left foot was worth two, and a header got you three. To add to the confusion, Ally would chop and change the teams, and you would be switched from one side to the other as the fancy took him. He always claimed to know exactly what the score was, but he was just making it up, and years later he claimed in a conversation with me that he had deliberately set out to confuse us in training and to wind us up, so that we would learn to remain calm when refereeing decisions went against us. Oh really? Goalkeeper Bobby Clark was the only individual who managed to sort out the confusion at training, because after every legitimate goal he would make a mark on the pitch with his studs. Bobby's scoreline would be 3-2, while Ally would work it out at something like 24-21.

During the long, hot summer of 1976 I got to know Ally a lot better, as I was one of the few players who remained in Aberdeen rather than heading off on holiday. I lunched with him at a hotel in the city, and he kept saying that he was sure we would win a cup and challenge well in the league. I tended to deflect his rash predictions, but I started to gain in belief as we sat chatting, and by the end of the meal I was also of the opinion that Aberdeen Football Club could win a trophy in the coming season. In saying that, I did not foresee that it would be the first trophy on offer in 1976-77 that I would hold aloft as captain.

The successful Scottish League Cup campaign started on August 14, 1976 with a 2-0 home win against Kilmarnock. I missed the match through injury, and the club were so delighted that Joe Harper had returned to the fold from Hibs, that he was appointed captain for the day. He repaid the compliment by scoring within four minutes to set up the win, secured when Arthur Graham knocked in the second. I also missed the away win over St Mirren and the home victory against Ayr United before coming back for a four-goal rout of St Mirren. In our following matches we drew with Ayr United and lost to Kilmarnock, but still stood on top of the group with nine points, three more than Ayr. It was in our quarter-final match against Stirling Albion that I began to believe that our name might very well be engraved on the cup. In the first leg at Pittodrie, we won 1-0 thanks to a Joe Harper goal, but they beat us 1-0 in the return, and we had to go to a replay at Dens Park on a cold October evening. It was not a match to remember, but we played to our full potential and won 2-0 to set up with a semi-final meeting with Rangers at Hampden Park. Our performance there was the best that I had witnessed from an Aberdeen side since making my first-team debut under Jimmy Bonthrone three-and-a-half years earlier. We were simply magnificent, and Rangers did not get a look-in as Jocky Scott completed a hat-trick and Joe Harper and Drew Jarvie added to the tally as we ran out 5-1 winners. Ally MacLeod ran on to the pitch at the end jumping up and down like a madman, and we were so desperate to view the television recording of our famous victory that we delayed our return north so that we could relive the dramatic events at the BBC television studios in Glasgow.

The Scottish League Cup final against Celtic on November 6, 1976 was a match that caught the imagination of the public. Newspapers were full of stories about whether a team such as Aberdeen, featuring in the culmination of the competition for the first time since 1955, could beat the mighty Celtic, who were making a remarkable 13th consecutive appearance in a League Cup final. Ally was very superstitious, and did not wish to change his habits despite wearing the same blue suit to all the League Cup games and avoiding a haircut since the tournament started. His wife, Faye, wasn't too keen about the well-used suit and the unkempt hair gracing a televised cup final, but Ally got his way. Not for the first time. This was my first cup final as a club captain, and I was still only 21. I received sound advice from Bobby Clark, who told me to soak up the occasion, as I might never get the chance to play in a major final again. As I led the team out on to the Hampden turf, I tried to savour every moment. I took a deep breath and looked to see where my family were sitting in the stand, and gave them a wave. I was delighted that Bobby Clark was following me out, as it had been touch and go whether he would play. He had broken a bone at the base of his thumb, and had missed our league match against Motherwell before the final. It was only a few hours before kick-off that Ally MacLeod decided to take the risk to play him, and he took the field with his hand strapped up. The other big talking point was the fact that Dave Robb, who had been one of our top performers that season, had been dropped to the bench. He was clearly peeved that he was not in the starting line-up, and he greeted the news with a face like thunder, but he was to have the last laugh. The match was a close-run affair, and we went behind when Kenny Dalglish was brought down in the penalty-box by Drew Jarvie after 12 minutes. Kenny got up, dusted himself down and scored from the spot, which made it difficult for an inexperienced side; and we needed to get back into the game pretty sharpish. Drew made up for the penalty gaffe with the equaliser after 25 minutes, following good work by Joe Harper and Arthur Graham, but we were really up against it in the second half. Celtic kept coming at us, and we were a bit fortunate to survive their onslaught and to take the game into extra-time. Within two minutes of the restart, we were ahead again, Arthur Graham, Joe Harper and Jocky Scott combining superbly to set up Dave Robb, who had come off the bench fortuitously to replace Drew Jarvie. From then on in we defended bravely, and when the final whistle blew, I was in dreamland and about to lift my first piece of silverware as captain of Aberdeen Football Club. It was a magnificent feeling. I climbed the steps at Hampden to receive the Scottish League Cup, turned to the massed ranks of Aberdeen fans and lifted the trophy, one-handed, towards them. The place erupted. It took us hours to make our way from Hampden because we were celebrating so much, which meant we arrived late for our victory party at the Station Hotel, Perth. We dined superbly, tucking into the standard footballers' fare of prawn cocktail followed by steak. Pasta and the notion of a balanced diet to enhance health and fitness were absent from the menus of most footballers back in the 1970s.

Bobby Clark went all Mystic Meg on me at the dinner, claiming that he had dreamed during the previous night that Dave Robb would come off the bench and score the winner. They had shared a room at our pre-match base, a hotel on the south side of Glasgow, and he confirmed to me: 'It was written in the stars.' According to Bobby, he had told Dave when he wakened on the morning of the game that he would play a major role in winning the trophy for Aberdeen. Dave had merely laughed, acknowledging that it was more than likely that he would be left on the bench. Now if any other player had come up with such a story, he would have been ridiculed, but because Bobby was such an honest citizen, I knew that he had not made the whole thing up just to impress. We were accorded an incredible reception in the city of Aberdeen the following day. We paraded the trophy through the streets, and tens of thousands turned out to cheer our achievement. On the day of the celebration parade, I admitted to the press and to our support that I thought we had been lucky to win the final against Celtic. What I did not reveal were details of my pre-season chat with Ally, when he convinced me we could win a trophy. The power of positive thinking?

The League Cup final victory elevated Ally's standing in the game, and inevitably the suggestion arose that he might move to pastures new. I knew that he and his family were happy with his Aberdeen posting, but events can move fast in football. He had been at the club for only 18 months when Willie Ormond resigned as Scotland manager, and Ally became the first choice to replace him. The first I heard about it was in May 1977, when we visited what was then known as Yugoslavia to play a friendly against OFK Kikinda. On the flight to the Balkans, Ally had been a bit more excitable than usual, if that were possible, but we put it down to the fact that we had finished the season with the League Cup in our possession, and that he was satisfied with picking up his first trophy as Aberdeen manager. I contributed to a newspaper column at the time, as did Drew Jarvie, and we were informed by journalists that the SFA had approached Ally to be the next Scotland coach, so I understood why he was distracted. I asked him straight if he was leaving the club, and he did not shirk an answer. He responded by saying that he was in two minds about the national job, and would probably not make a final decision until after our game against Kikinda. The match was a meteorological disaster, and we lost 2-1. If we had not travelled so far, I'm sure it would have been cancelled, as we were lashed with rain, and the pitch was dappled with puddles. On the last night of the trip before we left Dubrovnik Airport, the players had a drink with Ally in the bar. He did not say much, but we just knew that he had made up his mind to leave. On the flight home, he opened up a bit more and confirmed that he was about to become Scotland manager, but asked us to keep things quiet until the SFA announced the appointment officially.

At times Ally MacLeod had been a difficult and frustrating manager, but I wished him well. After all, he had chosen me as Aberdeen captain, and for that alone I would always be in his debt. He must have looked on me as someone on whom he could rely during matches, and I like to think I did not, ever, let him down. When news of his departure was confirmed, he decided to throw a big party at his house at Milltimber to say goodbye to friends and to the players and staff of Aberdeen Football Club. He had spared no expense. Bunting festooned the streets, streamers were cast all over the place, loud music filled the air and some great food was laid on. Heaven help any neighbours who had not been invited. We were issued with straw hats as we arrived, and I thought to myself: 'Was Victory in Europe night like this for the soldiers?' Ally announced that he had a little going-away surprise for us. I envisaged a big picture of the team with the Scottish League Cup, but I was nowhere near being right. Ally stood up, asked for quiet, then he brought out bottles of slivovitz, a Yugoslavian brandy made from plums, which you might have used as paint-stripper. Decent slivovitz I consider to be quite palatable, but this hooch was horrific. Each of us was presented with a bottle as a gift from the opposition during our bonding exercise in Yugoslavia, but none of us drank the stuff, let alone brought it home. Ally had stashed away a few bottles in his suitcase, though, and he informed the gathering that every member of the Aberdeen first-team squad had to drink a glass to celebrate him getting the Scotland job. I would be first up as captain, and I could not refuse, but it was not a pleasant experience.

Despite the slivovitz, I made a speech on behalf of the players, and I recalled the curious running challenges that the manager had issued to the club secretary, Jim Rust. Ally saw himself as a clone of Emil Zatopek, and fancied himself as a long-distance runner. The Czechoslovakian hero had won 5,000-metre, 10,000-metre and marathon gold medals at the Helsinki Olympics in 1952, and in the 26-mile-plus race he strode away from Jim Peters of England with a killer burst. Ally liked to think that he possessed a devastating burst of speed, and he challenged Jim Rust to a couple of races, six times round the track, for a bet. He took it so seriously that he would arrange for the reserve team to spectate, joined by a few members of the first team who were mug enough to waste their time. Why did he do it? I think he thought it was a good idea to keep spirits up. In my chosen few words at Milltimber, I also reminded him of the day that he nearly killed me. Being a passenger in Ally's car was not for the faint-hearted. One evening I was heading to Banff with the manager and Jim Rust, who was in the front seat, to attend a supporters' club function, and it proved to be the usual white-knuckle ride. As he drove, Ally would turn round to converse with me as I cringed in the back seat. On the road north at Inverurie, he negotiated a set of temporary traffic lights perfectly well, but on the return journey he decided to turn around to chat just as he neared the lights again, at a bend under a rail bridge. As he prattled on, he missed the bend completely at maybe 60mph, and ended up storming towards a cornfield. I thought I was going to die, but the driver managed to hit the brakes and pull up before we crashed. Jim and I were badly shaken, but Ally did not blink an eyelid. 'Oops,' he remarked, then reversed out of the cornfield on to the road with not another word. That incident summed up Ally, as did his leaving party, which was a bit weird and over the top, but fun with it. He had entered Aberdeen with a bang, and he departed in much the same way, and I was relieved that I had survived his impetuous driving habits to wish him well.

Ally MacLeod was a nice guy who embraced incredible enthusiasm. He uttered some wildly ambitious statements, but few people stopped him or told him to think a bit before he spoke out. He was a guy who lived on the edge, and his manner was extremely nervy, despite the fact that football followers thought of him as extremely confident. I sat next to him on numerous occasions when he had to make a speech, and you might have assumed that talking to a big audience would have been his forte. He was effective at public speaking, but he became most anxious beforehand, tore up lots of napkins before he got up on his feet, and always broke out in a sweat. Though some of his antics caused me puzzlement, he was a real football person who got around and spoke to people about Aberdeen Football Club, promoted it at every opportunity and treated the fans really well. And he did his best to inspire us to play attacking football.

To sum up, Ally MacLeod was a loose cannon with a heart of gold, who lifted Aberdeen Football Club and helped us to win the Scottish League Cup. I will not forget him, nor his mad ideas. It was symbolic that during Ally's only full season in charge at Pittodrie, we were decked out in a red strip with a white stripe down the left side. This was a departure from the traditional all-red kit, but it was fitting that Aberdeen's most eccentric manager should plump for the team's most eccentric garb. Who could possibly follow?

ON THE SPOT WITH ALLY'S ARMY

Poor Ally MacLeod still gets the blame for suggesting that Scotland could win the World Cup in Argentina in 1978. You were not bound to believe him, yet most of the country seemed to agree with his prediction. It wasn't his fault, well not entirely, that supporters considered him to be the new Messiah of Scottish football. I certainly did not believe that we could win the World Cup, though a 100,000-strong contingent of the Tartan Army believed enough to turn up at Hampden and in and around Glasgow to see the squad march off on their great adventure.

I was one of the six players on stand-by for the World Cup, but Ally decided to take Gordon McQueen of Manchester United instead. Gordon was a brave defender, but he was injured and did not play in South America. If he had pulled out, I would have been there, and maybe would have been able to tell the players: 'Don't get too carried away with Ally's enthusiasm: he's always like this.' Unfortunately, I did not get the chance to issue such advice, but Martin Buchan, the Manchester United player who went to the finals, told me on his return that it had been a difficult experience. He revealed that after he arrived at the hotel in Argentina, he had approached Ally and told him that he would leave his door open, in the hope that some intruder might enter his room while he was away, and decorate the place!

Martin also informed me, without identifying the individual player, that one of the substitutes in the memorable game in which Scotland beat Holland 3-2 had been terrified that the national team would qualify for the next stage of the finals, and thanked God that we did not. 'I want to get home,' was that player's heartfelt summation of the bad trip endured by some members of the party.

5

PAID ANOTHER FIVER A WEEK!

'When a man like Billy McNeill says you are part of his plans, you pay attention'

Nowadays the appointment of a manager is a slick presentation, with an announcement rolled out on the internet and via press conferences and interviews, 24-hour telly, the lot. That certainly was not the case when Billy McNeill took over at Aberdeen Football Club. Bizarrely, I heard about who our new gaffer was over a portable radio when I was perched on the roof of a house in Roslin Street, Aberdeen, converting a loft. I nearly fell off in reacting to the news, for I had been told that the favourite to succeed Ally MacLeod was none other than Bertie Auld, who was at Partick Thistle. You read that correctly: Willie Miller, the Aberdeen captain who had lifted the Scottish League Cup with one mighty hand during the previous season, spent part of the summer of 1977 working with his mate, Jimmy Skinner, mending roofs and undertaking loft conversions. Imagine Steven Gerrard, Neil Lennon, Barry Ferguson or John Terry telling their respective managers that they would be working as joiners or in other trades during the summer to make some extra dosh. It would never happen, for the money sloshing around in football these days is so great that players only need to worry about their golf swings, when they are not obliged to train or play. They are wrapped up in figurative cotton-wool, and I very much doubt that a top-class player would be allowed to climb on to his roof to fix even his television aerial, never mind tackling redevelopment of a loft.

I had taken up the job with Jimmy because I was on a

£50-a-week basic wage and was now married to my wife Claire and we needed the cash. We qualified for win-bonuses, but obviously they were not available during the summer when games were absent from the agenda. Our season had finished in April, and most of my team-mates had gone on holiday or to visit relatives.

Working as a joiner kept me active physically, but I undertook pre-season training on my own to get ready for the first day of work under Billy McNeill. The way that Billy strode on to the training pitch that first morning made it evident that he was a man deserving of respect. However, it was also evident that, when we met, I held out more respect for him than he did for me. That observation is not meant to sound nasty, merely to stress that I had to prove to him that I deserved to retain the club captaincy. I had to prove that point to the new boss, and Billy had his doubts, with my dislike of training creating a distinct problem. He felt that, as captain, I should throw myself 100 per cent into running round the park and into the dreaded press-ups. That was never going to happen. As for after training, he was aghast that the players scattered to the four winds and did not eat together at the club. I usually ate in my digs or got stuck into pie, chips and beans at a nearby café, but Billy, quite rightly, thought it better that we should enjoy tasty food together, and thereafter a hotelier delivered a selection of sandwiches to the club at lunch-time. We sat down together over our meal and discussed all things football. It was an important, yet simple, step towards improving the eating habits of the team, and it developed camaraderie.

We were drawn to play Rangers in our first Premier League match of the season, and to observe Big Billy, a Celtic legend, walking on to the Pittodrie pitch sporting a red shirt and an Aberdeen Football Club tie created a rather strange sight before kick-off. I feared that his association with the Parkhead side might cause him problems with Aberdeen supporters, but they took to him straight away. But then we beat Rangers 3-1 in his first game as manager, and went on a notable early-season league run, which included defeating Celtic in Glasgow in the new manager's first encounter with the club for whom he had performed with such distinction.

We fared less well in other competitions, and were forced out of the Scottish League Cup and UEFA Cup by the end of October 1977. We approached the League Cup hoping to retain the trophy, and after beating Airdrie and Cowdenbeath, we came up against Rangers. The tie was played over two legs, and the Ibrox part offered one of my worst experiences in an Aberdeen jersey, for we were hammered 6-1, and I was left shell-shocked. It must have been hard for Billy to stomach, and he swore that we would beat them in the return, and beat them well. That we did, by 3-1 at Pittodrie, but it took a while for the Ibrox drubbing to be expunged from my system. In the UEFA Cup competition, we played well away against RWD Molenbeek and came away with a 0-0 draw. They may have been relatively unknown outside their home nation of Belgium, but they had made it to the UEFA Cup semi-final the previous year, only to be denied by Athletico Bilbao on the away-goals rule. I thought that we could at least match them in the return leg in Aberdeen, but they played out of their skins. They scored just after half-time, and when Drew Jarvie equalized, I thought that we could sneak another goal. We threw caution to the wind and even I joined the attack, but our strategy backfired and Molenbeek regained the lead six minutes from time to put us out of the tournament. At least we could concentrate on our league campaign and on the Scottish Cup competition, which was not due to start until February of 1978.

By the end of October, a 4-0 away win at St Mirren, who were being managed by Alex Ferguson, thrust us to the top of the league two points ahead of Dundee United, and Billy was being hailed as a Messiah by some fans. It was the kind of start that the new manager had dreamed about, but the ensuing weeks demonstrated that we had a long way to go before we could consider ourselves to be realistic title contenders. We lost at home to Hibs and away to Rangers, and could only draw at

home to Clydebank, who were bottom of the table. As I got to
know Billy McNeill, I learned that though he was strongly
competitive, he was a genuinely nice guy, and his man-management was second to none. I can still detect that compassion and
ability to articulate football matters clearly whenever I hear him
on radio or television. An example of Billy's communication
skills came when he called me aside for a private chat on the
Wednesday before a match against Dundee United at Pittodrie.
We walked round the track at a time when I was haggling with
the club over the terms of a new contract. I was keen to stay, but
I was not earning a substantial amount and was seeking a salary
that reflected my responsibilities as captain. I even reminded him
that, on the day that I had learned of his appointment as manager,
I had been up on a roof working as a part-time joiner to boost my
income. He looked me in the eye, then put an arm round my
shoulder and stuck out his chest, and presented succinctly the
reasons why I should re-sign: I was part of his plans. The fact that
he wanted me to continue to work for Aberdeen Football Club
was a big boost to my morale, as we had not previously discussed
whether he wished me to stay. When a man like Billy McNeill
says you are part of his plans, you pay attention, and by the time
we had strolled a lap of the track together, he had convinced me
to sign a new contract, though not for the big pay rise that I had
wanted. Because of Billy's power of persuasion, I agreed to
remain at Pittodrie for an extra £5 a week, which took me up to
a basic income of £55 a week. With my new contract agreed,
albeit for what seems a paltry increase these days, I could
concentrate on my playing career.

A match that took place soon after I had signed a new deal was
against Hibs. It was eight days before Christmas, and we lost 2-0,
and the reason that I recall the occasion so vividly was because
Billy had decided to try me out in midfield. He admitted later
that this had been a mistake – the experiment of playing me out
of position was not repeated by any other Aberdeen manager –
and he rapidly returned me to central defence for our next
match, which brought on league leaders Rangers. It was the

biggest match of our season to date, as we were five points behind our opponents and could not afford to fall further behind. I was back in defence alongside Willie Garner, and we did not put a foot wrong and ran out 4-0 winners, and were back in the title race. Because we had a chance of winning the league, Billy demanded extra effort and discipline from all involved, and when a few players let him down over the New Year period, he acted swiftly. His disciplinary action against Willie Garner and Bobby Glennie led to Alex McLeish, who was still in his teens, making his Aberdeen debut playing beside me in defence. We had beaten Clydebank 1-0 away on Hogmanay, and Billy had told the players that he did not mind if they indulged in a few drinks that evening, provided they did not go over the score. I am not sure of the exact circumstances, but perhaps Willie and Billy celebrated too much. Billy felt that they had overstepped the mark at a vital time of the season, and that was all that mattered. They were established players, but were dropped for the match against Dundee United on January 2, and when Alex McLeish came in for training on New Year's Day, Billy told him that he would be making his first-team debut against United. There was no way that Alex would have been included in the team if Willie Garner had not stepped out of line, and it was a brave decision by Billy to count on such a young individual for such a tough fixture. Big Eck did not let the manager down and played superbly alongside me, never allowing the United strikers to get a kick. He had bags of confidence for one making his debut, and emerged as our man of the match in the 1-0 win. Afterwards Alex was buzzing, and rightly so, and he hoped that he would get a run in the first team. Billy had other ideas; Alex was a fine player, but the boss felt that he was one for the future at that juncture. Billy had made his point to Willie Garner and Bobby Glennie by dropping them for a game, and he was canny enough to realise that with a league title there to be won, it would be better planning to include experienced men when the going got tough. That reflected no shame on young Alex, and he would make a significant break-through all in good time.

In the first months of 1978, we were playing some vibrant, attacking football, and my particular highlight came against Hibs on February 25. We might have been 3-0 up at the time, but allow me to recall that my right-foot volley into the corner of the net took me back to my days as a schoolboy striker. It went in like a bullet, and offered the goalkeeper no chance. With eight league matches left, we were lying just a point behind top-of-the-table Rangers, who were on 42. With four games remaining, we were two points in arrears, and it transpired that the destination of the title would not be ascertained until the final day of action. Our final home match, our penultimate fixture of the league campaign, brought St Mirren to the Granite City on April 22. Their manager, Alex Ferguson, was positively beaming after his team had taken a two-goal lead after just 10 minutes of action. We managed to wipe the smile off Fergie's face in the second half, when Joe Harper marked up a hat-trick, and I weighed in to give us a 4-2 win. Thus, in our final league game on April 29, we had to beat Hibernian at Easter Road, and hope that Rangers would slip up at Ibrox against Motherwell. I was confident that we could beat Hibs and felt relaxed going into the game, partly because the destination of the league title was not entirely in our hands. We performed badly, as it happened, and though we went ahead through Ian Scanlon, Arthur Duncan scored for Hibs with three minutes left to hand the title to Rangers. Our supporters had been muted for most of the second half, which drew me to conclude that Rangers must be beating Motherwell. It transpired that the Ibrox men had controlled the game, and had not been in any trouble on their way to a 2-0 victory.

The outcome came as a bit of a disappointment, but I was not too downhearted as we had the chance to gain our revenge in the Scottish Cup final the following week. An impressive run towards Hampden had seen us overcome Ayr United, St. Johnstone, Morton and Partick Thistle, and the big talking point was whether Gordon Strachan should be named in the Aberdeen line-up for the big day. Wee Gordon, who had signed in

November 1977, was just starting to make his mark, and Billy McNeill was uncertain whether to play him. In the end, the manager decided not to include Gordon, and Billy believed that constituted a mistake that might have cost us victory in the final. I don't agree. Yes, Gordon would have made a difference, but so many of us were off form on the day that even the skilful wee man would have struggled to inspire us. We just did not get going, and we were one down at half-time after Alex Mac-Donald had scored, and Derek Johnstone made it two in the second half. With barely five minutes left, we managed to make some sort of impact with a crazy goal. Steve Ritchie mis-hit a shot which looped over the head of goalkeeper Peter McCloy. Nicknamed 'The Girvan Lighthouse' because of his exceptional height, Peter was so desperate to keep the ball out of the net that he dived backwards, but missed it completely, then swung from the crossbar like a funky gibbon might do as the ball plopped into the goal in what seemed like slow-motion. This put pressure on the opposition, but it proved too little, too late. Rangers had won the domestic treble, and success in the Scottish Cup final capped a great season for them. For my part, on the coach heading away from Hampden I swore to myself that I would *never* allow a team that I was captaining to freeze on a big occasion. That was what happened against Rangers. We had let down ourselves and our supporters, and it was my responsibility on the field of play to ensure that did not happen again. It is acceptable to be beaten by a better team, but not performing to your full potential is inexcusable.

I felt especially sorry for Billy, as winning the Scottish Cup against Rangers, of all Scottish clubs, would have made a perfect ending to his first season in charge. After Hampden we were all heading our separate ways for the summer, and I said goodbye to Billy, wished him well and assured him that we would reach more cup finals and would be challenging for the Premier League again in the season to come. He agreed, and we held a most positive discussion about the future. At the time I hoped that Billy would be with us for a good few years but, as it turned out, the Scottish Cup final had been his final match in charge of Aberdeen Football Club. A few weeks on, he received an irresistible approach to return to Celtic as their manager, and the moment I heard that news, I knew that he would be leaving. Billy was a young and ambitious manager, and I like to think that it was only the lure of Celtic that took him away from Pittodrie. I had surmised that he would use the Aberdeen manager's job as a stepping-stone, but I did not think that he would be ready to take the next stride so rapidly. It was a blow to lose Billy so soon, and I was not too keen on having to prove myself all over again to yet another gaffer. Whatever my thoughts on the matter, no-one could foresee that the new incumbent would revolutionise Aberdeen Football Club, and transform the team into a major European force.

6

FERGIE'S HAIR-DRYER TREATMENT

*'His comments created a siege mentality in the dressing-room,
and Alex Ferguson knew exactly what he was doing'*

Alex Ferguson? A young manager on the up. Not another one! All the managerial changes since I had joined Aberdeen Football Club had been a real pain to live through, and it was a sobering thought that Alex was to be our third manager in just over two-and-a-half years. In saying that, Billy McNeill's successor hit the ground running. He was straight-talking and didn't suffer fools gladly, a trait that I appreciated, but some players did not. They thought that the Glaswegian was too abrasive, and the dressing-room was divided over his managerial merits. Fergie was only 35 when he took over, and I was his 23-year-old captain. It was strange to have such a young man in charge, especially when you considered that he was just two years older than our goalkeeper, Bobby Clark. I tried to break the ice at Alex's first training session by reminding him that we had come up against each other in a friendly when I was a 17-year-old striker with Peterhead, and he was with Falkirk. He had no memory of that encounter, so I was damned if I was going to flatter him by telling him I thought he had played a good game.

Now Alex had left St. Mirren under a cloud after a row with the Love Street board, and the fall-out from that seemed to bother him for much of his first season in charge, and he appeared restless. It was obvious that he would not settle until that matter had been resolved. Like Billy McNeill, Fergie was not sure if he should keep me on as captain of the club. In his eyes I was a bit slow and poor at training. I would have to show him that I was worthy of a place in his team, which was not a good start with the new man. But Teddy Scott, who had bolstered morale and kept the team together after the departures of Jimmy Bonthrone, Ally MacLeod and Billy McNeill, appreciated my talents. Teddy, who hailed from Ellon in Aberdeenshire, served as reserve team coach, kit man and as club sage. In addition, he was kitted out with an excellent football brain, knew instinctively what was best for Aberdeen Football Club, and I respected him greatly. His response to Fergie's query about my aversion to training was: 'Just you wait till Saturday at 3 o'clock to see how good Willie is.' Ah, the good old days when we kicked off at 3pm every Saturday.

As Teddy suggested, what counts is performing for 90 minutes when it matters, but the boss reflected the strongest personality of any individual that I had met in the football sphere, and as I was no shrinking violet myself, we did not hit it off immediately, professionally speaking. He had definite ideas about how he wanted his team to play, and nothing and no-one would stand in his way. For instance, after he had watched me taking part in a few bounce games at Pittodrie, he called me into his office and said that he thought I defended too deep. I took on board what he said, but Fergie did not really change the way that I operated on the park, as I recognised my strengths and my weaknesses more clearly than anybody. If I had pushed up to the halfway line on every occasion that he asked me to, we would have been struggling to win as many games as we did. And I would have been struggling for breath. I was not quick, but I read the game pretty well and defended soundly in and around the penalty-box. Being asked to push up during games happened time and time again – not just under Fergie – and I grew sick of it. Thus, it was a battle of wills to begin with between Alex Ferguson and me over how deep I should defend, and Willie Garner was dragged into the debate. Fergie maintained that the other Willie and I should push out a bit more, though he did accept that we needed more strength in the midfield to allow that to happen. Through the ensuing years, Fergie's teams were primed to attack with the defence pushing out as quickly as possible, and at Aberdeen he started to use that system employing Willie and me as his football guinea pigs. Eventually I was trusted to play my own game, partly because when he bellowed at me to push up the park I more or less ignored the orders. Because of that I was not his favourite person in the Aberdeen squad in his early days at Pittodrie. (Years later, he told me that he felt I had under-estimated myself and should have pushed out more, as I had the talent to dictate the game even more than I did. Looking back, I can see his point of view, but as a young man I was as stubborn as he was).

Because friction existed between us, I felt that I needed help to handle the new manager, and I turned for advice to Bobby Clark, who had served as captain before I was appointed by Ally MacLeod. Bobby was an elder statesman and, as noted above, only a year or two younger than Fergie, and he provided a sane and intelligent voice in the dressing-room. He urged me to remain calm, to keep playing to the best of my ability and, most importantly, not to mention to anyone that I was worried I might be stripped of the captaincy. Another factor that riled me early on was the way that Fergie constantly compared me to Jackie Copland, with whom he had worked at St. Mirren. He wanted me to play like he did. Jackie deserves high praise, as he was a great player in his day, but his name proved to be the one that I did not wish to hear emanating from Fergie's lips. Jackie was signed by Fergie when he was St Mirren's manager in November 1976, and he was looked upon as a model profes-sional. He started out at Love Street as a striker, just as I had done at Aberdeen, and ended up playing sweeper, wearing the Number 6 jersey and being appointed club captain, just as I had done at Aberdeen. Though he was 29 when he was at his peak at Love Street, Jackie played a big part in securing the first division title for St Mirren, and Fergie was right to hold him in the utmost esteem. I, too, had a lot of respect for Jackie, but the way that Alex Ferguson carped on and on about him got on my nerves. When we played in any practice game, Fergie would remark to me: 'That was a good clearance, but Jackie Copland would have found a man with that pass.' Or: 'Not bad, Willie, but Jackie Copland would have used the ball better out of defence.' I can reflect now that Fergie was using his example just to wind me up and to make me determined to raise my game. At the time, though, it drove me mad every time he mentioned *that* name. I was the Aberdeen captain, had confidence in my own ability, and I did not feel that I should be compared to a player from another club, especially one such as Jackie who, with all due respect, performed well at a lower level of senior football. I did not feel, either, that I needed to be wound up, as I was committed to Aberdeen Football Club and was fully behind Fergie as manager. My ambition was to convince him that I should remain his captain, and constant references to Jackie Copland were certainly not required to achieve that. It got to the stage that, whenever the moniker was mentioned, I would aim a dirty look at Alex Ferguson, a stare that I perfected through the years. Things got too much with the spectre of Jackie hanging over me at every practice game, so I resolved to bring matters to a head and to confront the gaffer. In a frank discussion I assured him that I was 100 per cent behind him, and did not need wound up to make me play any better. Though the boss always tends to have the last word, at least he listened to me. He did not apologise, but the name Jackie Copland did not arise again. I always thought I was the better player anyway!

It was clear that I wasn't the only player who was struggling to get used to the Ferguson methods. The manager detected some dissent in the camp, and decided to take us away for some team bonding, though it was clear from his choice of venue that it would not be fun all the way. He took us to Gordonstoun, the noted private school near Elgin, which could count the Duke of Edinburgh and the Prince of Wales among its old boys, and it was certainly no holiday camp in the country. Indeed, it was an austere place, and being there was a bit of a shock to the system for all of us. What the boss enjoyed was the fact that Gordonstoun was away from the prying eyes of the public and press, and he could get on with training in peace. He could work on set-pieces, and shout and bawl at us as much as he liked. The out-of-the-way setting allowed him to push us to the limit, and the move proved to be a Ferguson masterstroke, though it did not feel like that at the time. We were accommodated in single beds in a big hall, similar to army barracks, and if it was bad enough having to share a room with a team-mate on foreign trips, it was 100 times worse being stuck in a great hall with every other member of the Aberdeen first-team squad. It was funny for, oh, five minutes, and the basic facilities on offer sparked a revolution. I made it clear whenever I went back to Gordonstoun – which we used regularly for pre-season training, with Fergie revelling in what he described as getting back to basics – that I wanted at least to share a room, and not to be forced to kip in a hall. As captain I got full support from the rest of the lads. We did not relish dining like schoolboys and missing out on our beauty sleep because of the significant level of snoring.

But at least the introduction to Gordonstoun provided me with my first taste of cricket, an experience to remember. After donning my whites, I was ordered by Fergie to open the batting with him. I had not wielded a cricket bat in my life, and I expected to be pretty useless compared to some others in the squad. Guys who attended school in Aberdeenshire and Ayrshire, for instance, were taught cricket at school and enjoyed it. Walker McCall, Neale Cooper, John Hewitt and Bryan Gunn could play a bit, but cricket was not on the curriculum in Glasgow schools such as my alma mater, so neither Fergie nor I had a bloody clue about technique. We headed for the wicket and he made clear that he would dictate the tactics in cricket, as in football, with the declaration: 'Right, I'll shout.' Even with a limited knowledge of the game, I knew that it was usually the man who hit the ball who made the initial call to run or not to run. Fergie was having none of that. I connected with a delivery and cracked the ball what seemed a hell of a way. I don't know how I managed that, but Fergie shouted at me to run, which I was doing anyway. As I was heading to the other end of the wicket, though, he shouted:

'Stop, go back.' He had barely moved from his crease, despite shouting to me to run, and he left me high and dry. Stranded in no-man's land. Bobby Clark hit the stumps, and I was run out for a duck. The gloves came off, the bat was thrown down and I aimed a dirty look at my so-called batting partner as I traipsed back to the pavilion. My strop led to mass hilarity among the ranks, and on a clear day I can still hear them laughing at me, Fergie and all, to this day.

Another abiding memory of Gordonstoun is of big Doug Rougvie attempting a technique known as an Eskimo roll in a kayak. The object is to return the craft to an upright position after rolling it underwater for 360 degrees. Big Doug thought it sounded easy, though because he stood more than 6ft tall, I did not think that he would go near a kayak for the simple reason that he would find it a tight squeeze. On top of the size issue – the kayaks at Gordonstoun's swimming pool were designed for use by teenage laddies, not husky central defenders. Doug was not the most coordinated of blokes, but he insisted that he could pull off an Eskimo roll, despite the fact that he had not taken to a kayak previously. We all stood round the pool ready for a laugh at his expense, and observed the kayak capsizing and Doug's head vanishing beneath the water. A few seconds passed, then a shoulder appeared and the kayak rolled to the upright position, but flipped over again beneath the surface. It was clear that Doug could not bring off an Eskimo roll, and worse, could possibly drown. I led the rescue group that jumped in to get the big man above the water and out of the swimming pool. We dragged him to the side, and he sat there looking sorry for himself and for all the world like a giant, nearly-drowned rat. Doug being Doug, he was back up on his feet pretty soon, as if nothing had happened, but I doubt that he went near a kayak again.

It was during our initial visit to Gordonstoun that Fergie first told us that to be successful we must beat the Old Firm in Glasgow, and that was one of his main goals in his first season in charge. Up until that point, the general thinking within Scottish football was that the Old Firm would always rule the roost. With all major finals being played at Hampden, they enjoyed the added advantage of not having to stray far for the big matches. Alex kept telling us about teams from the past that had challenged the Old Firm: Hibs and Hearts had come to the fore in the 1950s, Dunfermline did well in the 1960s, and Kilmarnock had won the league in 1965. He said that we could do the same, and challenge the Old Firm on a regular basis. He had some fine players on the books when he arrived at Pittodrie, including Gordon Strachan, Alex McLeish and Stuart Kennedy, and preseason motivation sessions at Gordonstoun gave even the top performers more self-belief. In my case he was preaching to the converted. I had been a member of Aberdeen teams that had beaten Celtic and Rangers in Glasgow, and had lifted the Scottish League Cup in 1976-77 after we had overcome Celtic at Hampden. Inspiring that winning mentality among all individuals at the club was Fergie's main aim. He would make use of just causes to unite the players, and at Aberdeen he maintained that the media had a west coast bias, and that everyone favoured Celtic and Rangers. Merely a means of inspiring his players at Pittodrie? He believed every word that he said, and he was absolutely right, and things have not changed. Some might argue that a bias towards the Old Firm does not exist, but it is palpable, and Fergie was merely stressing the fact.

The first game that we played after returning from the initial foray to Gordonstoun was a pre-season encounter against Tottenham Hotspur. I had been looking forward to the friendly for a long time, as Argentines Osvaldo Ardiles and Ricky Villa were expected to play. Unfortunately, as they were the first South Americans to sign for Spurs, the club had problems with the relevant paperwork, and they missed the game. I doubt that they would have had much influence on the result had they been eligible, for Aberdeen were on fire and won 3-1. Bobby Clark broke a knuckle, and unfortunately was not available for our first Premier League match of the season, against Heart of Midlothian at Tynecastle on August 12, 1978, which we won 4-1. It is memorable because it coincided with Jim Leighton's Aberdeen debut, and I recall feeling sorry for Jim because he let one in after only four minutes when Eamonn Bannon scored. I was concerned that the early setback might undermine his confidence, but I need not have worried. After Hearts' goal, the flow developed into one-way traffic in the opposite direction, and we kept the ball well away from Jim, and ran out easy winners. The few times that we allowed Jim to touch the ball, he did well, and I joke with him to this day that he spent much of his Aberdeen career not doing that much, because Alex McLeish and I were adept at keeping the ball away from him.

After that match, and just before a 3-1 win over Morton at Pittodrie on August 19, Pat Stanton arrived to become Alex's number two. My working relationship with the gaffer was still in its early stages, and I thought that Pat might be more understanding and take my side on a few matters. After all, I kept reminding myself, I was club captain. Wrong yet again, for like Alex, Pat harboured doubts about my commitment to training. Pat was quiet and self-contained, while Alex was vocal and passionate, and they formed a complementary managerial team. Both were real football people, and I had great respect for them. Pat had come to Aberdeen with a fantastic reputation as a player with Hibs, Celtic and Scotland. Fergie had met him at an SFA coaching school at Largs, and they had maintained their friendship, as their philosophies on football were similar. From my point of view, Billy McNeill had been first to take a pop at my lack of interest at training, then Fergie had raised misgivings, and along came Pat to have his dig at me. By this time I had perfected my answers, employing what Teddy Scott had told Fergie: that I should be judged on my actions from 3pm on Saturday. I said that to Pat, but it did not wash. He thought that I did what was asked of me, but felt I was a bit too casual in my approach on Monday and Tuesday at training, and did not put enough into the drills. He kept telling me that, as captain, other players looked up to me, and I should be training harder than anyone. I told him I had been through all this with Fergie, but said I would explain my philosophy to him just once. Yes, I told him, I may start slowly at training on weekdays, but it was a strategy designed to make me peak on match-days. (The fact that I ended up playing for 18 years indicated that I had adopted the correct strategy). I did pride myself on the fact that I never missed training, so at least I could say that I had a certain dedication. I might not be doing much, but I did show up, and as for setting a good example, I would do that on a Saturday afternoon. Anybody could look good in training, and how often has a manager commented pre-match that his team had been brilliant in training all week, only to see them humped a few hours later? Looking good in a high-pressure situation was what mattered! My routine was preparation, training, sleeping and eating properly, and I told Pat that I was not the only person who didn't like training: Kenny Dalglish, one of the greatest players produced in Scotland, hated it. So I was in good company.

After watching a few games, Pat saw that though my attitude towards training had not altered, my performances on the field more than made up for that. As with Fergie, he seemed to accept my explanation, and did not broach the subject again. Pat was the last coach at club level to bother mentioning my lack of interest in training, though Jock Stein gave me a few stares when I worked with him at international level. Clearly the word must have got round that I wasn't for turning on the matter, and I would advise coaches to heed the views of players the world over: dull and boring training routines make participants lose interest and shut off. I certainly found that happened to me at times, and it is up to coaches to keep things fresh. If the training regimes had been interesting, I would not have moaned so much, but endless runs and gym work were distinctly *boring*.

With the boss and Pat off my back on the issue of training, I could concentrate on playing. Our fifth league game of the season, against Rangers at Ibrox on September 16, 1978, demonstrated that Alex Ferguson's mantra that we could compete with the Old Firm was getting through to us. Ibrox was being reconstructed at the time, and a surreal atmosphere surrounded the proceedings. Rangers took the lead six minutes before half-time when Alex Forsyth scored with a penalty, but we continued to believe that we could achieve a positive result, and in the final minute Dom Sullivan equalised. We were delighted to leave Ibrox with a draw, but Alex was not so happy. He took me aside, and he told me as club captain that he was heart-sick at the way the players had talked before and after the game. He had heard us discuss the need to slow the game down to try to frustrate the home crowd and make it hard for Rangers, while he believed that we should not adopt such a negative approach. We should go out and try to beat the opposition, rather than thinking that a draw away from home was the best we could achieve. The rest of the team, quite reasonably in my opinion, felt that taking a point at Ibrox was a worthwhile result, and the atmosphere in the dressing-room when we returned from our chat was reasonably upbeat, which made the manager even more angry. Fergie told us to a man that we should show more ambition, and never be happy with a draw, regardless who we were playing.

I was beginning to work out how the Ferguson mind worked. I felt that though deep down he would be happy with a draw against Rangers, he would not admit it, and wished to keep us on our toes. He used psychological tactics in such a way that he got under our skins and made us believe that we had to raise our expectations – and that we should accept nothing but a win. An indication of his influence over the team showed three matches later, on October 7, when we played Celtic at Pittodrie, and handed out a hammering. We were three goals up after 33 minutes, thanks to Stevie Archibald, Joe Harper and Drew Jarvie. Tom McAdam scored for Celtic just before half-time, but another strike from Stevie made it 4-1 at the final whistle. We experienced a topsy-turvy time with Fergie in charge during that first season, however, and things blew up a bit after a home defeat to Hearts on October 21. We were dreadful that day, and the follow-up was a whispering campaign circulating in the city that players and manager were not seeing eye to eye. We still had a lot to learn about each other, without question, and at that stage I had my doubts about whether Alex would stay as manager, as he was taking time to settle, and our results were not altogether brilliant. We were not enjoying much luck, either. For instance, we played Rangers at Pittodrie on November 18, and should have beaten them easily. Joe Harper missed a penalty, and Peter McCloy pulled off a string of great saves, a shot from Stevie Archibald being the pick of the bunch, and we had to settle for a no-scoring draw. After a comprehensive 4-1 win over Hibs, we went to play Celtic at Parkhead, and came away with a 0-0 draw. Such results showed that Alex had the ability to get us up for big matches, and that he could instill genuine confidence in his team. In contrast, we could struggle against less notable opposition, and during that first Ferguson season, we failed to achieve consistency. A fixture that I remember clearly was against his old club, St Mirren, on February 24, 1979. We had played them the previous October in Paisley, and had been beaten 2-1, and on this occasion we drew 2-2. You might think a scoring draw was a decent result, but we were two goals up through Stevie Archibald and Gordon Strachan and cruising after an hour's play. Then Frank McGarvey pulled one back by lobbing Bobby Clark, and Ian Scanlon was sent off after a clash with McGarvey, a dismissal that put us on the back foot. To make matter worse, in 70 minutes I was given my marching orders for a challenge on McGarvey, and to this day I would argue that it was one of the worst referring decisions to which I was subjected in my career. I was sent off three times during my time in football, twice for challenges on Frank McGarvey, and once for kicking Roy Aitken. That sending-off against St Mirren was the most unjust, as in my view Frank took a dive and the referee, David A Murdoch, was conned. To make matters worse, the Love Street team equalised near the end through Jackie Copland. The very same Jackie Copland that Fergie had banged on to me about in training when he first took over as Aberdeen manager! Jackie scoring to make it 2-2 was a bitter pill to swallow as I watched, with a face like thunder, from the touchline. It was a dreadful refereeing performance, in my opinion, one of the worst that I have experienced, and I could understand Fergie's fury towards the official after the match. He ended up being reported to the SFA for his outburst, but I am convinced that his criticism of Mr Murdoch was more than justified. I felt really bad about being sent off, despite the fact that it was a miscarriage of justice, as I knew that Alex was fretting going into the game, as his father had been ill for a long time. As I trudged off the field after being sent off, he was standing there on the touchline in a daze. That day, he was not the Fergie I knew. However, throwing away a two-goal lead in a football match and me being sent off were put into perspective after the final whistle when the boss was told that his dad had died. It made us all realise how unimportant events on the pitch that day had been.

He did his best to remain focused in matches immediately after his bereavement, but I could tell that the loss of his father affected him deeply, and it took him a while to get over it. In the circumstances, the boss needed all the light relief that he could come by, and he got a bit of it a few weeks later in a match against Dundee United at Pittodrie. Tussles with Jim McLean's team were never light-hearted affairs, but what remains in the memory about this one was our novel playing strip. Lots of friends were in the crowd, and they remind me that on the day Aberdeen were playing in an all-white strip – on a snow-covered pitch. They said that all they could make out was my black hair and moustache, the rest of me blending into the background thanks to the snow-white gear. I would not dare put forward as an excuse for a 2–0 defeat the fact that we couldn't tell each other apart in the snowy conditions! The other league match that sticks in the memory from that period was against Morton on a wet April evening in Greenock. We won by the single goal, scored by Neale Cooper, but the significance came with the fact that Mark McGhee made his debut. He missed two first-half sitters, but enough was on show that night to confirm that Fergie had made an astute signing. We were inconsistent until the end of the season, our chances of winning, or even challenging for the league long gone. We finished fourth with 40 points, four behind Dundee United, five behind Rangers and eight adrift of Celtic, who were crowned champions once again.

Despite the inconsistency which undermined our efforts in Alex Ferguson's first season with Aberdeen Football Club, I felt that we had a team who would do well in cup competitions. That did not prove to be the case in the European Cup-Winners' Cup, but competing did give us much-needed European experience. We made the draw despite the fact that we had lost the previous year's Scottish Cup final to Rangers. The Ibrox club had also won the league, which put them into the European Cup, so we entered via the back door, and our first tie was against Marek Dimitrov of Bulgaria on September 13, 1978, four weeks into the league season. The first leg was played in the aptly-named Stanke, an absolute tip of a city, so grim that we called it 'Stinky Stanke'. The food, the hotel and the weather were universally awful, but apart from that, it was just fine. When we took the field, the rain was pouring down, and the conditions were appropriate for synchronised swimming. To add to our discomfort, a jazz band played by the side of the pitch throughout the match, and I wanted to stick the tuba player's instrument where the sun don't shine, as he was making such a racket. Willie Garner unfortunately broke a leg in the second half, to be replaced by Doug Rougvie, but we played pretty well throughout the game, and were sitting at 2-2 after Drew Jarvie and Joe Harper had scored. However, in the last minute Jim Leighton was clearly impeded, and Ivan Petrov scored to give the Bulgarians a slender first-leg lead. By coincidence, the home team's other two goals were fashioned by his twin brother, Verislav. The second leg, two weeks later on September 27, was a nervous affair. Roared on by a crowd in excess of 21,000, we kept on the attack until John McMaster expertly chipped a ball through to Gordon Strachan, who scored superbly to take the pressure off. Drew Jarvie netted with 15 minutes left, and when Joe Harper scored to make it 3-0 with nine minutes to go, I knew that we had booked our place in the next round.

Next up were Fortuna Dusseldorf, a workmanlike but not unbeatable West German team, who were in the same position as Aberdeen in that they had lost the 1978 German Cup final, but had been admitted to the Cup-Winners' Cup as runners-up. Their best player at the time was an up-and-coming youngster, Klaus Allofs, who went on to score West Germany's winning goal against Scotland in the 1986 World Cup. In the first leg in Germany on October 18, 1978, we were simply awful. We started badly, losing a goal on 15 minutes after the ball took a deflection off John McMaster's head and into the path of a delighted opponent. We did not recover, and lost 3-0. After the match, a naive Alex McLeish urged Alex Ferguson, who was wearing a hang-dog expression, to cheer up. Sharp intakes of breath all round as we waited for the explosion, but to give the gaffer his due, he decided to go easy on young Alex, though it was evident that he was desperate to have a real go at him. Asking Fergie to cheer up after a 3-0 reverse was not the best idea in the world, though it was a product of the innocence of youth. Suffice to say that Alex McLeish never again suggested to his manager that he should cheer up in defeat.

Big Eck had started playing in central defence beside me occasionally because Willie Garner was a long-term casualty after breaking his leg against Marek Dimitrov. He was also cast in midfield, but it became apparent that McLeish and Miller had the makings of an effective centre-back partnership, despite the fact that we had suffered an off-day against Fortuna. We stayed over in Dusseldorf before flying back the next day, and were expected to go straight to bed with tails between our legs after a pathetic performance. A few players went out to a disco, though, and stumbled back to the hotel to be greeted in the foyer by an irate Fergie. He read the riot act to those involved, and made it clear they could go drinking in club time only *after* they had actually won some silverware for Aberdeen. On the flight home, the manager had another blast about our poor performance, and emphasized sternly that he would not tolerate such a poor showing in the return. For my

part, as captain I would not allow my team to perform so badly
again.

Bobby Clark, who had been out of the side with a fractured
knuckle, returned to goal at the expense of Jim Leighton for the
home leg, and it was probably the quietest 90 minutes that
Bobby had spent on the field as we laid siege to the Fortuna
Dusseldorf end. They defended well, and it took us until the
54th minute before Chic McLelland broke them down, then a
goal followed three minutes later thanks to a great effort from
Drew Jarvie. We were just one goal behind on a 3-2 aggregate
with Pittodrie on tenterhooks. The fans anticipated more, but
the Germans defended for their lives, and how they managed to
keep the score to 2-0 remains a mystery. Drew Jarvie came close
a few times, Stevie Archibald had a header brilliantly saved, and
Joe Harper hit a shot wide when it looked easier to score. It just
was not our night, and despite playing well we were out of the
Cup Winners' Cup. Although we had gone down narrowly, we
had learned a lot. West German football was on a high at the
time, their players were technically much better than we were,
and the Bundesliga was the best in Europe. To our credit,
Fortuna Dusseldorf went all the way to the final of the competition that year, losing to Barcelona by 4-3 after extra-time.
Against Fortuna I came up against quicker, more street-wise
strikers than I had met in the Scottish League, and it was an eye-
opener to note the gulf in class between some Scottish forwards
and the West German variety. I maintain that facing West
German sides prepared us for our famous match against Bayern
Munich in the quarter-finals of the Cup Winners' Cup in 1982-
83, but more of that later.

The early rounds of the Scottish League Cup were fought out
when we were also involved in the Cup-Winners' Cup, and we
acquitted ourselves well in the domestic competition. I had
begun to appreciate that Fergie's ability to get teams up for
big matches would make us a combative cup team, who would
never give up. We were granted a bye in the first round because
of our European matches, and in the second round we beat

Meadowbank Thistle easily, by 5-0 in the first leg in Edinburgh and 4-0 at Pittodrie. In the third round, an Ian Scanlon goal saw us win 1-0 away to Hamilton Academical, then we destroyed them 7-1 at Pittodrie, Joe Harper adding another a hat-trick to his superb scoring statistics. In the quarter-finals, we came up against my old boss, Ally MacLeod, who had left the Scotland job after the debacle of the 1978 World Cup to return to Ayr United. We drew 3-3 in the first leg at Somerset Park, where Steve Archibald was sent off, but beat them 3-1 at home to make it through to the last four. We were due to face Hibernian in the League Cup semi-final, which was scheduled for Dens Park on December 13, 1978. Hibs had a good team at the time, and we accepted that it would be a close encounter. More than 21,000 people packed into Dens Park that night, but the semi-final did not offer much to cheer about, at least within the 90 minutes. I felt that we dominated proceedings, but failed to take our chances, and I was getting bad vibes about the outcome. The first period of extra-time produced a stalemate, but a minute into the second period, Stuart Kennedy produced a magnificent lob to give us victory. It had not been a pretty sight, but we had scraped a victory to take us into the final against Rangers.

You will recall that we had played Rangers in the Scottish Cup final at the end of the previous season, 1977-78, and had simply frozen on the day, losing 2-1 after a below-par performance. This time I was determined that things would be different. We booked into a hotel in Largs on the west coast to prepare, but we were hit with a pre-match problem that no-one had expected. Ian Scanlon was a fine performer, but an individual who fell in and out of love with football. Unfortunately, one of the times that he fell out of love with the game came on the eve of our Scottish League Cup final, which was not good timing. He told Alex Ferguson that he simply did not want to play, as his head wasn't right. You can guess what Fergie wanted to do with his head! We ended up playing Steve Archibald, Joe Harper and Duncan Davidson upfront, with John McMaster sitting in midfield behind them. It was an attacking line-up confirming that Fergie was a promoter of positive football, a leader of men who set out to try to win rather than to frustrate the opposition.

It transpired that the final was a bad-tempered affair, with bad tackles flying in from kick-off, and bad fouls punctuating the action. Derek Johnstone went through Stevie Archibald within the first few minutes, which curtailed his involvement, though he did soldier on until the final whistle. I was relieved to note that we did not freeze in the heat of battle, and gave as good as we got. We took the lead through Duncan Davidson in 58 minutes, and I felt that we could go on and win, but we were on the receiving end of some bad luck, and some bad refereeing. With 12 minutes left, Bobby Clark signalled to the bench that he was struggling with an elbow injury, and our physio, Brian Scott, wanted to take the field to treat him. While this was going on, a shot from Alex MacDonald, which would normally have been easily covered by Bobby, took a wicked deflection off John McMaster into the net. It was a lucky goal that we did not deserve to lose. The match deteriorated into a bit of a rough-house, and a total of six players were booked. Tempers were high, and Doug Rougvie was sent off for allegedly fouling Derek Johnstone. Big Doug was raging, claiming that he had not touched Derek, and that the Rangers player had made a meal of the challenge. Either way, his dismissal was a turning point, and it was backs to the wall for us after that. Just when I thought we would take the match into extra-time, up popped defender Colin Jackson to head home the winner for Rangers. I felt that we were unfortunate, and that we could have taken the game into extra-time, at the very least, but for the inability of the referee to allow Bobby Clark to be treated before the first Rangers goal, and the unjust dismissal of Doug Rougvie. Although Fergie did not make a big deal to the media about the sending-off, it gave him something to work with when influencing his players. The Old Firm are at it again/they get all the 50-50 refereeing decisions/newspapers are biased towards Celtic and Rangers. I got used to the mantra, and agreed with it.

His comments created a siege mentality in the dressing-room, and Alex Ferguson knew exactly what he was doing.

PEGGING BACK THE OLD FIRM

Many football aficionados that I have spoken to through the years believe that the bad atmosphere during that Scottish League Cup final of 1979 set the tone for future ill-feeling in games between Aberdeen and Rangers. Certainly, I felt a keen sense of anger over the defeat and Doug Rougvie's sending-off, but I cannot accept that one game caused all the friction. In the dressing-room, Doug was so angry at Derek Johnstone that Alex Ferguson had words with the Aberdeen backroom staff, who were ordered to make him calm down. That order was not just for Doug's sake, but for the sake of Derek Johnstone. Knowing Doug, he would probably have gone looking for Derek to seek, shall we say, an explanation for his on-field behaviour. We were all irate afterwards on behalf of Doug, a big, honest chap. I had been close to the incident, and I thought that Derek Johnstone had made the most of the challenge.

Whatever the rights and wrongs of that one incident, it was that match that made all the players of Aberdeen Football Club realise that we had to be very much better than either Celtic or Rangers to have any chance of winning in Glasgow. The refs were influenced by the home crowds, which Fergie had mentioned to us time and time again, and it was something that I firmly believed. Now don't give me the nonsense that they are not swayed by the support. I'm sorry, but they were, and coming to terms with that fact was a significant pointer for us to accept. It got to the stage, after that League Cup final defeat, that we would travel down to Glasgow almost hoping against hope that the officials would turn out to be fair.

I got the name of being the refs' best friend over the years by back-chatting to them, but I was simply sticking up for my team. I respond to any accusation that I spoke too much to match officials by stating that Celtic and Rangers fans needed to work out in their own minds the reasons why Aberdeen came to beat them regularly under Alex Ferguson. The best that they could come up with was that I influenced the referees! Of course, the officials wouldn't be influenced by 50,000 home supporters shouting for decisions for the home team, would they? No, they would be persuaded by Willie Miller instead. Aye right!

Celtic and Rangers fans in that era simply could not accept that we had developed into a better team, and they had to find a scapegoat: off the park it was Alex Ferguson, on the park it was Willie Miller. But because the referees were influenced by Old Firm followers, we had to be not just better than Rangers and Celtic, but much, much better.

After that Scottish League Cup final defeat, we aimed at being capable of travelling to Glasgow carrying a bit of arrogance with our kit, for Celtic and Rangers and their fans don't like arrogance, but you needed some of that to win cup finals in Glasgow. We wanted to build things under Alex Ferguson to the point where the Old Firm would be frightened that we were heading down to play them in their home city, because they could not handle our style of play. That point was reached by Aberdeen Football Club, as the continuing story makes clear . . .

In the 1978-79 Scottish Cup competition, we started with an easy 2-0 win over Hamilton Academical, a game in which I got on to the scoresheet. After Gordon Strachan had made a telling run from deep, his shot wasn't held by the Hamilton goalkeeper, and when the ball came my way, I made no mistake. A poacher's goal. The second was the work of Joe Harper, a genuine striker, but my finish from within the six-yard box put Wee Joe to shame. In the fourth round we beat Ayr United 6-2 at Pittodrie, and their having Jim McSherry sent off made our task all the easier. For me the quarter-final match against Celtic at Pittodrie was one of the early turning points in Alex Ferguson's reign at Aberdeen. Obviously our best chance to proceed in the tournament was to beat them at Pittodrie, but we went behind to a John Doyle goal in 25 minutes. Joe Harper equalised a minute later with a great volley, but we could not nail the winner, despite our best efforts. Commentators assumed that we would be beaten in the replay at Celtic Park, but we had other ideas, and by now Fergie had given us so much self-belief that we went down to Glasgow believing that we could beat Celtic on their home turf. Well, most of the team did. Our plan was to take the game to Celtic, to keep pressing them and to try to get down the flanks. We did that in style. Some 37,000 fans were present on that March evening in 1979, and the Celtic contingent gave their team a huge welcome when they walked on to the pitch. It was the days of the Jungle, the sector of Celtic Park occupied by diehard fans, who were passionate about supporting their team, but who over-stepped the mark at times. They did so in this match, stirring up the most vile and scary atmosphere that I had played in. We were roundly booed from the minute we walked out to warm-up to the moment that we finished the game.

An incredible noise greeted the kick-off, but two minutes later the place was almost silent because Joe Harper had set up Duncan Davidson to score. Stevie Archibald put us further ahead after 13 minutes, and though Celtic clawed one back via Bobby Lennox in the 63rd minutes, we held on to record a vital victory. Part of the reason for our success was the fact that after Dom Sullivan went off injured, we brought on Alex McLeish to man-mark Tommy Burns. Alex followed Tommy everywhere, and performed with high credit in such a high-pressure game. I knew that Alex was a great defender and terrific in the air, and in that performance against Celtic he confirmed that he was also an expert in marking his man. In my comments earlier, I criticised referees for caving in to pressure from Old Firm fans, but credit is due to Ian Foote, who took charge that evening, for an outstanding, unbiased performance under incredible pressure. He kept his nerve throughout. At the end of the 90 minutes, we tried to celebrate our success in style, but Celtic fans would not allow such an open display of arrogance, and cans, bottles and other missiles rained down from the terraces. Trouble spread to the stadium tunnel, and a Celtic player – I don't know to this day who it was – took a swing at our goalkeeper Bobby Clark, and caught him smack on the chin. Bobby, a big bloke, didn't go down, but the Celtic player was obviously not man enough to hang around to take the matter further, as the culprit did not own up and disappeared into the Celtic dressing-room. I had my suspicions that the assailant was a defender, but could never prove that.

That was the victory that confirmed our self-belief that we could travel to Glasgow and beat the Old Firm on their own patch, even under great provocation. Fergie always believed that we could do it, but some of his men needed convincing. That evening meant that we were all believers from then on. Unfortunately, even the best of combinations can have their off days, and that happened to us in the Scottish Cup semi-final against Hibernian at Hampden on Wednesday, April 11. We had gone from the high of winning at Parkhead to being kicked out of the tournament in a relatively short period. Only 9,900 spectators were at Hampden, and there was a distinct lack of atmosphere. We didn't help matters by throwing away a one-goal lead. Stevie Archibald had put us ahead, but Gordon Rae and Ally MacLeod, who converted from the penalty-spot just before half-time, gave Hibs the win. It was the most disappointing match in which I had featured during the first Ferguson season.

My relationship with Fergie, which had been improving slowly, changed completely after a match against Partick Thistle at Firhill that April. By dint of his tough character, Alex Ferguson was a difficult man to get to know, and among the reasons we did not bond immediately was the simple fact that he was the manager and I was the club captain, who had been appointed by the previous boss, Ally MacLeod. We were not too sure how to take each other, and despite overcoming the demands to play like Jackie Copland and misgivings over my attitude to training, a tension between us was still evident until the match against Thistle. We had been playing five at the back, and in my opinion the system wasn't working. At half-time I told the gaffer that we had to switch tactics, or we would end up losing. Mouthing off was a sign of my frustration, as I felt that I was not on my best form, and the defence was struggling to deal with the Thistle attack, which was led by Jim Melrose. At half-time the scene was just like a pantomime. Alex told me to shut up, I told him I would not. He told me to shut up again, I told him that I wouldn't once more, and so on it went. A red rag to a bull! Fergie raged at me, and I can't blame him. I had taken him on verbally in the dressing-room in front of the team, and criticised his tactics. He had every right to be mad at me, but I don't regret the outburst. As club captain I had to get my views across – I was the manager out on the pitch once the whistle had signalled the kick-off. Fergie didn't like my outburst, and I suppose there could be only one winner, and I actually feared that my Aberdeen career would be over. Instead, the opposite happened. That row was a defining moment in our professional relationship, and it was as if we knew that we could push each other to a certain limit, and no further. I got away with my outburst because I had Fergie's respect. That was the key. The fact that he did not drop me from the team suggests that he recognised my worth in standing up to him. And there are times in life when you *must* stand up for what you believe.

Although I did not criticize his tactics again after the confrontation at Partick Thistle, we had a good old staring match soon after, this time at Pittodrie. I had come in after a game played in the rain, and I was soaking. We did not lose, but he was not happy with the team's performance. As was his wont, he started to criticise the team one by one, starting with those nearest to the dressing-room door. I changed next to the showers, so I knew that I would be last in line for a bollocking. It seemed as if it would take him 20 minutes at least to get along to me as he shouted at each man in turn. His debriefing had lasted for 10 minutes when I stood up and said: 'Gaffer, I'm freezing. I'm going for a bath, and if you want me, I'll speak to you in there.' As I walked towards the ablutions, the dressing-room fell silent, the boss stopped his rant, and told them all to follow me into the bath. I didn't have too many head-to-heads with Fergie apart from these incidents, maybe because there was a mutual respect, and maybe because he knew that I could be trusted and was completely on his side. I think he knew that if he had given me the hairdryer treatment, he would have got the hairdryer treatment back. That was not bravado on my part or Alex backing down. It just showed that he was a shrewd judge of character. He knew the people to shout at, the people to leave alone and the people to put an arm around.

TURNING ON THE VERBAL HAIRDRYER

The hairdryer treatment can be defined succinctly as a nose-to-nose confrontation between Alex Ferguson and a first-team player, usually at the end of a match, sometimes at half-time. We would all be seated, and I could tell by the dark look when he entered the dressing-room whether or not he was on the warpath. He would select his victim, and the rest of us would prepare for the action, just like on the film set for a horror movie. He would walk up to his chosen unfortunate, look straight into the poor guy's eyes, then let fly. It would be an absolute blasting, and hairdryer treatment was a perfect description.

Fergie might have released a verbal volley right into the countenance of the player involved, but it was controlled aggression. I don't recall getting the treatment, and other senior players also tended to escape his wrath. Gordon Strachan, Mark McGhee and Jim Leighton may have been selected in their early days at Aberdeen Football Club, but they tended to chirp back. Mostly it was younger players that the gaffer wanted on keep on their toes who were his targets, and a lot of the dressings-down were for effect, to show everyone present in the dressing-room who was boss. As if we didn't know. The hairdryer treatment may have involved only one cringing character at a time, but the ripple effect guaranteed that the rest of the team got the message.

Alex McLeish and I changed side by side in the dressing-room, and when Fergie started, we would look at each other . . . and sigh. But we knew to keep out of the way when he was in full flow, which was never a pretty sight.

7

WE ARE THE CHAMPIONS!

'Eighteen days in April changed our season, and the nation's attitude towards Aberdeen Football Club'

It takes a good team to win domestic cup competitions and a great one to lift league titles, and Alex Ferguson considered that his Aberdeen team were great, rather than good. I did not totally share his optimism that we would win the championship in 1979-80. A great side? I thought we were a bit too inexperienced to be talking about winning titles. It was the manager's second season in charge, and we were far from being the finished product. We could string together some excellent results, but we needed to be more consistent, a quality we had striven for in the past. With Fergie at the helm, though, anything was possible. For the first time in my career, however, I could not shake off a niggling knee injury during pre-season, which meant missing the first league game against Partick Thistle. I was kind of glad that I was not included in the line-up, for just before the final whistle Alex McLeish handled in the penalty-box, and Colin McAdam scored the winner from the spot for the Jags. Afterwards Fergie didn't go off the deep end, as I thought he would. He was pretty calm, and when I arrived back in Aberdeen I realised why. I picked up the *Green Final*, the *Aberdeen Evening Express* sports paper, and the boss was quoted as saying that he thought we would have a very good season. He stopped short of predicting that we would win the league, but I knew that he thought we could achieve that.

I returned to the ranks for our next match against Hibs, which we won 3-0, and victories followed over Dundee United,

Morton and Rangers. The manager's bold prediction about a successful season may not have been far-fetched then, but just as we were riding along on the crest of a wave, we put in a dreadful performance against Celtic at Pittodrie. Tommy Burns was sent off for a bad challenge on Gordon Strachan, but even short-handed they managed to beat us 2-1. The boss was furious, and had a real go at us after the match. We responded positively, and put together another winning run. In mid-November Joe Harper was injured, and it looked as if he would be out for the rest of the season. I spoke to Fergie, but he was not too perturbed because he felt that Joe was past his best, and that we had better strikers at the club, such as Steve Archibald and Mark McGhee. In the final fixture before Christmas 1979, we beat St. Mirren 2-0, and though the match itself was not remarkable, it was an important day because John Hewitt made his debut for Aberdeen Football Club, and he went on to fulfil a significant role for us. After the 16th game of the season, we were fourth in the Scottish Premier League, which put us six points behind leaders Celtic with a game in hand. We had played well up to that point, but Celtic looked a solid outfit, and would be difficult to catch. In our third game of the New Year, we met them at Pittodrie and drew 0-0, which was a missed opportunity. That meant the gap between the teams had grown to 10 points, though we had completed three fewer fixtures. I knew it would be a big ask to make up the points, but on the other hand, being so far behind the Glasgow side meant pressure on us was less, while they were expected to remain at the top. Fergie drove us on with dogged determination, and slowly but surely we started to close the gap. Some people were now talking us up as championship contenders, and after we beat Dundee 3-0 win at Pittodrie on March 19, we were right back in the picture. 'They are getting worried,' Fergie said to me after the match, and he was absolutely right.

Eighteen days in April changed our season, and the nation's attitude towards Aberdeen Football Club. We were due to play Celtic at Parkhead twice in the league during that period. First against second with the stakes extremely high: two games that have gone down in Aberdeen folklore. After all, not many teams head for Parkhead and beat Celtic once, let alone twice. The first meeting, with nine games of the season left, took place on April 5. We simply had to win to have any chance of catching them, and we started superbly well and took the lead through Drew Jarvie, who was set up by Mark McGhee. Johnny Doyle equalised before Mark put us ahead again, but we still had more than an hour to hold out. Roared on by the vast majority of a 40,000 crowd, Celtic laid siege to our goal, but big Alex McLeish played a blinder in defence, and we kept them at bay. I thought we were about to emerge with a vital victory, but Bobby Clark, who had been performing heroics in goal all afternoon, brought down Frank McGarvey in the penalty-box. Bobby Lennox was one of the most experienced Celtic men, and you would always fancy him scoring, but Bobby, clearly feeling guilty about giving away the penalty, made amends with a magnificent save. Not for the first time. I was the first to pat him on the back, and the first to shout at everybody else to remind them that we were 2-1 up with the league title at stake. 'Concentrate!' I hollered, and by God, they did. We held on to inflict Celtic's first home defeat of their league campaign, and to secure a result that knocked the stuffing out of them.

A 2-1 win over Dundee the following week put us three points behind Celtic with seven games to go, and we now had a superb chance of lifting the championship. Fans pored over the record books to check when Aberdeen had last won the title: it was in 1955, which was a hell of a long time ago for such a proud club. We endured a few hiccups in the run-in, one of the worst performances coming against Hibs on a windy April evening. They had the late, great George Best in their line-up, and I was facing him for the first time in my career. Playing against such a world-class footballer should have been a thrill, but the experience proved to be most disappointing because George was well past his best, a shadow of his former brilliant self. Indeed, it was sad to witness him being unable to replicate the skills that had made him one of the most engaging characters to grace a football field, and he contributed little to Hibs' efforts, apart from being booked. We struggled to break them down, though, and Gordon Rae broke away to put the Easter Road side ahead in 66 minutes. After that they shut up shop. They were trying to avoid relegation, but I felt that any team that included George Best should not be resorting to passing the ball back to the goalkeeper at every possible opportunity with more than 20 minutes of a match left to go. Best joined in the negative tactics, and my abiding memory is of him passing the ball back to goalkeeper Jim McArthur from the half-way line, twice, to try to preserve the slender lead. Justice was done when we grabbed an equaliser through Andy Watson with 10 minutes left, but the 1-1 draw came as a distinct body-blow to our championship hopes.

I was left fuming, partly because we should have taken all the points, and partly because I thought the fans had been cheated by Best's poor performance. To his evident surprise, I had a go at him in the tunnel as we trooped off, for playing so negatively. We had a crowd of 16,000 at Pittodrie that day, 4,000 more than in our previous home game against Dundee, and I'm sure that most of the added support had come to enjoy a glimpse of the George Best magic. Most disappointing, and all rather sad that the spell had vanished forever. I still respect him as a brilliant player, but he was well past his sell-by date while in Scotland, and his performance that evening made me vow not to play beyond my time. Once I felt that I could not play to the best of my ability, I would retire immediately.

Although we were dropping points, Celtic were starting to feel the inevitable build-up of tension too, and they were faltering badly. On the day that we overcame Kilmarnock 3-1 at Rugby Park, we were delighted to hear that Celtic had lost to Dundee, by a margin of 5-1. I have reminders of our match against Killie, thanks to the tabloid headlines that highlighted a predicament which faced me in the second half. I had given away an early penalty, from which Kilmarnock scored, and this had cancelled out a strike from the spot by Gordon Strachan. We got our act together, and Mark McGhee and Stevie Archibald made it 3-1 by half-time, but as play progressed I developed a thigh strain, which was most uncomfortable. Alex Ferguson noted that I was in a bit of trouble, and inquired whether I wanted to come off, as he felt that matters were under control and wanted to keep me fit for later challenges. I was so focused on beating Kilmarnock, that I decided to soldier on, and I managed to get through to the final whistle without aggravating my injury, though I finished with heavy bandaging over my thigh. The tabloids described me as 'Captain Courageous', which led to me being the target of much ribbing from my team-mates. The fact that I did not want to leave the field demonstrated my commitment to the cause, and any man who represented Aberdeen Football Club that season would have followed my example. Such was the respect for Fergie that had been instilled in us during his time in charge, that any combatant would have soldiered on for our field-marshal, regardless of injury.

Next came the second episode of our April double-header against Celtic. Showdown time! Some observers believe that this was the clash that signalled the dawn of the Ferguson revolution at Aberdeen. It was the fifth match from the end of the season, we were level on points with Celtic, and Alex had drummed into us once again the fact that we had nothing to fear from the Glasgow team. He stressed to us, not that we needed reminding, that we had beaten Celtic on April 5, and we could better them again in Glasgow. The fixture was set down for a Wednesday evening in April, and on the coach journey to Glasgow, Fergie referred constantly to morning newspaper articles that claimed we stood no chance at Fortress Parkhead. The headlines maintained that Celtic could not possibly be beaten on familiar territory by the same team within 18 days. Fergie reiterated that we could stick the words right down the throats of those biased, west-coast journalists, enter Celtic Park with our heads held high, and leave victorious. He forecast that if we took an early lead, the home supporters would become restless, and we could take advantage and go on to win the game.

Doug Rougvie certainly took to heart Fergie's advice about not being scared of Celtic, or their frantic followers. While the rest of us warmed up together in front of the ranks of Aberdeen supporters, Big Doug exercised facing the notorious Jungle, which housed the most hostile Celtic fans. They shouted all sorts of obscenities, but Doug carried on with his routine as if they did not exist. When we returned to the dressing-room, Fergie delivered an epic team talk, which left me in no doubt that we were a better team than Celtic, and that we could succeed again in this daunting setting. I was really fired up as we gathered in the tunnel, and was convinced that we had the ability to win the match and the Premier League title. We also had Gordon Strachan on our side, and I felt that his magical contributions could tilt the balance in our favour. He had been performing magnificently in the league run-in, and seemed to relish the high-pressure matches. It was no surprise that on the evening the wee man was a revelation. We scored through Stevie Archibald after just nine minutes, the script that Fergie had set down, but we conceded a goal two minutes later via a George McCluskey penalty. We were then awarded a penalty, for which Gordon was handed the responsibility to put us back into the lead. I would have bet my last tattered pound note that he would have scored from the spot, but Peter Latchford pulled off a fine save. When some footballers miss penalties in vital matches, heads go down and they hide for the rest of the proceedings. Absolutely no chance of such an outcome with Gordon Strachan on the rampage. The penalty failure simply made him angry with himself, and he went on to cover every blade of grass as he turned in a top-class performance. Just on the stroke of half-time, Mark McGhee put us deservedly ahead as we had been dominant up to that point. It was fitting, as a follow-up, that Wee Gordon scored the decisive third goal, as he had been our man of the match. Victory thrust us to the top of the table above Celtic on goal difference. Each team had accumulated 42 points with four league games left to contest.

It is no exaggeration to proclaim that Aberdeen beating Celtic twice at Parkhead within 18 days sent shock waves through Scottish football. We were caught in the spotlight. Our next match was against St Mirren, who were third in the league and enjoying an outstanding season, but the tumultuous roar that greeted me from a 20,000-strong Pittodrie crowd, as I led the team out, proved that our followers believed we could lift the title. Their backing spurred us on, and our nerves were calmed after Ian Scanlon and Doug Rougvie scored to give us a 2-0 half-time lead. The second half was a formality, we had another victory under our belts, and were now three games away from the Scottish Premier League Championship. Dundee United, Hibs and Partick Thistle stood in our way. Dundee United at Tannadice proved a tough proposition, as they had not lost a goal in almost 16 hours of league football. It took a magnificent, 30-yard shot into the corner of the net from Gordon Strachan to give us the lead, and while John Holt equalised for the Tangerines, that single point maintained our advantage over Celtic. We now had to aim to overcome Hibs at Easter Road, and hope that the feisty St Mirren would hold Celtic to a draw in Paisley. If that happened, we would be champions.

The build-up to the match in sunny Leith was incredible, and Fergie did his best to relieve the pressure and to deter reporters who camped outside Pittodrie. They wanted to ask us the same old question: did we think we would win the league? What a daft question as we all *knew* we were going to win the league. I certainly knew that, under Alex Ferguson, Aberdeen Football Club could beat anyone, anytime, anywhere. As captain I felt a responsibility to ensure that the tension was dispersed for younger team-mates, so that they could concentrate on the forthcoming game. Hibs were heading for relegation that season, so it was fortuitous that we were facing the worst team in the league, and we also knew that our opponents were introducing to the fray a young goalkeeper, Dave Huggins, as regular Jim McArthur had been ruled out with a hamstring injury. The game proved a stroll for us. Steve Archibald and Andy Watson put us two up by half-time, and a double from Ian Scanlon and one from Mark

McGhee made it 5-0. As we were doing the business on the pitch, our travelling support had their ears pinned to radios broadcasting the commentary on how Celtic were faring at Love Street. They wanted the Glasgow team at least to drop a point, which would hand us the championship. In the second half, when we were cruising to victory, I was shouting across to them for confirmation of the score. A groan went up ten minutes from time, and I thought that Celtic must have put one in. A roar so soon afterwards confused me, and my first thoughts were that Celtic had been awarded a penalty, and had missed it. As it turned out, Celtic *had* been granted a penalty by the referee, but after consulting his linesman, he had overturned his own decision. What a let-off. It remained 0-0 in Paisley when our match finished, and after an uncertain interlude, our fans erupted in celebration. The Celtic game had finished 0-0, Aberdeen were Scottish Premier League Champions, and I felt a sense of wondrous achievement. We celebrated on the pitch, chanting 'Here we go, here we go,' and thoroughly enjoyed our moments of glory. The boss was jumping all over the place, hugging anyone who would accept his embrace, but I was shedding tears of joy with most of the senior players and heading back to the dressing-room to be interviewed by Scottish Television's Arthur Montford. He was the likeable presenter of the long-running programme *Scotsport,* and I presented my views on our title win as the champagne flowed. Arthur moved on for the views of Alex McLeish, who claimed that he was speechless, but proceeded to talk for ten minutes about our victory. Our Alex was never a shrinking violet.

I was particularly pleased that Bobby Clark had been in action between the goalposts when we clinched the championship. He and I had each played 35 league matches that season, and I must say that he was one of the greatest professional footballers that I was honoured to have as a colleague during my career. No-one deserved a league-winners' medal more than Bobby, who had preached to me that anything was possible, from my very first experiences at Aberdeen Football Club. The fact we that had triumphed in the league paid due tribute to his sermonizing, and his goalkeeping skills.

The coach trip back up to Aberdeen was great fun. We were singing songs, and even Stuart Kennedy, who was not a big drinker, was gulping down the bubbly. However, we did not gain possession of the Premier League trophy until the season had ended, officially. The SFA did not convey the silverware to the Easter Road fixture, and the basic principles of arithmetic dictated that it was still possible for Celtic to overhaul us – if Partick Thistle were to beat us by 10 clear goals at Firhill in the final league game. In the event, we drew 1-1 and ended up with 48 points, one more than Celtic, and I received the championship trophy from my former secondary school teacher, David Letham, who was involved with Queen's Park and was a leading light in the SFA.

Winning the championship had demonstrated our ability to play consistently, and the achievement was all the more admirable considering that we had to get our act together after mixed performances in cup competitions that season. We had beaten Arbroath, Meadowbank Thistle and Rangers over two legs to reach a Scottish League Cup quarter-final against Celtic. In the first leg, a 3-2 win at Pittodrie, Steve Archibald put together a hat-trick by scoring one goal with his head, one with his right foot and the other with his left. Thankfully, newspaper headline-writers concentrated on Steve's variety act rather than my stint as a stripper as I was reduced to my underpants on the park after I had ripped my shorts. More than 24,000 were present that night to witness my embarrassment, but my underpants were *clean,* honest. In the return leg at Parkhead, we won 1-0 thanks to a goal from Mark McGhee, and I kept shorts, and underpants, on. We beat Morton in the semi-final 2-1 thanks to a goal from Mark and another from the penalty spot by Gordon Strachan to set up a final against Dundee United. They had come to the final by a relatively easy path, and had not been drawn against a Premier League team on the way. It's just a shame that it was such a poor final, as it was the first time in 16 years that neither of the Old Firm sides had featured. It finished 0-0, and the closest we got to breaking the stalemate was when a header from Willie Garner rolled along the Dundee United goal-line before stopping in the mud and being cleared by Paul Hegarty. The replay at Dens Park was a disaster. To start with, I led the team out to the wrong end, and we found ourselves warming up in front of United supporters rather than our own. I had not done that before, neither did it happen again. The pitch was heavy and didn't suit our passing style of play, and Alex Ferguson confided after the game that maybe he should have forgotten his principles, and ordered us to play the long-ball game. Whatever the reasons, we were well beaten, a double from Willie Pettigrew plus one from Paul Sturrock sending the Scottish League Cup to Tannadice.

Our Scottish Cup campaign ended with a semi-final defeat to Rangers, but it made for an interesting tournament from my perspective. On the day of our first cup-tie against Arbroath, newspapers carried stories that Bristol City were about to make a bid for me. They were struggling near the foot of the English first division, and it was made known that they were interested in taking me south. No official bid came in, but I knew that some informal contact had taken place, and almost certainly I would have turned them down. They were a worthwhile side then despite their placing in the league, and they included a sizeable contingent of Scots exiles in their ranks. I had been on trial with them when I was 16 and had found Bristol to be a pleasant city, but in the long run my heart remained at Aberdeen. With the possibility of moving removed from my horizon, I went back to enjoying my football on the park, and that showed in our fourth-round match against Airdrie at Pittodrie. We won 8-0, and if I say so myself, I scored the goal of the game. Gordon Strachan provided the cross for me to make contact with the ball by scissors-kick for a spectacular goal, especially coming from a defender. I entered the semi-final versus Rangers convinced that we could win, as we had played them six times that season and had yet to lose. Unfortunately, it turned out to be lucky seven for them, a goal 15 minutes from time by Derek Johnstone enough to see them through.

Our involvement in the UEFA Cup competition that season ended with first-round defeat by Eintracht Frankfurt, which was no disgrace, as they could call on six West German internationalists, such as Bernd Holzenbein and Jurgen Grabowski, who had experienced victory in the World Cup finals of 1974. I had to laugh at the name of their South Korean striker, who scored in the 1-1 draw in the first leg at Pittodrie: Cha Bum Kun was a player of quality. Eintracht won the second leg in West Germany 1-0 through a goal from Bernd Holzenbein, and Cha Bum Kun hit the bar in another outstanding performance. He was the only player that I observed beating Stuart Kennedy for pace, though I doubt that Stuart would admit that.

In all, cup disappointments were far outweighed by finishing season 1979-80 as Scottish Premier League champions, but one championship would never be enough for Alex Ferguson. He called us together before the summer break, and emphasised that he expected us to be sharp and alert and ready for pre-season training. He assured us that he had been proud of our efforts, but felt that we could enjoy even greater success. I was not about to argue.

8

TAKEN APART BY LIVERPOOL'S GREATS

'Next person I hear laughing gets fined £10'

My dream of playing in the European Cup was about to come true. Winning the Scottish Premier League had presented me with the significant honour of being the first captain of Aberdeen Football Club to take his team into Europe's most prestigious tournament. In stating that proud fact, I should not have been the first skipper to do so, if justice had prevailed a quarter of a century before. Aberdeen won the league championship in 1954-55, which by rights should have guaranteed their passage into the first European Cup competition, which was due to be held the following season. Dave Halliday, the Aberdeen manager at the time, was keen that his club should participate, but it was invitation-only as no criteria had been drawn up for entry. Thus Harry Swan, chairman of Hibernian who also chaired the SFA, put his team forward for the tournament rather than Aberdeen. Hibs fans might argue that their club had been playing friendlies in Europe for years up to that time and that, unlike Aberdeen's ground, Easter Road was equipped with floodlights, and thus the team deserved a place in the European Cup. But as league champions, Aberdeen should have gone without a doubt, and should have received the kudos for being the first Scottish team to take part. Not fair!.

When I returned to Pittodrie for pre-season training, I tried to put thoughts of playing in the European Cup to the back of my mind. With difficulty. The entire north-east of Scotland was looking forward to our first participation: we were in with the big boys now, and I was adamant we would not let anyone

down. Appearing in the European Cup was the ultimate accolade, but as I tuned into the radio in the Pittodrie dressing-room,
I was not that impressed when I heard that we were due to play
Austria Memphis. They were a competent side, but this was no
glamour tie. It was a moment to savour, nonetheless, a piece of
football history, and when I ran out on to the Pittodrie turf to
face the Austrians on Wednesday, September 17, 1980 in front of
20,000 expectant fans, I was tingling with anticipation. Alex
Ferguson had briefed us in his usual thorough fashion and told us
to be patient, as our opponents had a reputation for being
difficult to break down and fast to counter-attack. We went
into the lead on the half-hour mark through Mark McGhee, but
Memphis started to play, and had their chances. Walter Schach-
ner was their danger man, but luckily for us his shooting boots
had been left back home, and he missed a couple of gilt-edged
chances. A single-goal lead was insufficient to take to Austria and
feel confident, but I had a hunch we could defend well and
frustrate them in the return leg. Their stadium held 37,000
people that night, most of them clearly expecting an easy home
victory, but by the end they were booing the home team. We
thoroughly deserved to travel home with a 0-0 draw, and our
performance in Austria proved that we were fit to defend well
under any circumstances. It was important to have one European
Cup victory in the locker, as the going would get much tougher
as the competition progressed, and the identity of our second-
round opponents made that abundantly clear.

Liverpool were the leading side in Europe in that era, no
question, and perhaps one of the greatest teams created in the
history of British football. We would go into the tie as overwhelming underdogs, which was fair enough, for they had Ray
Clemence in goal and other men of rare quality in Alan Hansen,
Kenny Dalglish, Graeme Souness and Phil Thompson. The
Anfield club had won the European Cup in 1977 and '78, were
world-beaters on their day, and Aberdeen would have to be at
the top of their game to have any chance of success. Newspapers
lapped up the notion of *'The Battle of Britain'* in pre-match

publicity with Liverpool promoted as firm favourites to shoot us down, and immediately after the first leg kicked off at Pittodrie on Wednesday October 22, 1980 before a packed house, the gulf in class became all too evident. We made a dreadful start, and went a goal down within five minutes when Craig Johnson found Terry McDermott, who managed to squeeze the ball past goalkeeper Jim Leighton from an acute angle. John McMaster was then badly fouled by Ray Kennedy, and forced to leave the field injured, which disrupted our tactics. The foul resulted from one of the worst challenges I had witnessed, and John missed the rest of the season, but we did manage to limit the score-line to 1-0, which frankly flattered us. Liverpool had played superbly well, and our fortunes did not improve in the second leg on Guy Fawkes Night, when the only fireworks burst forth from our opponents, and we were torn apart. Their opening goal came when I sliced a corner kick into my own net to give them the lead seven minutes before half-time, and at the break we were all a bit deflated until Drew Jarvie, without a hint of irony, declared: 'Right lads, three quick goals, and we are back into this game.' I'm ever the optimist in the business of football, but I could not follow that outrageous argument. The fact that Drew thought we could get back into the game was an indication of his positive attitude, but our Anfield dream died pretty quickly for Phil Neal, Kenny Dalglish and Alan Hansen completed the scoring to put us out of the European Cup. We had hardly kicked a ball over the two legs, and were outclassed. Totally. At the time we made all the right noises about being able to bounce back, but it came as a fundamental blow to our collective confidence. The boss had influenced us to think that we could beat anybody on our day, but the sad truth was that Liverpool were streets ahead. They passed the ball better, and upfront took the chances that came their way. We had a *lot more* work to do before Aberdeen Football Club would be treated seriously on the European stage.

The boss, of course, took it as a personal insult that his team had been beaten so badly, and on the coach bringing us home from Merseyside, his face was like thunder. We sat ever so quietly at the back of the bus, realizing that even chatting amongst ourselves would send him into a fury. A few players fell asleep eventually, and we thought that Fergie would have nodded off as well, so some of us started chatting, with the odd joke being thrown in by big Alex McLeish trying to lift the gloom. When Fergie heard laughter, he roared: 'Anybody who can talk after a display like that has no place in my team. Next person I hear laughing gets fined £10.' Guess what? We did not open our mouths all the way back to Pittodrie. But then I maintain to this day that no set of opponents could have lived with that Liverpool team, and our defeat should be placed in an appropriate context. In all our away matches in domestic competitions in that season of 1980-81, we did not lose more than one goal, which added up to an enviable record. Thus Liverpool's achievement in putting four goals past us at Anfield was quite superb.

As well as being dumped out of the European Cup before Christmas, our interest in the Scottish League Cup ended with defeat by Dundee in a quarter-final replay. The only highlight in the latter competition was standing gawping on the pitch against Berwick Rangers on August 30, 1980 when our goalkeeper, Mark de Clerck, drop-kicked a clearance from his penalty-box . . . and the ball came to rest in the opposition goal. I recall that the pitch was so hard that I was wearing Adidas Samba training shoes, and I followed Mark's rocket soaring over my head, the ball bouncing just outside Berwick Rangers' box and clearing the unfortunate goalkeeper, who was off his line, and landing in his net. Mark set off on a lap of honour when he realized, with amazement, that he had scored, and we gave chase in congratulatory mode. For the record, we returned north celebrating a 4-0 success after Stuart Kennedy, Gordon Strachan and John Hewitt also scored, but Mark's sensational goal is the one that will always be remembered. When he came into the team, I teased Jim Leighton that he should try to score from a kick-out. It soon became evident that he could hardly reach the halfway line with his efforts, let alone score at the other end, and Mark de Clerck's example was ammunition for endless wind-ups, which Jim took well.

We also failed to make a big impression in the Scottish Cup, going out in the fourth round to Morton, but obviously our main aim was to defend our Scottish Premier League title, but we blew hot and cold during what turned out to be an indifferent season. Things started well with an away win over St Mirren, and Alex Ferguson's face was a picture of satisfaction at the end, as it was the first win that he had secured at Love Street since ending his employment there. Fergie's assistant, Pat Stanton, left soon afterwards to become manager of Cowdenbeath, and a special character named Archie Knox joined Aberdeen Football Club. Archie shared Alex's passion for the game, was an excellent coach and a tough taskmaster, and he never let up. He appreciated hard work, and if you stepped out of line, you faced retribution. It was a nightmare for me to begin with, for when Archie turned up at morning training, he was so loud and full of life that he drove me daft. Here was me not looking forward to training in the first place, and Archie Knox looming large in the dressing-room full of vim and ready to go, his big voice booming with enthusiasm. I complained that his bark was too painful for me to deal with first thing in the morning, and pleaded with him to allow me to retreat into a wee corner to get changed for training as far away from him as possible. He just laughed, and the noise remained at sergeant-major pitch. Even when Archie was angry, it was funny. He would throw down his tammy, and storm off in the huff when things weren't going his way. Fergie and Archie were cut from the same cloth, and it was hard-wearing stuff, but I did not have a run-in with the latter in all the years that he and I worked together. Maybe that was because Fergie was so dominant and dealt with the flak. Among my fond memories of Archie was his stunned reaction when I informed him that I had originally operated as a striker, for he claimed that I was far too slow. Soon after he joined the coaching staff, however, I scored with a 25-yard rocket, which put us ahead against Morton on September 6, 1980. We won 6-0, and my biggest pat on the back at the final whistle was delivered by Archie.

Though our form on the pitch was indifferent, our fighting

spirit was not in question. For instance, we had fallen behind 2-0 down at half-time against Celtic at Pittodrie on September 27, and were in receipt of a fearsome Ferguson rollicking at half-time. He made it clear that we were letting ourselves down, but we were good enough to go back out and retrieve the game. We did just that, and though it took an own goal from Tom McAdam to set us on our way, a strike from Mark McGhee gave us a deserved 2-2 result. We could dig deep when necessary, and one of our best players from that season was Walker McCall, one of the first Scots to play as a footballer in the United States. He had left Aberdeen to join the Atlanta Chiefs, and on his return to Pittodrie on November 1, he hit a hat-trick in a 4-1 win over Airdrie. In his next match against Celtic at Parkhead on November 8, he performed with brilliance and scored two goals to give us a 2-0 win. Unfortunately, few remember Walker's exploits, because they came on a day that a crazy Celtic fan ran on to the pitch to attack Gordon Strachan. The wee man was playing exceptionally well, and one can but speculate that the culprit was feeling frustrated, and thought he would try to 'get' him. I'll never forget Gordon's surprised look as he spotted the chap running towards him, followed by a couple of policemen. I feared the worst and we all looked on in horror, apart from Doug Rougvie, who was off like a shot to help out. As it happened, the police officers apprehended the invader before he could molest Gordon, and before Big Doug had a chance to intervene. I remember Celtic's Danny McGrain noticing the fan closing in and going to aid Gordon, which came over as a fine gesture from an opponent. But then Danny is a true gentleman, and rendering assistance was in keeping with his true character. After the unfortunate incident, we offered Wee Gordon some good-natured ribbing about what might have happened if the Celtic fan had got up close. Would he have kept running away or stood his ground? Knowing Gordon's gift of the gab, he would probably have talked his way out of the predicament.

A few weeks later, it was my turn to be at the centre of dressing-room taunts. Colleagues had reason to wind me up –

because I scored four own-goals within five weeks, a record that
was most unwelcome. As reported earlier, I had leaked an own-
goal against Liverpool in the European Cup tie at Anfield, which
was embarrassing enough, but I hit a purple patch for howlers in
league appearances. Poor Jim Leighton was on duty in goals on
each occasion, and it was a supreme test of our friendship when
he had to pick the ball out of the net so many times after it had
been diverted there by me. My first own-goal in the league came
against St Mirren at Pittodrie on October 18, 1980. It was 1-1
when Frank McDougall collided with Jim Leighton and me. I
don't know to this day what Frank, a striker, was doing away
back in his own penalty-box, but the ball rebounded off my leg,
and trickled into the net. Some newspaper accounts awarded the
own-goal to Frank, but I admit to the last touch. Thankfully,
Mark McGhee bailed me out and scored twice, and John
McMaster had been on target earlier, so we emerged with a
3-2 victory. Own-goal Number 2 in the league came against
Airdrie on November 1, but we were 4-0 up at the time thanks
to Walker McCall's outstanding contribution, so that error was
quickly forgotten. Number 3 was recorded on November 22
after 35 minutes' play against Kilmarnock at Rugby Park, and
nearly cost us the league game. Alex McLeish saved the day with
an equaliser in the final minute. The common denominator in all
four disasters, of course, was that Jim Leighton was between the
sticks, so there is no doubt in my mind that he was to blame! In
taking the mickey out of Jim, I must make clear, in all seriousness, that though it took a while for us to develop an understanding after he broke into the team, we fitted together well
once he had settled. He was the best shot-stopper that I played
with, and though he was not the most agile of keepers about the
penalty-box, he was a master of pulling off one important save
after another in vital matches. I am proud to say that me, Jim
Leighton and Alex McLeish formed a terrific defensive triangle.

Two days after Christmas 1980, I did manage to place the ball
in the correct net in our 4-1 win over Celtic at Pittodrie, and at
that stage we were three points ahead in the table with one game

in hand. However, a string of disappointing results followed, including a 1-0 defeat at the hands of Rangers at Ibrox, and by the end of January we found ourselves one point behind. In the coming weeks, Celtic pulled away further, and long before the end they had the championship sewn up. We finished in second place, seven points adrift. After winning the league championship in 1980-81, merely finishing runners-up and doing so badly in cup competitions came as a huge downer. Looking back, I can but emphasise that losing so emphatically to Liverpool in the European Cup knocked the stuffing out of us, and had an adverse affect on our season overall. We did our best to get back into our stride, but the damage had been done. Fergie seemed like a bear with a sore head as the season wound up, and he was still apoplectic that we had been taken apart by Liverpool. He was adamant that, if we drew an English club in the UEFA Cup in the following season, we would beat them. Thoughts of revenge were very much on Alex Ferguson's mind.

9

A FULL SET OF MEDALS TO POLISH

'Big Eck curled a sublime shot into the top corner of the net'

The 1981–82 season was bound to be special for me, as I had been granted a testimonial to mark my ten years' service with Aberdeen Football Club. I could barely believe that a decade had passed since the nervous teenager from Glasgow had walked into the front entrance of Pittodrie, but the vast majority of professional memories had been positive, and at the age of just 26 I had plenty of good years left in me. I was pretty young to be granted a testimonial by the club, and it was an honour that I could not turn down: the outstanding services of Bobby Clark and Joe Harper had been recognized previously. At the same time, it did prove an awkward period personally, as Sunderland had made an offer to me to sign and had put together a worthwhile financial package, and I did feel rather guilty even considering a move with my testimonial game coming up. I would have been a fool not to consider seriously a move to Tyneside, as Sunderland had pulled out all the stops to attract my signature. Alex Ferguson was aware of that when we talked about it, and the manager accepted that I had to think long and hard about the offer. Ultimately, loyalty to Aberdeen's fans and my great respect for Fergie combined to convince me that I should turn down the offer.

With my future settled once more, I could relax a bit and enjoy the exciting events organized to mark my testimonial year. It was great fun watching my time at the club being showcased in a *This Is Your Life*-style tribute set up by my testimonial committee, which included Lord Kirkhill, Sam Rennie, Sid Barry, Sandy Dey, George Ramsey, George Wyatt and Jim Anderson and which was performed by the comedy team, Scotland the What. They did a grand job all around, the highlight being a match against Tottenham Hotspur arranged for Pittodrie. Although I was on the losing side in my testimonial game, which ended 1-0, the occasion was good fun, and at least I played. I make that point because Bobby Clark and Joe Harper had missed contributing to their respective matches because of injury. Around 11,000 spectators turned up to my main event, which featured former Aberdeen favourite Steve Archibald, who was now banging them in for Spurs, as well as Steve Perryman, Glen Hoddle and Graham Roberts. A little-known Tottenham man named Garry Brooke scored with a penalty eight minutes from the end to clinch victory in what was a hotly-contested affair for a testimonial. It happened to be my 451st appearance in Aberdeen colours.

When the season–proper got under way, I was determined to lead the team to more silverware, though 1981-82 did not start too well. We won our Scottish League Cup section with nine points from six games, ahead of Kilmarnock, Hearts and Airdrie, and in the quarter-final hammered Berwick Rangers, but we came up against Dundee United in the two-legged semi. Matching up the clubs inevitably produced tight encounters, and looking back at their side from that era explains why. Hamish McAlpine, Richard Gough, Paul Hegarty, David Narey, Eamonn Bannon, Paul Sturrock and Davie Dodds were among the top players in their squad, and they were well drilled by Jim McLean. We made a stirring start to the tie, and I was delighted with our 1-0 win at Tannadice on Wednesday, October 7, 1981, a victory made all the more sweet as United were going for their third successive Scottish League Cup triumph. A headed goal from Peter Weir made the difference, and I was confident that we could finish the job at Pittodrie. Unfortunately, that did not happen. I was at fault for Paul Sturrock's first goal, Jim Leighton lost his footing at a vital time to allow him to score a second, and Ralph Milne netted for 3-0 to push us out of the tournament. I put that defeat down to bad luck, for nothing seemed to go right on the park. Fortunately, under Fergie Aberdeen Football Club did not have to endure many off-days.

After that crushing disappointment against Liverpool in the European Cup in the previous season, we had to do well in the UEFA Cup to ensure that the English press and public took us seriously when it came to European competition. We had been subjected to much criticism from south of the Border after our heavy defeat at Anfield, and we were desperate to demonstrate our true capabilities. For that fundamental reason I was keen to draw an English side in the UEFA Cup, and I was delighted when we were paired with Ipswich Town in the first round. They just happened to be the UEFA Cup holders, having beaten AZ 67 Alkamaar of the Netherlands in the final, and they featured players of the calibre of Mick Mills, Terry Butcher, Frans Thijssen, Arnold Muhren and Alan Brazil, who were at their peak. We were facing a difficult challenge, but post-Liverpool Fergie was relishing the perfect opportunity to confirm to the English football fraternity what we could do. I also felt that we had the players to beat any opposition when the team clicked, and I was in the zone, to use an apt American expression, when we faced Ipswich for the first time at Portman Road on September 16,1981.

It turned out to be a night to remember, and we proved resilient early on, though Frans Thijssen put Ipswich ahead on the stroke of half-time. During the break, the bosss told us that he felt we could achieve at least a draw, and we should take the game to Ipswich from the re-start. This we did, and a Peter Weir cross was flicked on by Alex McLeish to John Hewitt, who grabbed the vital equaliser. That 1–1 draw away from home was a huge confidence booster, as we had become only the third team to avoid defeat at Portman Road across 24 European ties. We knew that, by rights, we should be cast in the role of firm favourites for the return at Pittodrie, but surprise, surprise, the English press disagreed and tried to claim the result at Portman Road as a fluke. They claimed that the Tractorboys, to quote the East Anglian team's agrarian nickname, had suffered an off-night, and would more than redress the balance against the Dons way up in Scotland. Manager Bobby Robson got in on the act, claiming that we had shot our bolt at Portman Road, and would be beaten at Pittodrie. You can guess Alex Ferguson's reaction to that observation. Suffice to say that he made it clear that we would win the match, come hell or high water! We certainly did not need lifting for the second leg, as the players were also outraged that many down south had not taken seriously our outstanding form in drawing at Ipswich. They harked back to our defeat against Liverpool, and how we had ridden our luck at Portman Road. Frankly it all got a bit boring. And it made me *so* angry!

On the night of September 30, 1981 at Pittodrie, we were ready to take Ipswich Town to the cleaners, as they say. We were favoured by a break after 20 minutes when John Wark fouled Gordon Strachan in the penalty-box, and the wee man stepped up to convert the penalty. They equalised after Neale Cooper had fouled Eric Gates to allow John Wark to score from the spot, and at half-time the teams stood level. Thereafter, Peter Weir played one of the best spells of 45 minutes that I have seen by an Aberdeen player. He was in magnificent form despite being up against Mick Mills, an England internationalist. He gave Mick a real run-around, turning the defender inside out, and creating chance after chance for our strikers with some superb crosses. When they did not make the most of such opportunities, Peter took centre-stage and scored two magnificent goals, using a different foot for each, to deliver a deserved 3-1 win. We could have had a fourth, but Paul Cooper saved another Strachan penalty. The Ipswich Town players, Bobby Robson and the English media hardly realized what had hit them. It was a win that I relished deep down, as it showed English football and the pundits that Aberdeen Football Club deserved respect. In saying that, the respect emanating from England was hard to detect . . .

○ ○ ○

THE SASSENACH SUPERIORITY COMPLEX

It is my firm belief, based on long professional experience, that regardless of how well Scottish teams perform, the English will continue to think the Scottish game is of a poorer standard than what is on offer down south. They will give us no credit whatsoever. It does not seem to matter how well we do against them.

You can go back over matches involving Scottish and English teams, such as Celtic versus Leeds, Rangers v Leeds, Celtic v Liverpool and Celtic v Manchester United at Parkhead, where the Scottish team emerged victorious, but for which no genuine, lasting praise was given to the winners. Try to convince the English that we have even half-decent teams is impossible. You are wasting your time.

I have met Bobby Robson, who quite rightly was knighted for his services to football, when attending charity dinners through the years, and I kept reminding him of how easily we beat his beloved Ipswich Town. The first time we met, a few years after the match, he claimed that he did not recognise me, but maybe that was because my hair was disappearing as quickly as Ipswich's chances of beating us that night at Pittodrie. We were first introduced by Alex Ferguson who, with a big smile, announced me as his captain when Aberdeen beat Ipswich, adding: 'You must remember that night, Bobby,' By which time Fergie was laughing. I would urge Scots fans to do the same.

O O O

After the highs of the match against Ipswich Town, our next UEFA Cup tie was not one to set the pulses racing. Arges Pitesti were hardly a household name even in their native Romania, and we did not know what to expect. the boss drummed it into us not to be complacent, and it was good advice, because there was a slight danger we might let ourselves down if we did not approach this challenge correctly. Thus our attitude in the first leg was spot-on, and by half-time we were three goals up thanks to Gordon Strachan, Peter Weir and John Hewitt, and we should have won by more. The second leg is one that I remember, not for the quality of the football, but for Fergie's tea-cup throwing exploits at half-time. Pitesti was in Romanian farming country, an isolated spot that was as dreadful as any of the places I had experienced during my time in football. In a statement similar to the one that summed up conditions in Bulgaria on an earlier European expedition, the food was awful and the hotel was rotten. It was like taking a step back in time, though no tuba was present on the touchline to add to our disorientation this time as it was when we played in Bulgaria. It seemed as if we were overcome by the general malaise that gripped the place and we were clearly out of sorts early on, and played very badly. We were two goals down at half-time, and I don't have to tell you that a stern-faced Fergie met us at the dressing-room door. 'Sit doon,' he shouted as he slammed the door shut before laying into us for failing to get our act together, and for being complacent. He said we were slow and lazy, and he accused us of leaving our brains in the dressing- room. He was absolutely right, but he was winding himself up more and more, and kept glancing at the tea-cups set out on a table in the midst of the dressing-room. Once he spied them, I knew it would be time to duck, for crockery would start flying pretty soon. Right enough, the cups were soon crashing into the dressing-room wall, and as each drinking vessel shattered, his face reddened more and more, and I thought he was about to explode. This was a serious outburst, but considering we were two goals down to a team that we should have been tearing apart, his anger was justified.

FLYING TEACUPS AND THE URN STRIKES BACK

Through the years I had watched the boss kick a variety of items, such as kit-hampers, in frustration when we were failing to provide the goods, and I could never work out how he did not break his toes while venting his wrath. In the dressing-room in Romania, a big tea-urn was placed on the table. It was a massive item, and after he had sent the teacups flying, the manager turned his attention to the urn. He gave it a forearm smash hoping it would fly off the table and smash on the floor, but it didn't

*move. Not even a centimetre. But did it hurt his arm! He grimaced in
pain the moment he came in contact with the tea dispenser. I was sitting
among shattered cups trying to stifle my laughter. You could see his face
turn to a shade of pale, but he was doing his determined damnedest not to
show that he was in pain. He just kept on talking, but I could see that all
he wanted was for us to get back out on to the pitch – so that he could yell
out in agony in private.*

*That was the day the tea service got its own back on Fergie, though I'm
sure that, as one who has since been dubbed a knight of the realm, he does
not act in such a fashion these days. A stray boot reportedly kicked into
David Beckham's face in the Manchester United dressing-room was
obviously a one-off. Still, for those who had not experienced teacups sent
flying in the dressing-room, just as for those who went through the hairdryer
treatment for the first time in days of yore, it would not be forgotten.*

Although I thought the incident had come over as somewhat
comical, Fergie's outburst had the desired affect on the young
players confronting Arges Pitesti. I was the senior figure and
captain, and I needed no reminder that we were in danger of
crashing out of the UEFA Cup. But a lot of youngsters were in
the dressing-room, too, and Fergie thought they needed booted
up their backsides, in a manner of speaking, after their dismal
first-half performance. His shock tactics, teacup missiles and all,
had the desired affect, and a penalty from Gordon Strachan then
a goal five minutes from time by John Hewitt gave us a 2–2 draw.
Our performance still had not pleased the gaffer, but by the end
he had calmed down a bit, and the arm that he used to swat the
Romanian tea-urn seemed to be less painful.

Our aggregate win meant that Aberdeen Football Club had
ventured into the third round of a European competition for the
first time. For a club with such a proud history, that amounted to
a dismal record, and few followers of football gave us much
chance of proceeding further after we were paired with Hamburg, a team with a formidable reputation. Franz Beckenbauer,
who was 36 at the time, had long been associated with Bayern

Munich, and many outwith West Germany thought that he had played for that club alone. On the contrary, he enjoyed an Indian summer with Hamburg and continued to show glimpses of greatness, though he was well past his prime when we met at Pittodrie on November 25, 1981. Taking on Hamburg was a critical test, and we were able to emphasise during the 90 minutes that we had signed up some exceptional young players, who would enjoy bright futures. The pick of the bunch was Eric Black, who had made his league debut earlier that season as a 17-year-old against Dundee United, and who marked the occasion by scoring a fine headed goal to give us victory.

Fergie's adage was that if a player was good enough he was old enough, and he handed Eric his chance against Hamburg. He could afford to take risks by bringing in young players, because he had stability in other areas of the team in the shape of me, Alex McLeish, Stuart Kennedy, Mark McGhee and others. With experienced guys on hand, young players could be introduced and would be well looked after. Mark was a rock upfront, a big physical presence, and that eased the burden on Eric and other budding strikers attempting to break through. Eric duly scored our opening goal against Hamburg, and ironically the more experienced players were drawn into errors. Stuart Kennedy, who was usually thoroughly reliable, lost possession at the edge of the area after a mix-up with Jim Leighton, allowing Horst Hrubesch to swoop to score their equaliser. Hrubesch proved to be a real handful, and Alex McLeish confided later that he was one of the most difficult opponents he had faced. German newspapers described him as *Das Kopfball-Ungeheuer,* literally *the Header Beast,* because he was so effective in the air, and had been blessed with oustanding physical strength. In the second half Andy Watson put us 2-1 up, but unfortunately Gordon Strachan failed to convert a penalty award, which was to prove costly. John Hewitt made it 3-1 nine minutes from time, but Hrubesch popped up again with three minutes left: 3-2 it was, which left a huge hurdle to surmount in the second leg. The return at the Volkparkstadion was played out in freezing conditions with snow piled up at the side of the pitch. We were outclassed, pure and simple, and were three goals in arrears in 70 minutes, Mark McGhee claiming a scant consolation near the end. It was no surprise that Hamburg reached the final of the UEFA Cup that season, only to lose to IFK Gothenburg. The fact that they progressed to win the European Cup against Juventus in 1982–83, with Hrubesch operating in the striking role, also came as no surprise.

GERMAN LESSONS

The German strikers did not pass up that many chances, which meant that as a defender I had to be on my toes all the time. In Scottish league games, players failed to take the majority of opportunities, and maybe would score once for every three chances presented. For the guys at Hamburg, the ratio was more like two from three.

At domestic level, my tactic was not to commit myself in the tackle and to put the onus on the attacker to beat me, the rest of Aberdeen's defenders and finally Jim Leighton. Not easy, but I could not rely on that approach at European level against teams of the level of Hamburg. I had to be decisive in and around the penalty-box, and close them down straight away. You could not let them hit the ball from 25 yards as at home, because the German strikers had the strength and talent to strike home from outrageous distances. Nobody in Scottish football would get past me, Big Eck and Jim from long range, but the German front-men had the potential to do so.

The other phenomenon that I was made aware of was their movement in and round the box. Their one-twos were fast and difficult to halt, and I had to ensure that I matched the run of my man. I could not afford to switch off for a moment because if I did, the Germans would take full advantage of such indecision.

Certainly, the two games against Hamburg were the most significant European learning experiences of my career up to that point, and many other players at Aberdeen Football Club felt likewise.

Our league form that season was satisfactory overall, and we were among contenders for the title, though the campaign had started badly with a 4-1 defeat to Dundee United on August 29, 1981, and we were dogged by early inconsistency. The fact that Jock Stein, the Scotland manager, was viewing that reverse from the stand would not have helped my chances of making the national team. We were given a typical rollicking by Alex Ferguson afterwards, and I shuddered to think what Big Jock was thinking about me after that 90 minutes. Our next game was not much better, and we lost 3-1 to Celtic at Pittodrie. Poor Gordon Strachan had to put up with being chased again by a Celtic fan, who took exception to him scoring our goal. Gordon was a target for many opposition fans, simply because he was usually such an outstanding performer. At the start of the 1981-82 season, only Jim Leighton was on the top of his form week in, week out, and against Rangers on October 10 he pulled off a save from a penalty effort from John McDonald to help us to secure a 0-0 draw. I had given away the penalty. By mid-February, it was obvious that we needed to put together a sequence of positive results to have any hope of winning the championship. After a dull 0-0 draw against Dundee, who lay bottom of the table, we were eight points behind league leaders Celtic. That deplorable performance acted as a wake-up call, and we rallied superbly after that, 15 wins from 16 matches ensuring that we were back in the hunt in the Scottish Premier League. Success against Celtic on March 27, 1982 meant that we had narrowed the margin to four points with five games left, and we kept breathing down their necks until, with one game to go, we still had an outside chance of landing the title. To have achieved that position after such a sluggish start paid tribute to the never-say-die mentality that Fergie had dinned into us. The mathe-matical facts were that to clinch the championships we needed to win our final match against Rangers by five goals, and hope St Mirren would beat Celtic at Parkhead. A long shot it might have been, but at half-time we were four goals up on Rangers, and Celtic were drawing with the Paisley side. We still had a chance, but it was not to be as Celtic found their form to win the match by 3-0, and the championship.

We could still anticipate a Scottish Cup final against Rangers after an eventful tournament. Before we played Motherwell in our first match, we heard that Wolverhampton Wanderers were interested in making Alex Ferguson their new manager. That unsettled us, for we did not wish to lose his managerial skills, and I wanted the team to put on a show against Motherwell to emphasise what he would be missing if he departed Pittodrie. It turned into an exceptional experience for John Hewitt. We kicked off and the ball went back to Stuart Kennedy, who put in a long cross to John, who scored after 9.6 seconds. Incredible! The fastest goal in Scottish Cup history won us the tie. Next in the draw were Celtic, and we had home advantage. They had beaten us twice in the league at Pittodrie, and we were determined that would not happen again. John Hewitt again starred as our goal hero, though this time he waited until the 19th minute to net the winner. We were handed home advantage again against Kilmarnock in the next round and won 4-2, with Gordon Strachan adding two penalties within four minutes in the second half. In the semi-final we beat St Mirren, though it took us two meetings to see them off. Frank McDougall scored just after an hour, and we equalised through yet another penalty delivered by Gordon Strachan. The replay was arranged for Dens Park, and on a sodden April evening the pitch had degenerated into a quagmire, which rendered football skills almost redundant. Matters were settled because of goalkeeping mistakes. We scored first when Billy Thomson failed to hold a shot from Mark McGhee, but Frank McAvennie brought them level. Thomson was adjudged to be at fault for our second goal scored by Neil Simpson, but Doug Somner thrust St Mirren back into the game before an effort from Peter Weir gave us victory by 3-2, and passage into the final versus Rangers.

I was among three survivors with Stuart Kennedy and John McMaster from the previous Aberdeen-Rangers Scottish Cup final, lost in 1978 when Billy McNeill was manager. Those new to the thrill of being involved in a cup final included Neil Simpson, Neale Cooper, Eric Black and John Hewitt, who had already made distinctive marks on the team despite relative inexperience. On May 22, 1982 Hampden provided a day to remember, mainly for a magnificent curling shot into the net which, if it had been fashioned by a Brazilian, would have been hailed as one of the goals of the decade. The scorer was Alex McLeish. John McDonald had scored early to put Rangers ahead before Big Eck stepped into the breech. John Hewitt's corner was cleared to him just outside the penalty-box. Alex looked up and spied that Jim Stewart had strayed off his line, and curled a sublime shot into the top corner of the net. The match moved into extra-time, and we took complete control, with Mark McGhee, Gordon Strachan and Neale Cooper hitting the target to present us with an emphatic 4-1 victory, and the Scottish Cup. In the triumphant aftermath, I suggested to Alex McLeish that he had not intended to curl the ball so perfectly into the top corner, and that he was simply trying to cross it. He had the perfect riposte, reminding me that, three days prior to the final, we had spent an away day at Cruden Bay, which included a training session and a round of golf. During training he hit a free-kick which had curled into the top corner, just like its successor in the Scottish Cup final. I had no answer to that, and I must say that such skill was a perfect indication of Alex's ability on the ball, which many did not fully appreciate. Ultimate victory in the Scottish Cup completed my full set of domestic medals, adding to those from our Premier League Championship and Scottish League Cup success.

It was also a great day for our full-back, Stuart Kennedy, and not just for the football. Stuart was a film buff, and he met Hollywood star Burt Lancaster at Gleneagles Hotel, where our celebration party was booked. Burt had been resident there during the filming of *Local Hero*, and came across to inquire about the trophy that was resplendent on the table beside me. I told him that we had won the Scottish Cup for soccer, the term used by Americans to distinguish the sport from their brand of football, and he seemed pleased for us, though he did not seem that sure what soccer was. But Stuart collared one of his movie heroes for a chat, and I could not make up my mind whether my team-mate was more pleased to win the trophy or to chat to Burt Lancaster at the end of a wonderful day.

The Scottish Cup had been the holy grail of domestic trophies for me. I had started to visit Aberdeen as a schoolboy footballer soon after the 3-1 Scottish Cup victory over Celtic in 1970. The trophy was in the boardroom over that summer, and I sneaked in once or twice to take a look. The memory of the grand trophy being on view at the club, albeit fleetingly, stayed with me, and it spurred me on to believe that I could achieve major honours with Aberdeen Football Club. My faith in the team that Alex Ferguson had forged, plus beating Ipswich Town in the UEFA Cup tie, confirmed to me that I was part of an extra-special side. The medal missing from my collection was of the European variety, and while some might have thought that going all the way in such a competition was a pipedream, under Fergie's dedicated direction anything seemed possible.

10

A GLORIOUS NIGHT IN GOTHENBURG

*'Super-spy Archie Knox embarked on a mission to watch
Real Madrid against Valencia, where they lost 1-0'*

Gothenburg! Mention the name of the Swedish city to a supporter of Aberdeen Football Club, and wait for the broad smile to break out. That also happens to me, for beating the mighty Real Madrid to lift the European Cup Winners' Cup was the greatest night of my football career. And to think that I might have missed it, for at the start of the 1982–83 season I was out of contract, and Rangers had made a bid for my services. I was free to move and an offer was on the table, though financially it did not amount to that much. These were the days before the arrival at Ibrox of a big-spending manager in Graeme Souness, who might well have offered me five or six times my Aberdeen salary to move to Glasgow. But it was not to be, and Rangers came forward with £200 a week, exactly the same as I was paid at Pittodrie, but with an enhanced bonus system, though even that was not worth writing home about. Their manager, John Greig, said he would also make me Rangers' captain, and there was an unwritten rule that the man who wore the Ibrox armband received £40 a week from the *Scottish Daily Express* for putting his name to a weekly column. I would have been marginally better off, but I didn't fancy the move, despite John Greig doing his best to convince me otherwise. We had a detailed discussion by telephone, but I told him that I would not meet him face to face unless there was a chance that I would sign, as I did not wish to waste his time. My decision on whether to leave Pittodrie would be solely based on football, as the financial benefits were only marginally better. Would I be better off staying under Alex Ferguson or serving Rangers under John Greig? It was no contest, with all due respect to John. I had left Glasgow as a 16-year-old for a new life in Aberdeen, and I was very happy at how things had turned out. I was content professionally and personally, Aberdeen were a great side making strides under an excellent manager, so I decided to remain where I was.

Many Rangers fans could not fathom why I would say no to Ibrox. In their minds, and in those of Celtic supporters, these were bigger clubs, so why would I not wish to join one of them to progress? The difference for me was that I did not consider the Old Firm to be that mighty entity, for Aberdeen were winning trophies. Fergie wanted a definite answer on my future before he would play me again in Aberdeen colours, and because I didn't give him one immediately, he dropped me from Drew Jarvie's testimonial match against Ipswich Town on August 7, 1982. In the end, I asked the Aberdeen board for a £20-a-week rise to take me up to £220. They said no, but came back with £10 a week, and I accepted that, as I think that they had sussed out that I would stay, come what may, though such a small boost to such a limited weekly income seems pathetic nowadays. Though the boss wanted me to stay, he did not try to influence me too much. We had a chat or two, but he was always of the view that you were either with him or against him. He did tell me that the Aberdeen chairman had said I had no chance of getting a £20-a-week rise, and he was absolutely right. What bothered me, though, was that the club had the upper hand when it came to contract negotiations and transfers, and they did not have to tell a player whether other clubs had come in for you or not. That is why newspapers were vital as sounding-boards for other clubs to make public the names of the players they were interested in signing. I certainly could not rely on the Aberdeen board to tell me what was going on. Things have changed since then with the Bosman ruling, and the power in transfer negotiations lies with the player. After I made public my decision to stay, Alex

Ferguson did not say too much, for he was not about to massage my ego by telling me how delighted he was, but he did pose the odd fundamental question, such as: 'Why would you ever want to go to Rangers anyway?'

MONEY OR FOOTBALL?

Looking back, I have to laugh at signing a fresh contract as Aberdeen captain for an extra £10 a week, for years later when I returned to Aberdeen as director of football in 2004, I tried to attract a full-back to Pittodrie by offering him a substantial sum, but Southend United were willing to pay him three times as much. Aberdeen had the football tradition, Southend had the money.

Now, I can't blame a player for being attracted by an offer of big bucks, but sometimes you would hope that football rather than finance would be the main motivation for joining a new club. I was a case in point, a man who put football ahead of monetary reward. I could have left Aberdeen for more cash, but decided to stay. On the other hand, if I had headed off, I would have missed the greatest moment in the annals of Aberdeen Football Club.

Each detail of that successful European campaign remains firmly etched in my mind. I can remember all the twists and turns in the 10 games that we stacked up to get to the final, and the elation when I lifted the European Cup-Winners' Cup. It was our first European trophy in our 80-year history, and it is a significant chapter in the story of Aberdeen Football Club. The boss told me privately in advance of the tournament that he thought we might struggle a bit; he felt that so many big clubs were involved in the draw that that we would do well even to reach the latter stages. When I examined the list of teams entered I understood his concern, for some of the names were Barcelona, Inter Milan, Real Madrid, Bayern Munich, Austria Vienna, Paris St. Germain and Tottenham Hotspur. Jim Leighton, Gordon Strachan, Alex

McLeish and I had been on international duty at the World Cup in 1982, and were hoping for time off before the club season started to re-charge our batteries. We had to fulfil a preliminary Cup-Winners Cup' tie, which was a real pain, as we had to cut short our holidays to return to pre-season training. We were also involved in two Scottish League Cup fixtures before we took on Sion of Switzerland, who were a bit of an unknown quantity. Fergie and Archie Knox had watched them twice before we took them on, and though they made it clear they thought they were a competent side, I gained the feeling they were confident we could beat them.

I was certainly relishing the chance to play in Europe again, and I could not quite believe the start that we made to the campaign. We won the first leg 7-0, and Eric Black, Gordon Strachan, John Hewitt, Neil Simpson, Mark McGhee and Stuart Kennedy shared scoring duties with a Swiss defender by the name of Balet, who turned the ball into his own net. The day before the return match in Switzerland, club secretary Ian Taggart, chairman Dick Donald and our doctor, Bill Catto, decided to fly over the snow-capped Matterhorn in a light aircraft. Dick told me later that they were heading through cloud, and at one stage came within what seemed like touching distance of the rock face, and he thought they were bound to crash. A typical Aberdonian who did not betray much emotion, Dick admitted that he was mightily relieved when the plane landed safely. Two months later, the club was obliged to carry out the mournful duty of sending a telegram of condolence to the flying centre involved, after the same pilot and four passengers were killed on a similar flight. Being 7-0 ahead meant that the return leg was an irrelevance, and many local fans were obviously too embarrassed to turn up, as only 2,400 people were present in the stadium. Still, the second leg was a thing of beauty because of the enchanting alpine scenery surrounding the Tourbillon Stadium, and unusually I had plenty time to look around and take in the views across to the Matterhorn. It was one of the few games in my career in which I could afford to be distracted, because I knew we were home and dry even before a ball was kicked, though I did rally the troops from kick-off. Maybe I enjoyed the Swiss atmosphere a bit too much, and at times I did drift too far out of position. It was as if I was back to my days as a teenage striker, and I went up for corner-kicks and free-kicks at every possible opportunity. My poaching paid dividends, and I planted my name on to the score-sheet in our 4-1 win, heading in a corner from Peter Weir. It was my first goal in a year-and-a-half, John Hewitt contributed two and Mark McGhee completed the account, which brought a final tally of 11-1 over the two legs.

I felt that we had nothing to worry about in the first round-proper when we drew Dinamo Tirana of Albania, but I was proved wrong. We controlled the first leg at Pittodrie on September 15, 1982, but we struggled to score before finally taking the lead on the half-hour mark when John Hewitt scored. It was a lucky strike, as their goalkeeper spilled the ball from a shot by Doug Bell, and John was in like a flash. We should have built on that, but failed to do so, and any thoughts of overcoming the Albanians with the ease experienced in the previous round quickly evaporated. Fergie was in a dreadful mood after the game, and he had every right to be so. He complained that we had let our supporters down, and in ripping into us in the dressing-room left no doubt that we would have to improve 100 per cent in the return to have a chance of making it to the next round. Celtic had played in Albania three years previously, and Fergie had talked at length to their officials and to gentlemen of the press about the perils of visiting the rugged Balkan nation. Problems had arisen over visas, and as Aberdeen had found to our discomfort in other visits to the communist strongholds of Europe, the food had been shocking and the hotels of poor standard. It was assumed that conditions would turn out to be similar when we flew to Albania, so the club did everything to ensure we were well prepared. Dr Bill Catto gathered all the medicines that we would need plus lots of salt tablets, and we packed a hamper to ensure that we would eat well.

When I turned up at Aberdeen Airport, I encountered a bit of a shock as the newspapers were running stories about Albania being at the centre of a coup, complete with reports of tanks on the streets and fighting in the countryside. I climbed the steps into the plane with some apprehension after reading the news, and remember that in those days communications with some regions of the globe continued to be haphazard, so I would be unable to phone home, which meant that my family would be frantic with worry for our safety. We flew into Tirana Airport expecting mayhem, but all was quiet in the Albanian capital. As the coach made its way into the city, I spotted gun towers, but they were unmanned, and people walking by the side of the road were smiling at us rather than brandishing guns. Farmers with notably bad teeth waved from the fields as our bus sped by, but there was nothing to suggest that we had entered into the teeth of a battle to control the country. No tanks, no riots, no dissent. We checked into our hotel, and everything was fine. It turned out that 20 rebels had landed at a spot on the Albanian coast in three dinghys four days before we arrived, but they had been shot dead on the beach. That was the sum and substance of a coup that failed.

A telling memory of Albania was the profusion of leather coats, which most residents seemed to wear. There was one decent hotel, in which we were resident, thank goodness, and the other guests and the rest of the populace just stared at this party of strangers from faraway Scotland. We seemed to offer entertainment value, for Albania did not receive many foreign tourists. It was if we were imported for their entertainment, and the citizens of Tirana wandered around the town square at night to catch a glimpse of us playing cards in the lobby. Shadowy figures clad in leather coats gazed at us as if we had flown in from another planet. A very strange experience, and the match against Dinamo Tirana was as off-putting as the country. It was staged on September 29, 1982 in boiling-hot weather. It was 92 degrees on the Fahrenheit scale when we kicked-off at 2pm, and I was sweating from the moment that we took to the pitch. It was an uncomfortable heat, and I found it most difficult to get used to the oppressive atmosphere, but this was one of many football challenges in which the tactical acumen of Alex Ferguson shone through. He decided to play Gordon Strachan and Peter Weir as out-and-out wide men, as the pitch was extensive and in good condition. He told us to keep possession and to let our opponents tire themselves out by chasing the ball all over the pitch in the heat. It proved a masterstroke, and as the game progressed, Dinamo Tirana expended more and more energy and became increasingly fatigued, and we were in complete control. When the final whistle went at 0-0, we were delighted. From a personal point of view, I was euphoric because I would soon be departing from Albania, and after that trip I treated anyone dressed in a black leather coat with deep suspicion.

Our second-round match involved another foray into a land shaped by communism, against Lech Poznan of Poland. Archie Knox was handed the duty of compiling a dossier on the team, and he made clear that they had some effective individuals in their squad. He returned from his spying mission with an intriguing story about an official being assigned to him by the Polish Government everywhere he ventured. The country was subject to civil unrest at the time, with the shipyards of Gdansk a crucible for political change, and the Polish authorities wanted every foreigner to be kept under scrutiny. Was Archie Knox considered a significant danger to state security? Well, when he booked into his hotel, he discovered that his minder was intent on sharing his room, which was taking man-marking a bit too far! Archie did his job well under trying conditions, and he highlighted the men that Aberdeen had to watch with particular attention when the action began. The first leg went ahead in Aberdeen on October 20, 1982, and we won 2-0, but we should have scored at least four. Mark McGhee and Peter Weir scored, but we missed lots of other chances, Eric Black hitting the bar twice and Gordon Strachan striking a post.

When we arrived in Poland on November 2, 1982, the stories that Archie had related were obviously accurate. Anti-aircraft

guns were stationed near the airport runway, and some of the
official party who welcomed us on to Polish soil were kitted out
in military fatigues. Long queues for bread were evident, and one
could sense revolution in the air and a feeling of desolation in the
streets. Football, then, offered an outlet for the people's frustra-
tions, and a big crowd was attracted to the stadium for the match,
despite the fact that we held a 2-0 aggregate lead. That evening
we proved that we were becoming experts at travelling away
from home in Europe, and defending a lead. I thought that Alex
McLeish and I gave a great account of ourselves in not giving
their strikers a kick. The midfielders also put in terrific shifts, and
when Doug Bell scored after an hour, I realised that we were
again home and dry. Put in context, it was an outstanding result
in Poland, for only months later Lech Poznan went on to win
their domestic league. We had reached the quarter-finals of a
European tournament for the first time, and we were drawn
against the might Bayern Munich as a just reward.

Now Bayern could field footballers of class throughout their
team, and Fergie spent lots of time poring over their strengths
and weaknesses. He travelled to watch them perform on a
snow-covered pitch against Karlsruhe, who were near the
bottom of the Bundesliga. According to the boss, it did not
matter that the Bavarians were depleted, for they possessed great
strength in depth. In the run-up to the game he kept talking to
me about getting tight on Karl-Heinz Rummenigge, and it was
not a Ferguson trait to keep going on and on about just the one
player, or even to worry about the opposition in general. Fergie
and I resolved that I had to stay on my feet when facing
Rummenigge, and not dive into the tackle; if I did that, the
German would skin me every time. I didn't need firing up, but
Franz Beckenbauer, against whom I had played during the
previous season when he was with Hamburg, managed to get
my blood boiling anyway. Although he was not connected with
Bayern Munich at that time, he was quoted in Scottish newspapers before the game claiming that we were technically
inferior to Bielefeld, a team that Bayern Munich had beaten

5-0 the previous week. He also claimed that when a Scottish team played away from home in Europe, they were only half as good as when they performed at home. We managed to make him eat his words.

The first leg was away from home on March 2, 1983, and in addition to Rummenigge, they could field Paul Breitner, Dieter Hoeness – brother of the more famous Uli, who was Bayern coach – and Klaus Augenthaler, but we put on a great performance in the Olympic Stadium in Munich. Bayern, who bore an enviable European pedigree, were firm favourites to overcome Aberdeen in our 45th European match, though I do not believe that they under-estimated us. Whatever, we certainly matched them all the way, our key to our success lying in midfield. I thought that Doug Bell, Neale Cooper and Neil Simpson were quite magnificent. Neale was the star man in my reckoning, as he was lined up to mark the great Breitner; Doug and Neil man-marked their immediate opponents devotedly, and we deserved our 0-0 draw. To balance that, Rummenigge destroyed my film-star good looks, or at least I joked bravely to him that he had done so. In attempting one of his acrobatic overhead kicks in the second half, he missed the ball and cracked me in the face with such force that he knocked out my front teeth. I bear the dental legacy to this day in the shape of a bridge with four permanent false teeth. Rummenigge, who must have recognized that my years as the Aberdeen pin-up boy were over, helped me to look for my dislodged teeth, but in vain. It was one of my most surreal rituals on a football pitch. Here I was, having played in the first part of a European Cup-Winners' Cup quarter-final, searching for my dislodged front teeth in the mud at the Olympic Stadium with Karl-Heinz Rummenigge, an all-round star that I considered was the best player that I ever faced, who was fast, used his body well to shield the ball and was lethal when he had a chance to score – and who had been denied that opportunity by Aberdeen. Afterwards, he told reporters that he had been impressed by 'the one who lost his teeth and shouted a lot'. Me, I presume.

After securing that result, we had an outstanding chance to beat them at the second time of asking, and reaching the semi-finals. Bayern coach Uli Hoeness claimed that his team would win at Pittodrie, but I believed otherwise. He revealed that he had watched us beat Celtic 3-1 at Parkhead, and he thought that we were very fast and technically efficient, but could be overcome. Aberdeen's board of directors were extremely nervous about the outcome, and desperate that we should come up trumps, so that we could reap the benefits of a money-spinning semi-final tie. The return leg on March 16, 1983 turned into a marvellous night, and the capacity crowd of 24,000 who crammed into Pittodrie witnessed a game that has reserved a unique niche in the club's history. It remains my favourite Pittodrie encounter, and nothing comes close. In the lead-up, the men of Bayern Munich made it clear that they would score at Pittodrie, and they did so. But we scored more than they did in a classic struggle, in which fortunes flowed ebbed and flowed. Once again, tactics dictated by Alex Ferguson in the second half, when we were up against it, turned the tide in Aberdeen's favour. Klaus Augenthaler gave them the lead after ten minutes, and we endured some nerve-wracking episodes thereafter as they pressed for a second strike, that would have killed the game. We survived the onslaught, and Eric Black hit the bar as we fought our way back into contention. We deserved to equalise through Neil Simpson just before half-time, and when we entered the dressing-room for some respite during the break, the match was finely poised. Fergie and Archie sat us down and told us that we were only 45 minutes away from the biggest result of our lives, and that we had to go back out there and give our all. Alex was calm and eloquent at this juncture, and he struck me as being quietly confident. I shared his optimism, and even after a magnificent volley from Pflugler on the hour-match that left Jim Leighton with no chance, I felt that we could turn around a 2-1 deficit. It was at this point that Fergie pulled off another of his instinctive tactical masterstrokes. John McMaster came on for Stuart Kennedy, and John Hewitt replaced Neil Simpson in a double switch that paid dividends. Neale Cooper was moved to left-back to neutralise winger Del Haye, who was enjoying an outstanding game, Doug Rougvie slotted in at right back against the tall Pfluger, and John McMaster was invested with the responsibility of spraying passes from midfield to try to unlock their defence. With 14 minutes left, a training-ground set-piece brought forth a result. McMaster ran over the ball from a free-kick, and Gordon Strachan chipped it craftily into the penalty-box and on to the head of Alex McLeish, who out-jumped Augenthaler to clinch the equaliser. If the score-line remained at 2-2, Bayern Munich would go through as they had scored two away goals, and I knew that we must push forward, but I did not dare to think that we would grasp the winner so quickly. A minute after Alex had equalized, John McMaster was involved again and put in a cross for Eric Black, whose header was pushed away by goalkeeper Muller. John Hewitt was lightning fast in his reaction, and turned the ball into the net through the goalie's legs. The nutmeg was a signal for the Aberdeen fans to go crazy, and the players were in danger of duplicating that state of excitement. I tried to get them to calm down, as we had to see the match out, but it was an impossible job. Supporters were roaring us on, and as the minutes ticked away Bayern's despera-tion reached new heights and they threw caution to the wind, but the German team could not break us down. When the French referee blew the final whistle, Pittodrie erupted with joy at Aberdeen Football Club's most significant result up to that date.

It was a victory to cherish, but I did not realize how significant the triumph was until some years had elapsed. That night at Pittodrie set up the most intense atmosphere that I have ever experienced, and I still get a tingle up my spine when I remember the din made by the crowd at the final whistle – and Fergie's little dance on to the pitch. I was not present at Pittodrie in the 1950s when 45,000 fans roared approval or derision at their teams, but I have to say that in a more modern era I had not experienced an atmosphere like that, nor have I since that magnificent night. We had beaten Bayern Munich, an iconic organization who were predominant in a country where football was at its peak during that period, and which contained World Cup winners in their line-up.

After that triumph, I feared no-one in the football sense. I had learned much from West German teams, who tended to be superior to us, until we turned the tables on Bayern. Aberdeen could now go on to win the Cup-Winners' Cup after the way that we had reacted in the quarter-final. Other teams left in the mix were Waterschei, Real Madrid and Austria Vienna, and it was no secret that I was happy to play the little-known team from Belgium, then hoped to move on to contest a dream final with Real Madrid. Waterschei had beaten Paris St. Germain in the quarter-finals, so they were a force to be reckoned with. Fergie had travelled to examine their form against Bruges, and had been duly impressed by strikers Voordeckers, a Belgian internationalist, and the Icelander Gudmundsson. On Saturday, April 2, 1983, four days before the first leg against Waterschei, we lost to St Mirren at home in the Scottish Premier League. The boss hated losing to St Mirren, his former club, at the best of times, and that result put paid to any hopes that we had of taking the league title, which was eventually carried off by Dundee United. A capacity crowd turned up to watch our performance against Waterschei on the night of April 6, and fully expected that we would make up for the disappointment of our league campaign by beating the Belgian team, and take a big stride towards the European Cup-Winners' Cup final. The noise emanating from our support was phenomenal, and we responded by opening up at a great rate of knots, and within four minutes we had one foot planted firmly in the final. Eric Black scored after two minutes, then Neil Simpson beat three men for our second barely two minutes later. Mark McGhee claimed the third in the 67th minute, then Peter Weir's diving header hit home, two minutes after that. The visitors got a goal back, but a further strike from Mark McGhee made it 5-1.

One blow to our prospects in the second leg, which should

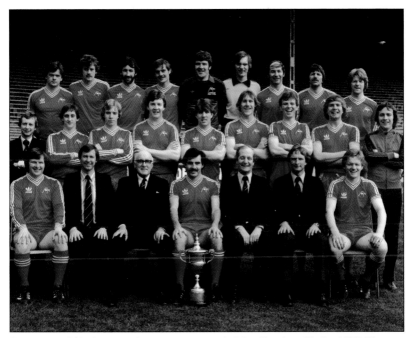

Champions. One of my proudest moments was helping Aberdeen lift the 1978-80 league title, the first time we had won the championship for 25 years.

The squad that won the European Cup-Winners' Cup and the Scottish Cup in 1983 along with club officials and of course the boss, Sir Alex Ferguson, gather at Pittodrie for an official end of season picture.

Sir Alex Ferguson and I study the great names on the European Cup-Winners' Cup as we parade the trophy through the streets of Aberdeen. Picture Courtesy of SNS Group.

Goal! Alex McLeish and I celebrate after my goal against Celtic secured us a 1-1 draw in April, 1985, a result which gave us the point required to ease us towards our third title in six seasons.

I was honoured to be asked to make a speech at the Aberdeen centenary dinner in October, 2003 which was attended by players and officials from past and present.

Sir Bobby Charlton, Sir Alex Ferguson and me with the crystal decanters presented to us by club chairman Stewart Milne and John Mitchell, managing director of Aberdeen Fabrication at the club centenary dinner in 2003.

I was in esteemed company as part of the BBC commentary team for the World Cup in France in 1998. The men behind the microphones included Gary Lineker, a bleached Ally McCoist, Martin O'Neill and master of ceremonies Dougie Donnelly.

Dougie Donnelly and I shared a microphone together on many occasions. Here are the two of us about to start commentating at the World Cup in France, 1998.

Drinking a toast to the Scotland World Cup squad before their World Cup match against Brazil. Dougie Donnelly and Ulrika Johnsson joined me at the Eiffel Tower in Paris to open the champagne. Later that evening Ulrika was beaten up by her then boyfriend Stan Collymore in a pub full of Scotland supporters.

The joy of my face is clear to see. Aberdeen are the European Cup-Winners' Cup winners. What a feeling! Picture Courtesy of SNS Group.

Left. The proudest moment of my football career. Lifting the European Cup-Winners' Cup is a moment I will remember forever. The smiles on the faces of Bryan Gunn and Alex McLeish and the look of bewilderment on the face of Gordon Strachan shows how much it meant to them as well.

Below. Ready for action. I lead the team out against Real Madrid in the European Cup-Winners' Cup final and am followed out onto the pitch by Jim Leighton and John McMaster.

It's much better wearing a trophy on your head than a hat! Here's me displaying the
Drybrough Cup which we won after a 2-1 victory over St.Mirren in August 1980.

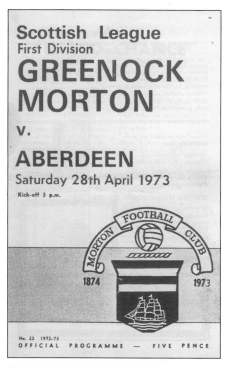

Left. With 37 minutes of the 1972-73 season remaining I was given my Aberdeen debut against Morton, but not as a defender but as a striker!

Below. On a match night and the now famous image of me as Cuban revolutionary Che Guevara flutters away in all its glory.

It's the start of the 1971-72 season, my first as a professional footballer. I'm seventh from the left in the middle row, in case you don't recognise me without my trademark moustache. Back then it was only Steve Murray, front row second left, who was man enough to sport facial hair.

I shake hands with Liverpool captain Phil Thompson before our European Cup match in 1980. Unfortunately the pleasantries ended there and then as they showed us no mercy, beating us 1-0 at Pittodrie and 4-0 at Anfield. To be fair to us nobody could live with them back then.

I tussle with Quentin Young of Rangers in a 1-1 draw at Ibrox on 12 January 1974.

ABERDEEN

Referee:
C. LO BELLOE (Italy)

1 BOBBY CLARK

2 IAN HAIR

3 JIM HERMISTON

4 EDDIE THOMSON

5 WILLIE YOUNG

6 WILLIE MILLER

7 ALEX WILLOUGHBY

8 DAVE ROBB

9 ARTHUR GRAHAM

SUBSTITUTES

....
....
....
....

10 DREW JARVIE

11 BERTIE MILLER

....

TOTTENHAM

1	Pat JENNINGS	6	Philip BEAL
2	Ray EVANS	7	Alan GILZEAN
3	Cyril KNOWLES	8	Steve PERRYMAN
4	John PRATT	9	Martin CHIVERS
5	Mike ENGLAND	10	Martin PETERS
		11	Ralph COATES

SUBSTITUTES

....
....
....
....
....

UEFA CUP
SECOND ROUND
FIRST LEG

Not so picture perfect. Aberdeen's first competitive home European match against an English club was played against Tottenham Hotspur in the UEFA Cup on October 24, 1973. We drew 1-1 at Pittodrie but were well beaten 4-1 at White Hart Lane.

Playing at my beloved Hampden Park against England in 1980. I went on to play 65 times for Scotland, twelve as captain.

An indication of the impact that our victory in the European Cup-Winners' Cup final made was shown by our elevation onto the front cover of *World Soccer Magazine*.

I was proud to play alongside Gordon Strachan, one of the greatest ever players to represent Aberdeen and Scotland.

We are the champions. My team-mates lift me shoulder high after we clinched the 1979-80 Scottish League title.

I look a bit pensive before our European Cup-Winners' Cup Semi-final first leg match against Waterschei of Belgium. I need not have worried as we hammered them 5-1 at Pittodrie.

Kick-off approaches in Gothenburg. I exchange pennants with Real Madrid captain Santillana before the biggest game of my life.

Duncan Davidson and I sign up for a promotional venture organised by Northern Scotland Co-Operative Society back in 1977.

have been a dawdle, was that Doug Bell was ruled out because of injury. Waterschei were terrified of the man, and no wonder. He had been our star performer against them at Pittodrie after Fergie had decided that he should be given the fullest opportunity to display his dribbling skills, which were similar to those of the legendary Celtic and Scotland winger, Jimmy Johnstone. Waterschei were bemused and harassed by his presence on the field, and they must have cracked open a few bottles of Belgian lager when they heard that Doug had been ruled out of the return. I was pretty relaxed, as I was convinced in my own mind that we had the semi-final sown up, but I was adamant that we should not do anything silly when we performed in Belgium. It was in contests such as these, that Aberdeen were supposed to win, in which I earned my corn as the skipper. We had a group of youngsters in the team at the time, and I had to make sure that they did not make the mistake of relaxing beforehand, believing that the hard work had been completed. But then I usually felt a bit more anxious when we were expected to win matches, and I felt the need to disabuse players like John Hewitt and Neale Cooper of the notion that we simply had to turn up to go through. I was a talker, an organizer who took deep pride in his team, and who worked hard to avoid blowing our chances. Waterschei played in the Belgian town of Genk, which was easy for our supporters to reach, and many made the trip on the assumption that they would partying. They were absolutely correct. We didn't see much of Genk, as the team stayed in Maastricht in the Netherlands, this being a region of Europe where various national frontiers converge, and we simply travelled across the border for the match, and passed a massive car plant at which were parked hundreds of Ford models. That I do remember, because we didn't see much beyond the hotel, the training ground, the football pitch and the car factory.

Before the game on Tuesday, April 19, 1983 each of us was presented with a box of strawberries. Handing over such items happened a lot in European countries, and as captain I received fruit, cheeses and flowers at various times in return for the more basic Aberdeen pennants and plaques, while the directors might make introductory gifts of whisky or tankards to opposition officials. For all of our attempts to ensure that we did not hand on-field gifts to Waterschei during the match, Alex McLeish and I slipped up and allowed them to score the only goal. Disappointing as it was to lose, the result did not take the shine off the fact that we had made it comfortably into the European Cup-Winners' Cup final. The aggregate was 5-2. On the other hand, what upset me desperately was the fact that Stuart Kennedy had suffered a knee injury that turned out to be much more severe that at first thought. He had taken a knock early on, but typically of Stuart, he thought that he would run off the discomfort, and he stuck out the 90 minutes, but afterwards was in real pain.

A CAREER DESTROYED IN ITS PRIME

The injury ended Stuart Kennedy's career there and then, which was a personal tragedy shared by everybody at Aberdeen Football Club, for he was one of our finest footballers. Appearing beside him in defence was a joy, and his play instilled great confidence in me. He was a great bloke and a true professional, and I would reckon that he was the club's greatest-ever full-back.

As a defender and captain, I never had to worry about Stuart. I did not have to tell him when to push out, when to get on the right side of his man or worry about him sleeping and being caught out by the left- winger. He was quick, extremely competent and a big loss on the park and in the dressing-room.

Stuart was a big personality, a big talker with an opinion on every topic, but you need that type of person in your team. He was also a great laugh, and kept winding everybody up: he gave Jim Leighton the nickname 'Bozo', though I'm not sure why. He was keen to ensure that players received worthwhile bonuses for cup runs, and to the club board he was known as the 'Barrack Room Lawyer'. A genuine team player, he also sported a moustache to rival my facial hair.

Some pundits maintain that fewer serious injuries afflicted professional footballers in my time, which meant that we could get by using fewer players. They claim that the game nowadays is quicker, and that teams are more athletic and yet more prone to injuries. That is true to an extent, as today's players are more finely tuned than we were. I wouldn't say that they are fitter, but it is true to say that my vintage of footballers came in all shapes and sizes.

○ ○ ○

Alex Ferguson did not return to Aberdeen with the main party from the Low Countries. The fact that we had played Waterschei on a Tuesday meant that he had time to fly to Madrid to watch the other semi-final between Real Madrid and Austria Vienna the following evening. He had travelled to the Bernabeau with members of the Scottish press on a fact-finding mission. The first leg had ended 2-2 in Austria, and in Spain Alfredo Di Stefano's Real Madrid team won 3-1 to secure their place in the final. When the boss returned home, he told us that he thought we had a great chance of winning the final, which was due in three weeks' time. They may have been six-times European champions and we were just two-times Scottish champions, and they may have had the likes of Stielike, Camacho, Santillana and Metgod in their team, but we also had some talented international players to call upon, and I shared Fergie's optimism, which became infectious. Super-spy Archie Knox embarked on a mission to watch Real Madrid against Valencia, where they lost 1-0, and with it their hopes of winning the Spanish league title. This meant that the only chance they had left for honours that season was to beat us and lift the European Cup-Winners' Cup. The build-up to the final was incredible. Aberdeen, and much of Scotland, were focused on the big game, and we were approached by a producer to make a record, which was released on the Cherry Red Record label. *The European Song,* which could not be described as a classic, included the lyrics:

McLeish and Miller and Strachan too,
Will lead us forward and take us through
Because we're going to do it
We're going to do it
We're going to do it for you.

The record release was supposed to be a big money-spinner, but I don't think we saw a penny. I can say that it was good fun making the record, and we belted out *The European Song* and its B side, *The Northern Lights of Old Aberdeen* (what else?) in the recording studio. I must admit that we were all a bit puzzled, though, when we heard the eventual release. I, for one, did not recognize any of the voices, and most of the production sounded as if it had been sung in tune, unlike the studio original. Maybe it had been dubbed, but what was certain was that supporters boycotted the musical work in their droves, although I know that a few individuals, sports journalist Robert Martin of the *Scottish Sun* for one, retained their copies in first-class condition. These were bought as mementos, but I don't believe that the intention was to play the songs. A wise move, I say.

The city of Aberdeen was at fever-pitch during the count-down, and shops the length of Union Street set up good-luck displays in their windows. Men and women walked around wearing Aberdeen shirts that they had bought to wear, and this gesture was a phenomenon long before the fashion was adopted as the norm among a significant sector of fans. Everywhere I went, I was patted on the back and given sincere encouragement. The final inspired many spin-offs, and one small business struggled to secure sufficient supplies of red ribbon to produce Aberdeen rosettes, such was the demand. The rosettes were produced at a little corner shop in Raeburn Place, Aberdeen, where four talented ladies led by Frances Carter worked flat out: pennants, badges, streamers, bookmarks, banners and car stickers were also included on their fast-moving production line.

Alex Ferguson left nothing to chance in our preparations. He made sure that the hotel selected for our vital stay was to his liking, and a few days before we left for Sweden, he called together the wives and girlfriends of team members. He tried to make the preparations as relaxed as possible . . . which included printing up a false itinerary for the ladies. It said that they would gather at Pittodrie at the crack of dawn, and leave by a bus which would transport them to Gothenburg in south-west Sweden via various points in mainland Europe. He told them to pack warm clothes, a toothbrush and a cup, and informed them that they would be accommodated in single beds in a big dormitory. They were not best pleased, until the gaffer assured them that the so-called arrangements were nothing more than a wind-up. He included serious intent in his message to partners, though, telling them politely that though they were invited to the game, he did not wish them to contact their husband or boyfriend. Any problems that they faced at home, or once they arrived in Gothenburg, would have to be handled by them and club officials. The players were not to be disturbed on any account. Doug Bell's wife was included in the ban on personal contacts, despite the fact she was pregnant at the time of the final, and if she went into labour, she was to call Fergie rather than her husband. The character who had put together various travel packages for the club and the fans was the larger-than-life travel agent Harry Hynds from Glasgow. He told me that he had started to book more than 1,000 beds in Gothenburg in December, after Lech Poznan had been eliminated in the fourth round. Following the tumultuous defeat of Bayern in the quarter-finals, he had booked six aircraft, and before the semi-final against Waterschei, he had moved in on some of the best hotels in Gothenburg.

Alex Ferguson tried hard to deflect the pressure from players and towards himself, but it was a difficult task, as European Cup-Winners' Cup fever had engulfed Aberdeen Football Club and their excited followers. On the Monday morning on which we left for Gothenburg, the manager held a press conference in the boardroom at Pittodrie to outline his thoughts on the forthcoming game. Archie McPherson, Gerry McNee, Ian Broadley, Allan Herron, Ally Guthrie, Alastair Macdonald, Ron Scott, Ken Robertson and Glenn Gibbons, a close friend of Alex, were among those that I remember filing in. There were not enough chairs to go round, so Archie and some others had to stand around the table taking notes. After the press conference, Alex went down to the docks to wave off the 500 Aberdeen fans who were setting sail for the final on the P & O ferry St Clair. We then made our way to Aberdeen Airport for the flight, and the contingent included the first-team squad, club directors, journalists and a handful of supporters. On Tuesday, players' wives and some of the Pittodrie staff went to Sweden by plane, and over three days leading up to the final, 59 flights carried nearly 5,000 Aberdeen fans across the North Sea: 28 flights carrying 2,500 supporters left on the day of the game alone, the first aircraft heading off at 6.06am. By two o'clock all flights had departed without a single delay. Aberdeen Airport kept meticulous records from that amazing time, and duty-free shop manager Louis Cowie reported that supporters spent £49,000 in duty-free on outward journeys, a tidy sum for 1983. Cowie's inventory showed that 2,000 four-bottle packs of Carlsberg Special Brew were bought plus 917 bottles of vodka and 165 bottles of white wine, while the whisky account showed 400 bottles of Glenfiddich and Glenmorangie sold plus 431 litres of Grouse. Confidence in the result was summed up by 66 bottles of champagne being carried to Sweden, and in-flight records reveal that 150 bottles of brandy and 200 bottles of gin were downed above the North Sea before touch-down in Gothenburg.

The team arrived in Gothenburg on Tuesday, May 10 and checked into a hotel with the unfamiliar name of Fars Hatt, set in the village of Kungalv. It overlooked a river, and looking at pictures of the white building in retrospect, it is clear that it would not have been a candidate for a top award in architectural design. Indeed, it appears as a concrete monstrosity, but I roomed with Alex McLeish and kept myself to myself for most of the time, strolling by the river or sitting in the room thinking or reading or listening to music. I slept a lot, too, and most of my team-mates through the years will tell you that that was one of my favourite activities. In contrast, Alex found it difficult to sit still, and roamed around the hotel nipping into the rooms of team-mates to find out what was going on, before he could be completely happy. Fergie had played down events so much to the team that it seemed as if we were facing just another cup final. It didn't mean that he was being blasé, but that he had gone out of his way to ensure that we were totally relaxed. Believe it or not, but beyond sleeping and otherwise relaxing, I had more fun in the run-up to the Real Madrid game than on most European trips. We enjoyed plenty of laughs, quiz-sessions and pretty easy training that was not too technical, and I did not feel under pressure. It was great man-management that certainly worked, as it put my mind at rest.

The idea to play things down had been planted in Alex Ferguson's mind by Jock Stein, who travelled with us to Gothenburg and proved a great help to the gaffer. It was an important move, as any manager facing his first European final needs all the help that he can get. Jock had managed Celtic to European Cup glory in 1967 and in Gothenburg he calmed Fergie down, and Fergie calmed us down. One ploy suggested by Jock was to try to lull Real Madrid into a false sense of security. He suggested that Fergie take a bottle of whisky as a gift to Alfredo Di Stefano, the Real Madrid manager, and to say to him that he was just delighted that his team were sharing a pitch with the great Real Madrid. Jock told the boss to attempt to induce in Di Stefano the impression that Aberdeen were in Gothenburg to make up the numbers. It was a hard thing for the boss to do, as he was hell-bent of leading us to victory, but he took on board the psychological diversions that Jock wanted him to use. Di Stefano probably did think that Aberdeen were there to make up the numbers, for we were not mentioned in the same breath as Liverpool, Barcelona, AC Milan or Real Madrid.

First impressions of the Ullevi Stadium were positive, though when we trained there in mid-afternoon on the eve of the game,

I felt that the grass was a bit too long and could do with a cut. Real Madrid arrived a few minutes after we had left the pitch, and some of the Scottish press representatives who had stayed to watch marvelled at their skills. Luckily, the scribes did not pass on that information to me or any of the Aberdeen players until after the final. After the training session, we returned to the Fars Hatt Hotel for a quiet team meal then a sports quiz organised by Alan 'Fingers' Ferguson, who was acting as the Aberdeen press officer for the final. Fingers had banned Fergie from taking part, as he claimed that he was over-competitive, but the manager would act as referee and adjudicate on any dodgy decisions. I was the captain of one team with Gordon Strachan in charge of our opponents in a question-and-answer session that was scheduled to last for about half-an-hour, but which went on much longer, mostly because each team claimed they were being cheated out of points. Fergie sat chuckling and making the final rulings, and as it turned out, the quiz score finished level and the outcome depended upon a tie-break. The question posed was: which Scottish club side has the most letters in their name, and how many letters are in that name? We were in quick as a flash with 19 letters making up Hamilton Academicals, but Fingers said that was wrong, and put it across to Gordon's team, who were a bit confused because they thought our answer was right. However they went for 18, which turned out to be correct, as the team's official title is Hamilton *Academical*. 'It's not a bloody spelling quiz,' I protested, with Fergie becoming more and more amused, just as I was became more and more wound up. He ruled that Fingers was correct in rejecting my team's answer, and announced that Gordon's team were the winners.

It is hard to believe now that most of the first-team squad of Aberdeen Football Club spent the night before the biggest game of their lives falling out over a sports quiz that did not finish until just before midnight. But then Fergie wanted to take our minds off the game itself, and he succeeded. Despite being furious at losing out on the quiz tie-break, I slept well and did not waken until 8am. The rain was a mere drizzle when I looked out of the window, which was an improvement on some heavy stuff that we had witnessed since our arrival. The quiz was still on my mind, and when I spied Alan Ferguson at breakfast, I approached and remarked: 'Thanks a lot, Bamber.' He laughed, and responded by saying that he was intending to take over from Bamber Gascoigne on the TV quiz show *University Challenge* when he returned home. I spent a relaxed morning, but tension was mounting among some less-experienced players, and Fergie was walking around in relaxed fashion calming nerves as best he could. A pinball machine was installed in a corner of the hotel lobby, and most of the players had a shot. There was precious little else to do, and hitting the controls hard and trying to tilt the machine dispersed some pent-up aggression. I preferred to walk, even in the drizzle. No last-minute worries arose over who would be playing, and the boss had announced his starting line-up to reporters the day before the final. However, legendary sportswriter Jimmy Sanderson was a bit confused by full names being quoted, and asked who this person *William Ferguson Miller* was. I knew that I would play, but I felt sorry for the injured Stuart Kennedy and Doug Bell, who would miss out. Fergie rated Stuart highly, and put him on the bench, though his severe knee injury would prevent him playing even for a few minutes. It was a goodwill gesture by the gaffer that was most touching. For Doug, missing the final was a huge disappointment, but he was a talented young player, and we all felt that he would have better times ahead. John Hewitt and Andy Watson had played from the start in the semi-final second leg against Waterschei, and they were on the bench.

Back at the hotel, Alex Ferguson, Archie Knox and press officer Alan Ferguson had decided to go for a run on the jogging track round the lake. Alan had completed a London Marathon a few weeks previously, and was probably the fittest, but Fergie and Archie were determined not to let him win. I watched the three as they came into view for the final stages, and Alan was elbowed out the way as his rivals ran towards the end of the jogging track and sprinted for the line. Both claimed victory.

Why was I not surprised? We left for the Ullevi Stadium at 6pm as rain pelted down, and in the dressing-room the manager delivered an emotional team talk. He highlighted the magnificent Aberdeen support that had travelled to Sweden by bus, train, plane and boat to cheer us on. We couldn't let them down. We couldn't let ourselves down. After such an inspiring oration, we were convinced that we would lift the European Cup-Winners' Cup. We formed a formidable group of men, who were managed by the best in the business. How could we fail? I was not nervous before kick-off, and I stuck to my ritual: shorts on, right sock, left sock, strip over head, boots. I walked slowly out on to the pitch soaking up the atmosphere. This was my moment, the one in which I recognised without doubt that Aberdeen Football Club would write their name in the history books.

We were certainly not intimated by Real Madrid despite the prestige that they carried, and Eric Black opened the scoring after a Gordon Strachan corner was headed towards goal. Eric, a predator in the penalty-box, steered the ball home after just seven minutes of the final. Alex McLeish made few mistakes during his playing career, but the heavy pitch and driving rain were factors which led to his misjudging a back-pass, which allowed Santillana to go one-on-one with Jim Leighton. Jim brought him down in the box, and Juanito levelled the scoring from the penalty-spot seven minutes later. I had to steady the ship in the ensuing period, as they came at us in full force. Indeed, the gaffer informed me later that for 20 minutes after that penalty equalizer, we had forgotten all that he had drummed into us in terms of keeping our shape. He was spot-on, as usual, and the Spanish side could have taken the game by the scruff of the neck at that time, and scored a few goals. Thankfully, they failed to do so, and we managed to calm down and to revert to our passing game. At half-time, the boss demanded more effort, more control and more patience. He wanted us to go out and be positive and to take the game to our opponents, and he altered the tactics slightly, in that Peter Weir was pushed further forward, and Mark McGhee and Eric Black were instructed to track back more. We did well in the second half, but lost Eric near the end with a leg injury, and John Hewitt, who had been unlucky not to be on the field from the start, took over. With eight minutes left on the clock, Peter Weir went past two Real Madrid defenders and passed the ball to Mark McGhee, who put in a left-foot cross which Augustin in goals came for, but missed. In a split-second, John Hewitt got his head to the ball to give us the lead. With the minutes ticking down agonizingly slowly, I gave away a free-kick just outside the penalty-box, though I did not believe that I had committed a foul, and protested. I was praying: 'God, please don't let them score with this free-kick.' If they had, I would have carried the blame for the rest of my life. I was not in the wall to defend the free-kick, but just off it ready to charge the ball. I ran towards it, but Salguero had got his shot away, and I turned anxiously to watch the trajectory of his strike. For a horrific moment I thought that the ball was going in, and it came as a massive relief, probably the most intense such feeling of my life, when it swept narrowly wide. All hell broke loose at the blast of the final whistle, and the moment is caught in the iconic photograph of reserve goalkeeper Bryan Gunn jumping off the Aberdeen bench closely followed by Alex Ferguson, Archie Knox and Stuart Kennedy. What people might not know is that Fergie, in his rush to celebrate, fell head over heels into a puddle after being accidently pushed by Bryan. He got up, steadied himself and ran as fast as he could on to the pitch – as manager of Aberdeen, the team from the north-east of Scotland who had triumphed over the mighty Real Madrid in the European Cup-Winners' Cup final. It took ages for officialdom to bring us the trophy. No orchestrated presentation ceremony had been arranged, as is done nowadays. No fireworks. No big build-up. But they did supply an old table on which to display the cup and medals. I received the trophy from a member of the Italian FA, who wanted to raise it to the heavens with me, and I had almost to wrestle it from his grasp to fulfil the captain's role, and to do the honours myself. When I laid hands on the

European Cup-Winners' Cup, it was the proudest moment of my playing career. I grasped the trophy in my left hand and turned to our ecstatic supporters, and as their ear-splitting roars rang out in the night air in Gothenburg, I realized full well what we had achieved. I examined the list of previous winners engraved on the trophy, and our name was now carved with pride among the greatest clubs in Europe.

I stayed on the pitch for as long as I could savouring the victory, running round the pitch with my team-mates. I was experienced enough to recognise that times such as these do not come around too often in the game of football, and they should be enjoyed to the fullest extent. I noticed, for the first time, the banners that had been draped around the stands: '*Peter Weir lays on more balls than Emanuelle*' was an allusion to a racy film of the time; a slightly-racist slogan aimed at our Spanish opponents, which would not likely be tolerated these days, declared: '*Doug Rougvie never lets a diago by*'; and the one which I most appreciated, and which was closest to home, read: '*Gordon Strachan gives out more majestic passes than Dick Donald*', referring to the Majestic Cinema in Aberdeen, which was owned by our club chairman. Other banners identified where supporters were based, such as Jock's Pub in Old-meldrum, and a huge offering identifying Dons fans from Peterhead. I had to be dragged off the pitch, and we stumbled into the dressing-room as high as kites. I did not need champagne to heighten the excitement, but that did not stop me partaking of a glass or two, or maybe three. Well-wishers crammed into the dressing-room to congratulate us, among them Jock Stein, who had helped our manager so much on the expedition to Sweden, and Ernie Walker of the SFA. Well done, boys! Mission accomplished!

Come the heroic morn, we gathered up Swedish newspapers as souvenirs of our achievement, and the consensus in print, translated for us by hotel staff, was that Aberdeen had deserved to win the final. During the flight from Gothenburg to Aberdeen, we supped champagne from the trophy and passed it round the cabin. The flight was rather bumpy – a reminder perhaps of our European campaign – but I did not care about flying conditions as I was elated, and hung over, in equal measures, which made for an ideal combination. We had been wonderfully supported in Sweden, and we were prepared for a stupendous welcome home, but I just did not expect the massive numbers who spilled on to the streets to greet our return. The plane touched down just before 3pm, and the minute we emerged we were swamped. Photographers and television crews met us at the foot of the aircraft steps, and airport staff cheered us through the customs area. Our personal luggage and kit were transported to Pittodrie immediately, and club officials arrived at the ground at about 3.30 to be greeted by 20,000 people, who were already camped inside the stadium. The team did not reach the ground until two hours later, which was a tribute to the patience demonstrated by our quite wonderful fans. Before that, the open-top bus snaked its way from Dyce through Bucksburn and via Queen's Road and Union Street towards Pittodrie. I had been on the go for 24 hours with little sleep, and by the time I reached the stadium, I was shattered and running on adrenaline. I wasn't the only one who was out on his feet, for Mark McGhee could not summon up enough energy to embark on a lap of honour on the Pittodrie pitch. We had put so much effort into beating Real Madrid, had celebrated in appropriate fashion afterwards, and we were mentally and physically drained. I crashed into bed later, and did not stir until mid-morning the following day. As I slept, Fergie and Mark McGhee, now refreshed, were at the quayside to welcome back the ferry St Clair, which had shipped fans back from Gothenburg. Browsing newspapers from that era shows that 493 passengers and 63 crew sailed to Sweden on the Monday afternoon before the final, and that Captain Mike Gray from Shetland brought the vessel safely back into Aberdeen Harbour to the sound of cheering from those on shore. The biggest tribute to the fans on the St Clair was that no trouble broke out, and not even a chair was damaged on the outward or inward voyages. I enjoyed one day-off in the wake of victory, and when I returned to Pittodrie I was met by hundreds of letters and telegrams from many parts of the world, which emphasised the enormity of what we had achieved. One message that I remember was a simple letter from a 67-year-old Gordon Slater from Birmingham. He had not written to a football club before, but felt moved to make contact because he was so excited about the way we had played against Real Madrid. A telegram was received from the Scottish Fishermen's Association, and a motion of congratulation was moved in the House of Commons by MPs including Robert Hughes, James Lamond, Dennis Canavan, Ernie Ross, Norman Hogg and Bob Cryer, and the legendary Liverpool manager, Bob Paisley, added his good wishes. Bayern Munich, the club that we had beaten in the quarter-finals, sent congratulations, which was a nice touch, as did a chap by the name of Alan Benton, who described himself as West Africa's one-man Aberdeen Supporters' Club. Robert Messer wrote from New South Wales in Australia to say that he had got up at 4am local time to listen to the game, and had never been so excited in his life. In the days before Internet access, it was exciting to receive telegrams from people such as Dons fans in up-state New York, who had watched the match on Channel 47, and had celebrated hard into the night. Academics calling themselves the Oxford Dons at Mansfield College, Oxford, were among those who wrote to me personally. I was on cloud nine, as were the other players, but we had to get back to earth quickly.

To be honest, I would have been happy if the season had ended there and then, but that was not the case, and only three days after victory in the European Cup-Winners' Cup – which brought each player a bonus of £2,000, though the money was secondary – we were down to play Hibs in the final Scottish Premier League game of the season, and we had to concentrate on the Scottish Cup final as well. The Scottish Cup had been put to one side amid all the excitement, but Alex Ferguson now had it placed firmly at the top of his agenda. He told us that we had two games left in season 1982-83, and he wanted 100 per cent concentration in both. We would have the rest of our lives to remember carrying off the European trophy, and should cast thoughts of our triumph into the backs of our minds in the interim.

Our game against Hibernian was an inherently difficult fixture, as we still had an outside chance of winning the league, but we had to hope that Dundee United and Celtic lost their final matches, and that we emerged with a win. The Hibs players applauded us out on to the pitch, and we duly returned their good wishes by giving them a 5-0 thumping. Dundee United and Celtic won their last fixtures, which meant that United were crowned league champions with 56 points, one ahead of Aberdeen and Celtic. We had to get ourselves in the mood again for a big occasion, as the following Saturday, May 21, 1983 we were due to play Rangers in the Scottish Cup final at Hampden, the fixture coming ten days after our heroics in Gothenburg, and seven days on from the Hibs match. It would be our 60th competitive game of the season. We had beaten Hibernian 4-1 at Easter Road in the third round, followed that with a 1-0 win over Dundee, squeezed past Partick Thistle in the quarter-finals, and overcome Celtic in the semi thanks to a Peter Weir goal.

Not surprisingly after our win over Real Madrid, Fergie decided to field the same team against Rangers at Hampden, though Alex McLeish was an injury doubt up to the morning of the final. It appeared as if we were suffering from an end-of-season hangover, and had played too much football, for our performance against Rangers was dreadful. The better chances fell to them, and with seconds of the 90 minutes remaining, Jim Leighton brought off a great save from Jim Bett to take the game into extra-time. Fergie agreed that we had under-performed, and we had to up our game to have any chance of victory. We reacted positively, and with four minutes left, Craig Paterson deflected a Mark McGhee low cross into the air – and Eric Black pounced to score the winner.

We had become the first team outside the Old Firm to win the Scottish Cup in successive years during the 20th century, but the boss was still furious about our overall showing. In a television interview, he claimed that Alex McLeish and I had been the only men who had performed to their full potential. Obviously that did not go down well, and the mood in the dressing-room was not as upbeat as it should have been, considering we had landed our second trophy of the season. Despite the manager's comments, I did not believe that I had displayed top form, and I had struggled to achieve the right frame of mind for Hampden after the euphoria of our successful expedition to Sweden. Alex McLeish and I probably had the experience to allow us to stay focused, but it was not at all easy. Though the build-up to the European Cup-Winner's Cup final had been as relaxed as it could be, the ensuing emotion of our Gothenburg exploits had taken its toll and affected the legs, especially of the midfield men who had run their hearts out against Real Madrid. Because of the manager's negative line, our Scottish Cup party in St Andrews was rather downbeat. He did concede later that he had been wrong to chastise the team, but his comments were an indication of his setting high standards, which he expected all his players to achieve. He cared deeply, and wanted our success to continue. After apologizing privately to the players for the critical remarks, Fergie returned to TV screens to make his apology a public matter. His retractions further enhanced my opinion of the man, as it took a big character to admit that he was wrong, especially one driven so hard as Alex Ferguson.

Certainly, supporters of Aberdeen Football Club must have been tempted to believe that our success would now be never-ending. For the second time within a fortnight, Union Street was thronged with fans cheering us on an open-top bus ride through the city, this time bearing the Scottish Cup. I was obviously lapping up all the success, and when we arrived at Pittodrie a welcoming crowd of 20,000 was again there in waiting. I was drained mentally and physically, but satisfied beyond expectation. It had been a long, hard but rewarding season, and I knew well from experience that Alex Ferguson would not let up, and once again would expect even more success in the season ahead.

11

THE GRANDIOSE HABIT OF CUP FINALS

*'The Super Cup may have looked rather strange, but I
desperately wanted to get my hands on it'*

Winning one European trophy might be good enough for some
footballers, but not for me. After lifting the Cup-Winners' Cup, I
found myself in exalted company. Only Billy McNeill, who
captained Celtic to European Cup success in 1967, and John
Greig, who fulfilled the key role for Rangers when they won the
Cup-Winners' Cup in 1972, had led Scottish teams to continental triumphs. I wished to go one better, and to become the
first Scot to captain a Scottish club to two European trophies. My
chance to mark up the double came in the final of the Super
Cup, which was played between the winners of the European
Cup and the holders of the Cup-Winners' Cup. After Celtic
won their European trophy, they played Racing Club of
Argentina in the World Club Championship, as the European
Super Cup had not been introduced, and they were beaten in a
play-off game. Rangers did take part in the Super Cup, but were
beaten in the final by Ajax. The Super Cup should, by rights,
have been described as the Super Shield, for at the pre-match
press conference before we faced Hamburg, the reigning European champions, the trophy was placed at the top table, and it
was shaped like a shield. The Super Cup may have looked rather
strange, but I desperately wished to get my hands on it. Only
Hamburg stood between Aberdeen proving that they were the
leading team in the European arena in that period.

In the first leg, played in Germany, we used our European
experience to take the sting out of the game early, and were

never in too much trouble. We played well defensively and managed to soak up everything that was thrown at us. They included in their line-up the West German internationalist, Felix Magath, and all their telling moves were inspired by him, but Jim Leighton was hardly troubled as we came away with a creditable 0-0 draw. The second leg took place on a rainswept evening at Pittodrie, and fans were taken aback when we ran on to the pitch after donning white shirts and black shorts, as Hamburg were kitted out in their all-red strip. We may not have felt at home in our odd uniform, but we did feel at home in terms of performance. Neil Simpson got on the end of a Peter Weir cross to score, and Mark McGhee netted a second to put us on easy street. We dominated the rest of the match, and coasted to a victory that ensured the name of Aberdeen Football Club would be taken seriously throughout Europe. Within weeks we were informed by UEFA that we had been named European Team of the Year for 1983 in a poll carried out by *France Football* magazine.

Our Super Cup victory had been achieved without the significant services of Stuart Kennedy, whose career-ending injury I recorded with sadness earlier on, and while followers of the game might say that no player is irreplaceable, Stuart was not far short of that description. Fergie struggled to fill the major gap that he had left behind, experimenting with a few other full-backs before settling on Stewart McKimmie from Dundee as a regular replacement. Billy Stark also joined us from St Mirren, as the manager continued to spend wisely. The Premier League campaign for season 1983-84 started well for me, and I scored in our 5-0 win over St. Johnstone, and did the same against St Mirren when the score-line was repeated. The writer from the *Aberdeen Evening Express* described my shot into the net against Paisley's finest as 'a thunderous drive from outside the box'. Who was I to argue? In contrast, events of Saturday October 29, 1983 brought me down to earth, for it was a day that could have undermined the incredible strides that we had made under Alex Ferguson. Reporters had been talking about Rangers seeking a new manager after making a dismal start to the season, and on the

morning of our game against Dundee at Dens Park, the story
broke that they would ask Alex Ferguson to take charge at Ibrox.
He had been the biggest single influence on my football career,
and I did not want my mentor to depart, and you will recall that I
had turned down an offer from Rangers the previous season
because I wished to continue to work with Fergie at Aberdeen.
As an example of our continued devotion to the man, the whole
team played superbly against Dundee, the 3-1 success keeping us
at the top of the league ahead of Dundee United, Celtic and
Hearts. Two nervy weeks passed before Alex revealed to us that
he would stay where he was: Rangers' second choice, Jim
McLean of Dundee United, also turned them down before
the familiar figure of Jock Wallace accepted the post. Sighs of
relief all round in the north-east of Scotland, for Fergie was
considered vital to Aberdeen's continuing success.

POSITIVE FACTORS THAT SWAYED THE BOSS

*Almost invariably, Aberdeen Football Club have reflected the high
standards of a well-run operation, and at the time the business was
being operated efficiently by Dick Donald, Chris Anderson and the rest of
the Pittodrie board. Alex Ferguson was not subjected to much, if any,
interference from them in carrying out the duties of manager to the best of
his remarkable abilities. He was allowed to get on with his job in relative
peace.*

*This positive but hands-off relationship with the club chairman and
board of directors would have helped to sway his decision to stay at
Pittodrie, rather than to take up a new appointment at Rangers. He also
had a group of talented players at his disposal and this factor also would
have counted in his decision-making.*

In tune with the widespread feelings of relief, the team turned in
outstanding performances to win our next fixture 3-0, by coincidence against Rangers. The following Saturday, November 19,

before our home match against Heart of Midlothian, we were the recipients of a special presentation by the SFA to mark our successes in the European Cup-Winners' Cup and Scottish Cup the previous season. Fears had been expressed that after our European exploits, we might suffer from a hangover in the following season, but that was not the case. By January 7, we were four points clear of Celtic in the Scottish Premier League table after 20 matches, and though wintry weather intervened and we did not play again until February 4, Fergie kept us on our toes during the interlude. We had an outstanding chance of winning the title again, and though we had no competitive games, he kept training at a high tempo and did not allow us to become complacent. He was on his own by this time, as Archie Knox had left to take over as manager of Dundee. This *was* a big loss to us, for Archie's football knowledge was second to none, though he operated in the shadow of Alex Ferguson. It took guts, though, to try to prove himself in occupying a manager's hot seat, and it would have been easy for Archie to stay on as an assistant at Aberdeen. Who would act as replacement to the trusted lieutenant? When his identity was revealed on February 9, I was somewhat surprised. The boss entered the dressing-room to announce that Willie Garner, my old team-mate, was to be his new assistant manager. Willie had been working with the reserves, and was a good coach. He had played at the highest level, and he had learned a lot from working with the boss and Archie, as we all had. I got on well with Willie, and there would be no problem being told by him what to do on the training field, though I had acted as his captain. I must say that, by that stage in my career, even the boss didn't have to tell me much, and the same could be said for the rest of the experienced players in the squad. A lot of us played on instinct, and one who fell into that category without doubt was Gordon Strachan. In my book, season 1983-84 saw him at the peak of his powers. He was a joy to play with, but must have been absolute hell to play against. Against St Mirren he scored his 100th goal for Aberdeen, and not surprisingly clubs in various European countries were keen to

attract his whirlwind energy and expertise. For instance, Cologne
watched him run rings around Motherwell on April 7, and he
scored another superb goal in a 2-0 victory. Many other clubs
were admiring the wee man from afar, and it was evident that we
would be struggling to hold on to his talent for much longer.

GINGER CAN BE HOT TO THE TASTE

*It is often said within the wonderful world of football that Gordon
Strachan is a bit lippy. My answer to queries about his attitude is: what
do you expect? Gordon is wee, ginger and Scottish, and that's how wee,
ginger Scots tend to act on the football field, and elsewhere. Gordon was
one of the most intelligent footballers that I played alongside. His vision
and his ability to bring other men into the game and to set up chances was
amazing to behold, as was his penchant for turning games to his team's
advantage with a one-off piece of brilliance.*

*For many years, he forged a great understanding with full-back Stuart
Kennedy, and having an individual of such talent behind him allowed
Gordon to take chances, knowing that Stuart would cover for him.
Gordon was a livewire who could read a game with rare clarity, and it was
no surprise when he eventually followed the management trail. Throughout his career at Pittodrie, he performed his duties displaying a broad grin,
and he was a magnificent example to up-and-coming professionals.*

With seven games left in the league, we were sitting at the top of
the table with 50 points, two ahead of Celtic, but significantly we
had played four games fewer. The title was well and truly within
our grasp, and we continued to pick up points until it became
clear that I had a wonderful chance to win the Scottish Premier
League Championship on my 29th birthday on May 2. We faced
Hearts at Tynecastle needing a win to take the title. It proved to
be a tight encounter, but a goal from Stewart McKimmie
delivered a 1-0 win, and the title. Earlier that day, I had been
informed that I was Scotland's Player of the Year, an accolade

that depended on voting among members of the Scottish Football Writers' Association, which was a great honour. Charlie Nicholas had won the award the previous year, and Paul Sturrock was the recipient before that. Billy McNeill, John Greig, Pat Stanton and Danny McGrain had been honoured in the past, so I had joined distinguished company. I did feel, however, that the recognition from Scotland's journalists had come a year late. After all, I had been captain of Aberdeen Football Club when they won the European Cup-Winners' Cup during the previous season: Charlie Nicholas had gathered the most votes after scoring lots of goals, but another Scot had lifted a European trophy! Billy McNeill and John Greig had received the honour after their teams gained European silverware, but for some reason I was not granted recognition immediately. Still, from 1980–84 I was playing at the peak of my powers . . . so the football scribes got it right eventually.

My other major hope that season was to retain the Cup-Winners Cup, but we fell just short. We managed to overcome Akranes of Iceland in the first round and Beveren of Belgium in the second, and in the quarter-finals we were drawn to meet the Hungarian team, Ujpest Dosza. Now for me Hungarian football had always been tinged with a bit of a mystique, the feeling dating back to when their national team, with the master Ferenc Puskas as captain, beat England at Wembley in 1953 by the amazing margin of 6–3. We played Ujpest Dosza in the Megyeri Stadium in Budapest on March 7, 1984, and like the Hungarian teams of old, they proved to be an effective footballing outfit. We missed chances and should have won, and how they managed to beat us 2–0 was beyond me, for we were the better side on the night. That was the one factor that made me think we could beat them, and beat them well, at Pittodrie. Alex Ferguson had certainly not given in, and he kept reminding us that we had come back from similar deficits before, and that we could do so once more. A crowd of 22,800 packed Pittodrie for the second leg on March 2, and I told my troops before kick-off that the game was there for us to win. They didn't let me down. We came out of the trenches at pace and laid siege on the visitors' goal, and Mark McGhee took the cue to accomplish a personal triumph, after passing up an easy chance in the first leg. He hit the target after 37 minutes, and played a blinder throughout, but for all our efforts it seemed that the game was slipping away from us. With two minutes left we were leading 1-0, which meant that we were behind on aggregate, and just when all looked lost, Mark popped up to score and to take the match into extra-time. Three minutes into the first period of overtime, Gordon Strachan put over a cross which eluded all but Mark, and he ghosted in at the back post to score the winner. A hat-trick fashioned by Mark McGhee ensured another tremendous night for us: another game to enter the folklore of Aberdeen Football Club.

I was sure that we could now pull off a unique double with successive Cup-Winners' Cup wins. In the semi-final we drew Porto, who were less well-known as a team than nowadays, and I felt that in the Portuguese we had probably drawn the weakest side left in the tournament. The other semi-final featured Juventus against Manchester United. Fergie travelled to check out Porto in action, and told us that they were quick on the break, and must not be under-estimated. We played in front of 65,000 fans in Portugal on April 11, 1984 and were under pressure for most of the game, Fernando Gomes' header in 14 minutes providing the only goal. Not a bad result away from home, but on the other hand they were a technically-efficient unit, and playing at Pittodrie would hold no problems for them. Mist was drifting in from the North Sea when the return leg kicked off, and that was a blessing in disguise for it helped to obscure a performance that was below par. We were outplayed, and when Vermelino scored with a superb chip with 15 minutes left to make the aggregate 2-0, our dreams of back-to-back European triumphs vanished into the East Coast haar.

As compensation, we had another Scottish Cup final to look forward to. We had endured tough times getting there, and in the third round had to depend on a replay to squeeze past Kilmarnock after drawing 1-1 at Pittodrie. I particularly remember the replay on February 15, 1984, because I scored, and also contributed to one of the goals of the season. Gordon Strachan played a one-two with me, performed the same meticulous manoeuvre with Eric Black, then with Mark McGhee, and finished off one of the finest-quality team scores that I have witnessed. My goal came next, and Peter Weir got the third in our 3-1 victory. Clyde were beaten in the next round, but in the quarter-finals we found Dundee United a tough proposition; after a goal-less draw at home, another Mark McGhee strike after just two minutes gave us victory in the replay. In the semi-final we beat Dundee 2-0 to set up a final against Celtic on May 19. Reaching cup finals was becoming second nature to Aberdeen, and I certainly did not book holidays around cup-final time, as I expected to be featuring at Hampden. Come the big day, we took the lead after a Gordon Strachan corner was headed forward by Alex McLeish to Eric Black, who volleyed the ball into the net. Five minutes before half-time, our mission should have been made easier after Roy Aitken was sent off for a foul on Mark McGhee. He was the first player to be shown a red card in a Scottish Cup final since Rangers' Jock Buchanan, and we should have killed the game after that turn of events. But much to my consternation, Paul McStay equalised with four minutes left. I had to dig deep to disperse my anger at the game going into extra-time, but we upped a gear and Doug Bell, who had already made a difference after coming on as a substitute, hit a post, and Gordon Strachan reacted quickly to pass the ball to Mark McGhee, who clinched the cup for Aberdeen.

The crucial goal was a fitting way for Mark to end his career with the club. I had known for a while that he was considering signing for Hamburg, as he was a powerful striker of the type that would do well on the Continent. He was a significant loss on various levels, for he was a firm friend and a tireless worker on the field of play. He made space for his colleagues, was unselfish in front of goal and was a deadly finisher, as he had proved by the procession of goals that had boosted Aberdeen's fortunes in various competitions. What I did not know for sure at the time, though my suspicions had been alerted, was that the Scottish Cup final victory over Celtic would also mark Aberdeen swan-songs for Gordon Strachan and Doug Rougvie. The relationship between Alex Ferguson and Gordon had been strained, to say the least, for much of the latter part of the season, and Fergie was not the only one to conclude that the wee man was for the off. Inevitably, the talk was to the effect that he would follow Mark to West Germany, most probably to Cologne. When he was sold to Manchester United, it came as an absolute surprise, but I knew Gordon would be a success at whatever club he played for. Big Doug Rougvie moving south to Chelsea was another disap-pointment, as he provided a big presence on the park. His leaving did not hit us as hard as the decisions of Mark and Gordon to move on, but we could have done without a triple whammy of that nature. Still, a remarkable triple whammy of European Super Cup, Scottish Premier League Championship and Scottish Cup marked a fitting final season for such distinguished servants of Aberdeen Football Club.

12

SUCCESSES COME WITH A PRICE

'Fergie just got on with the job of rebuilding his team'

The summer of 1984 was a difficult period for me. The transfers of Mark McGhee, Gordon Strachan and Doug Rougvie, a triumvirate of comrades who had shared a host of inspiring football moments with me, proved deeply unsettling. I kept my thoughts to myself, and attempted as captain to inspire a positive mood and to unite spirits in the dressing-room, as important business had to be addressed – which included playing in the European Cup in the coming season. But keeping things upbeat was easier said than done, as thoughts invariably turned to who might be next to take the high road away from Aberdeen. Our successes meant that a coterie of clubs were trying to tempt players away, and as Aberdeen did not hold financial reserves from which huge wages could be offered, conditions were relatively easy for predators. It was a difficult situation. On the one hand, the fans wanted us to keep winning trophies, but we had to do it with a team put together on a limited budget. I wanted us to go from strength to strength under Fergie, but I knew in my heart that the Gothenburg team was being dismantled piece by piece.

There was also no guarantee that the gaffer would remain in post, as lots of clubs were interested in benefiting from his winning ways. The latest to test Fergie's resolve were Tottenham Hotspur, who offered him a lucrative financial package to head south. In the end he turned it down, but how long before he said yes to a new employer? A manager losing the goal-scoring abilities of Mark, the midfield talents of Gordon and the physical presence of Doug would had every right to moan about his predicament, and to consider moving on, but the boss just got on with the job with rebuilding his team.

○ ○ ○

LOYALTY AND TRUST: KEY WORDS IN THE FERGUSON LEXICON

Team building was, and remains, one of a raft of abilities reflected on the Alex Ferguson CV. Two key words that I would associate with his style of management are loyalty and trust. He can suss out people out straight away, judge character and find out what makes them tick. At Aberdeen, he went out of his way to detect the strengths and weaknesses of a player on and off the park. He knew who he could trust, and who he could not. He put a lot of store in that word trust.

When he arrived at Aberdeen, Alex Ferguson had a big job on his hands, as he had inherited Billy McNeill's set of players. He moved some individuals on to make way for younger men, but did that as quickly and as painlessly as he could. He was not one to sack players, and depended on his good eye for football talent and tactical nous to decide where various individuals would fit into his side.

He also made use of an excellent scouting network, and was energetic in searching the country to target signings. But in developing a great Aberdeen team, the unfortunate follow-on was members of the squad being tempted away by big-money offers from clubs beyond Scotland.

Such is life!

○ ○ ○

Getting on with the job meant that Alex Ferguson brought in Frank McDougall from St Mirren in place of Mark. Billy Stark, who was already at the club, would replace Gordon, and Tommy McQueen from Clyde to fulfil Doug's role. Though obviously I was hoping that we would do well in the European Cup, my two major aims for season 1984–85 were to win the Scottish Cup again – I had lifted the trophy three times in a row, and was desperate to make it a quartet – and to retain the Scottish Premier League Championship. In our first game in the Scottish

Cup, we beat Alloa 5-0 at Pittodrie, recent signing Billy Stark making his mark early with a hat-trick. We squeezed past Raith Rovers 2-1 thanks to another new boy, Frank McDougall, scoring twice: I was particularly pleased that he did so, as I had given away a penalty that allowed the Kirkcaldy side to take the lead. The quarter-final was a stern test, as we drew Hearts at Tynecastle, where an Eric Black goal cancelled out a strike from Sandy Clark. In the replay, our cause was aided by Hearts centre-back Roddy MacDonald being sent off after just 15 minutes for elbowing Eric in the face. Billy Stark scored the only goal to set up a semi-final against Dundee United, which was to be played at the neutral venue, so it was back to Tynecastle. We should have won that game, but we could not put the ball in the net. John Hewitt came close and Billy Stark hit the inside of a post, but it wasn't our day. The game did have its lighter moments, and I experienced a career first: being kissed by an opponent. While they may do it a lot in Italian football, it was never the Scottish way, so allow me to set the scene for this momentous piece of play-acting . . . Billy Kirkwood and I had got caught up in an incident near the touchline, and were swearing and squaring up to one another. The referee pulled us apart. Hand-bags-at-dawn stuff it was, and we soon calmed down. Now, I knew Billy pretty well off the park, and both of us realised that we were acting like daft laddies, so to defuse the situation, he kissed me on the forehead. I did not return the compliment, but his friendly action, done for a bit of fun, took the nastiness out an incident which might have boiled over. Paul Sturrock put United ahead, and with Neale Cooper being sent off for a tackle on Ralph Milne, my dream of lifting four consecutive Scottish Cups was fast disappearing. Things got worse when Stewart Beedie scored for them after an hour to make it 2-0, but Davie Dodds was sent off soon after for fouling me near the touchline, and a glimmer of hope emerged. When Ian Angus scored with four minutes left, it was more than a glimmer. With a couple of minutes still to go, Maurice Malpas handled in the penalty-box, and we should have been awarded a spot-kick.

Apparently, the only person who did not see Maurice handle the ball was referee Hugh Alexander, and it was frustrating in the extreme to be denied a stonewall penalty, which would have given us the opportunity to equalise.

Suffering from what I considered to be a bad refereeing decision was a sad way to end our 23-match undefeated run in the Scottish Cup. At least we had made the semi-final of the competition, which was a considerable achievement compared to our pathetic efforts in the Scottish League Cup. We lost by 3-1 to Airdrie in our first match, and Ally MacLeod, who was now in charge of the part-timers, relished beating his former team. That defeat was bad enough, but worse was to follow in the European Cup.

The last time we had entered the European Cup draw, we had been dumped by Liverpool in the second round, but I felt we could do a lot better. We drew Dynamo Berlin in our first match, which was a tough prospect as they had won the East German championship six times in a row, and had reached the European Cup quarter-finals the previous year. Unfortunately, Frank McDougall was ineligible, as he was banned for four matches after being sent off when playing for his previous club, St Mirren, against Feyenoord. The first tie at Pittodrie on September 19, 1984 was closely contested. The East Germans were a well-disciplined side, and it took the aerial ability of Eric Black to break them down. He struck in the 33rd and 67th minutes, but we let in a goal struck by Schultz with eight minutes left, which returned to haunt us. Indeed, the second leg on October 3 was a match I would rather forget. Andreas Thom scored for the Berliners in the second half, but Ian Angus allowed us the draw level. At 1-1 we would have qualified for the next round, but with six minutes left, Ernst put them 2-1 up to take the game into extra-time. No more scoring was recorded in 30 minutes' overtime, though I came close with a chip-shot which hit the crossbar. And so the outcome depended on penalties.

Now at Aberdeen, I have to confess, we did not practise taking penalties, so in seeking volunteers for the job against Dynamo

Berlin, I could not find five men who fancied taking a spot-kick. All I could see were the backs of my colleagues, for no-one wished to be looked in the eye to undertake such an onerous responsibility in a high-pressure situation. I certainly did not feel the inclination to try to score from the spot, but as I had managed to muster only four volunteers, I felt that it was my duty to give it a go. Heroes to a man, Ian Porteous, Tommy McQueen, John Hewitt and Billy Stark all scored, and the East Germans missed one attempt when Schulz hit the bar. I was our final penalty-taker, and me scoring would see us through to the next round of the European Cup by a shoot-out margin of 5-4. I must say that I was not nervous as I walked up to take the penalty, but I committed the cardinal sin of changing my mind during the run-up. I had intended to put the ball into the right-hand corner, but drilled it to the goalkeeper's left instead. He guessed correctly and saved the shot. I felt absolutely dreadful, but we were not out of contention yet, and the outcome would now be decided by sudden-death penalties. Dynamo scored with their first kick, which meant that Eric Black had to equalize, but unfortunately he missed, and we were out. Now, I don't mind taking responsibility for errors in my playing career, but an urban myth has been perpetuated that I missed the penalty that put Aberdeen out of the tournament. I realised that I had been cast as the fall guy when a female member of staff at Aberdeen Airport unfurled a banner to greet our return from the Continent, which proclaimed: 'We *still love you, Willie*' To this day, people talk about my missed penalty that put Aberdeen out of the European Cup. But it was Eric Black whodunit!

Struggling in cup competitions would not matter so much to me if I managed to help the club to retain the Scottish Premier League title in season '84-85. We started our campaign with a home win over Dundee, and followed that with away victories over St Mirren and Dundee United. We beat Morton at Cappielow in the fifth game of the season. They were my bogey team, and I hated playing at Greenock. I had won only three times in ten visits to Cappielow, but this time we were never in trouble, and cruised to a 3-0 victory. Only Celtic and Dundee United got the better of us in the league before Christmas, and in the first game of the New Year, United beat us again, by 2-1 at Tannadice. That allowed Celtic to sneak closer, and though we remained top of the table with 33 points from 21 games, they were only two points behind at that stage. We stepped up the pressure, and by February had accelerated to eight points ahead of Celtic with 11 matches left on the fixture list. They did beat us at Parkhead, but we kept our nerve, and recorded victories over St Mirren, Dundee, Hibs and Dundee United. The crucial match for us featured Celtic again, at Pittodrie on April 27, 1985, which was the third-last game of the Premier League season. We needed a win to be sure of the title, but even a draw would leave Celtic with scant chance of gaining the championship, as we would have to lose our final two away games, and they would be obliged to overturn a goal difference of 13. Fergie ensured that we were fired up for the vital clash, as he wanted to win the title at home at Pittodrie as up to that point Alex Ferguson's teams had secured their championships away from home. The script did not go according to plan when, after 40 minutes, Celtic were granted a penalty, which I did not feel was warranted. I was close to the incident, and not for one moment did I consider that Billy Stark had fouled Mo Johnston, as the referee indicated. Roy Aitken scored from the penalty-spot, and we were required to chase the game. On the hour-mark, I went up for a free-kick from Ian Porteous, launching myself at the ball and out-jumping Roy Aitken, which was no easy task, to head it in off a goalpost. John Hewitt came close to claiming the winner near the end, but the 1-1 draw meant we were champions-elect.

We beat Hearts 3-0 in the second-last match, a hat-trick from Frank McDougall setting the seal on the destination of the championship. It was fitting that Big Frank should grab the glory, as he had put in some hefty contributions for us over the season, and had scored several other important goals. Our last league game was against Morton at Cappielow, and for the first time in my football career against my bogey team, I approached the ground wearing a big smile, for if I finished on the losing side once more, it did not matter. The arithmetic had worked out in our favour already. As it turned out, we won 2-1 to set a Scottish Premier League record of 59 points gathered from 36 games; second-placed Celtic were seven points behind. Thus Cappielow provided a perfect setting for our championship season, in which we won 27 games, drew five, lost four, scored 89 goals and lost only 26. Our first league championship under Fergie in 1979-80 had been a magnificent achievement, but I would maintain that to repeat the feat in 1984-85 without the considerable contributions of Mark McGhee, Gordon Strachan and Doug Rougvie, and with the team in transition, was worthy of equal merit. It showed that Fergie could work his magic despite changes in the personnel.

13

REWARDED WITH TWO VARIETIES OF SCOTTISH CUP

'We started with all guns blazing, and did not let our opponents settle'

As defending Scottish Premier League champions, great things were expected of us in 1985–86 by our supporters, and by Alex Ferguson, naturally. The manager told me that, as he had won the Scottish Cup and Premier League, he really fancied having a tilt at the Scottish League Cup, the domestic title that had eluded him thus far. He would have to fulfil that ambition with a sole addition to his squad from the previous season, but it was a significant addition. Jim Bett arrived from Lockeren in Belgium for £300,000, and watching him in training I knew straight away that he could be an important figure for us. Big players who would take responsibility were needed on the park, and Jim fitted that mould. Fergie could not wait for the season to get started, so that he could see him perform competitively.

In the Scottish League Cup, which had taken on board a sponsors' brand as the Skol Cup, we enjoyed a relatively-easy run to the quarter-final with victories over Ayr United and St. Johnstone. With the World Cup in Mexico to be played the following year, I was keen to impress international manager Jock Stein, who arrived to watch our quarter-final match against Heart of Midlothian at Pittodrie. Jim Leighton, Alex McLeish, Jim Bett, myself and other Aberdeen employees with international aspirations did well, and we won thanks to an Eric Black goal that set up a semi-final over two legs versus Dundee United.

They had knocked us out of the League Cup three times in recent seasons, and I was intent on ensuring that we turned the tables. As was the boss. We played superbly in the first leg at Tannadice, winning 1-0 thanks to an Eric Black goal, and we were equally impressive in the follow-up tie, a goal from Frank McDougall ensuring that we would make the final.

Our opponents at Hampden on Sunday October 27, 1985 were Hibernian, and Fergie's distinctive cough, a sure sign that he was nervous, was in evidence beforehand, and indicated just how keen he was to land the silverware that had eluded his grasp. We were in complete control from the start, to the extent the game was later described by fans as 'The 12-minute final' because of the short space of time it took us to score twice. Eric Black netted from a John Hewitt cross after two minutes, and Billy Stark added the other 10 minutes later. It was all over bar the shouting, and Eric scored again in the second half for an emphatic 3-0 victory. It was a tournament success of which I was extremely proud, for we had not conceded one goal in the six matches in the competition, and we had presented Fergie with a trophy to complete his domestic set. Just like my collection of medals, but I got there first. Success had been secured thanks to our experience of the big occasion, more than anything else. We knew how to handle Hampden finals, as we had played in a sequence of them, and teams such as Hibs were not used to such prestigious events. Indeed, we went out of our way to hit teams like Hibs quickly, to leave them shell-shocked with no way back. In that Scottish League Cup final, our policy was clear for all to see.

The boss may have targeted the Scottish League Cup, but I preferred winning the Scottish Cup, and I felt that Aberdeen should be involved in the end-of-season showpiece each year. Our initial involvement in '85-86 comprised an easy 4-1 win over Montrose on a snowy day: helpfully, they played in white, and you could hardly see their men! They failed to pick me up, allowing me to score the second of our goals with a header. Next up were Arbroath, who were beaten 1-0 thanks to a goal from Joe Miller, then we faced a tough quarter-final tie against

Dundee. The first match ended at 2-2, and we were lucky to come away with a draw. Just when things looked lost, an opposition error allowed John Hewitt to score the equaliser, which took the match to a replay at Pittodrie, and that did not prove any easier. Dundee went ahead, but Eric Black replied, and a spectacular curling shot from Peter Weir in the first period of extra-time pushed us through. The semi-final against Hibs at Dens Park proved an easier proposition, and we emerged on top from Fergie's seventh Scottish Cup semi-final in eight seasons by a margin of 3-0. On target were Billy Stark, Eric Black and Joe Miller. Hearts formed the hurdle that stood between us and another Scottish Cup final success. The Tynecastle club had been going for a league and cup double, but the championship was snatched from their grasp by Celtic on the last day of the Premier League season. That shattering setback had clearly knocked the spirit out of them, and they had been transformed into a shadow of the team that had run us close all season. Using the tactics that we had employed against Hibernian in the Scottish League Cup final earlier in the season, we started with all guns blazing, and did not let our opponents settle. Eric Black had been dropped after Alex Ferguson discovered that he had signed for French side, Metz. He had appeared in all three of our previous Scottish Cup wins, and was likely to be a big miss against Hearts, despite the fact that their confidence had taken a big knock. Fergie, though, was adamant that he would not be playing in the cup final, as he was departing. Right on cue, the rest of our strikers took charge of the script just when it mattered, John Hewitt striking after just five minutes, and following up with another goal just after half-time. Billy Stark made it three, and to add to Hearts' woes, their captain Walter Kidd was sent off for throwing the ball into John Hewitt's face. I must admit to having felt sorry for the Edinburgh club that day, for they had ended up with no silverware despite striving for league and cup. From Aberdeen's point of view, we had two trophies to show off from our season's exertions, and adding the European Cup to our haul that season would have a wonderful achievement. It was not to be.

Our new European expedition started in the far north with a 3-1 away win over Akranes in Iceland, and we went one better with a 4-1 result at Pittodrie. Servette of Switzerland turned out to be more difficult in the next round, and we had to be satisfied with a goal-less draw in the away leg before struggling at home in the return. It is an under-statement to record that we were lucky to get through, for twice they hit a goalpost, and our manager, who was never one to pour loads of praise on to the opposition, said he felt Servette's display was the finest that he had watched from a team visiting Pittodrie on a European mission. A Frank McDougall goal gave us a 1-0 win, but our performance was mediocre. Our next match was a quarter-final that I anticipated with relish – as did Jim Leighton, Alex McLeish, John Hewitt and other men who had been involved in our European Cup-Winners' Cup triumph over Real Madrid – for we had drawn IFK Gothenburg of Sweden, whose home was the familiar Ullevi Stadium. Although I was keen to play there again, we could spare no sentimentality about the trip, for Gothenburg were one of the form teams in Europe at that time. Their line-up had been put together by Sven-Goran Eriksson, who had just left and who would proceed to manage the England team some time later, and they had Gunder Bengtsson in charge when we played them. The first leg was down for Pittodrie on March 5, 1986, and it was a special date for me, as it would be my 50th appearance in European competitions. Before kick-off, a minute's silence was marked for the late Swedish Prime Minister, Olaf Palme, who had been the unexpected victim of an assassin's bullet in a Stockholm street. After that solemn overture, the period after kick-off proved that we were facing a side of quality. We had to battle for an early goal to try to put our Swedish visitors off their stride, and I was most surprised when that chance fell to me. I moved up for a corner-kick on the 16th minute, and when the ball was cleared towards me, I whipped it past their goalkeeper with my *left* foot. I had scored a few by means of right-foot shots and headers through the years, but sticking one in with my left was a rarity. They equalised through Tord Holmgren just before half-time, and they dictated most of the ensuing 45 minutes. We managed to score against the run of play through John Hewitt, but with a minute left Johnny Ekstrom rounded goalkeeper Bryan Gunn, who was playing for the injured Jim Leighton, to ensure a 2-2 draw for Gothenburg.

I obviously had a vast store of memories centered upon the Ullevi Stadium from our famous defeat of Real Madrid, but this time we would have our work cut out to come away with a positive result. We stayed in the centre of Gothenburg rather than outside the city, and the second leg, which was played on March 19, was something of a non-event. The hype leading up to the match and headlines which concentrated on the idea that we were returning to the stadium where we had enjoyed our finest hour, were more interesting than the run of play. IFK Gothenburg were happy to sit back and let us come on to them, which was a reasonable tactic considering that they had a 2-2 draw from Pittodrie tucked away. We tried our best, but simply could not break them down to clinch the goal that would have taken us through, and it was 0-0 at the final reckoning. The away-goals rule sealed our fate, and we could have few complaints about being knocked out, as Gothenburg were that bit more cohesive over two legs.

Despite winning the two Scottish cups on offer and making reasonable progress in Europe, our performance in the Premier League during 1985-86 was thoroughly disappointing. Indeed, my best memory was unfurling the SPL Championship flag for season '84-85 before our first match, which was against Hibernian. And the most poignant point of the league season was visiting Parkhead on September 14, 1985, soon after Jock Stein had collapsed and died after Scotland's World Cup qualifying match against Wales. Nearly 40,000 spectators packed Celtic Park to pay their respects to a one-off manager of clubs and his national team. Three Aberdeen supporters laid a wreath behind Pat Bonner's goal before the match, which Celtic won 2-1. We were joint top with Celtic and Rangers with 14 points after 10 games, but that was as good as it got. In the wake of Big Jock's untimely death, Alex Ferguson took over temporary responsibility for the Scotland team. He had been assisting Jock while toiling hard as our gaffer, and with a World Cup looming in nine months' time, the boss had no option but to grasp the joint managerial roles. He did not stint in his efforts at Aberdeen, and eight games later we were still leading the table with 23 points, one ahead of Hearts and two beyond Rangers and Celtic. Just before Christmas, however, we were knocked off the top after a defeat by Dundee United, and Fergie's rage was so intense that he was sent to the stand for arguing too much with the referee. Hearts won 1-0 at Pittodrie on January 18, 1986 to inflict our first home defeat in 13 months, and though I scored in a 1-1 draw at St Mirren on March 15, we were not playing well enough in league fixtures. Our hopes of retaining the Scottish Premier League Championship vanished when another defeat by Dundee United in April was followed by an away draw against Heart of Midlothian at Tynecastle. The match against Hearts was notable in one way in that it was the first league match in Scotland to be screened live on television. We were 1-0 up thanks to a Peter Weir goal from the penalty-spot, but John Colquhoun equalised to end our league hopes, faint as they were. Celtic beat Hearts for the league title on the last day of the season, and Dundee United squeezed past us into third place.

The two trophies, though, had been gained before the death of Aberdeen director Chris Anderson. Chris was a stalwart who had given the players and manager exceptional backing through the years. Though a victim of motor neurone disease, he turned up at as many games as he could manage up to the end. He contributed much to Aberdeen Football Club, and he enjoyed many days of glory in return.

14

AN IMPOSSIBLE ACT TO FOLLOW

*'Many were experiencing doubts about Ian Porterfield's
ability to drive us on to further glory'*

Throughout the eight years I spent with Alex Ferguson at
Aberdeen Football Club, he told me constantly that only a
massive club such as Manchester United would tempt him away
from Pittodrie. He was true to his word, and rejected approaches
by Wolverhampton Wanderers, Rangers and Tottenham Hotspur, but after the exceptional achievements that he had accumulated at Aberdeen, he could not keep saying no. I was not the
only one to believe that it would be only a matter of time before
his defences crumbled. He was an ambitious man, after all, and
had displayed managerial talent that would benefit any football
club. The Aberdeen board did their best to tempt him to stay,
and three games into the season and on the eve of a Scottish
League Cup match against Alloa, they announced that he was to
be made a club director. It meant that he would have one foot
in the manager's office, and one in the boardroom. It was a
commendable move by the board, and after his appointment we
had fresh hope that he would remain at the club as the driving
force on and off the field for many years to come. Despite the
elevation, the rumours persisted that he would be on his way
soon, and that Manchester United would be his destination.
Whatever, uncertainty over the gaffer's future coincided with an
indifferent start to the 1986–87 season.

We were beaten by Sion of Switzerland in the European Cup-
Winners' at the first time of asking, a defeat that was hard to
fathom because we had beaten that team 7-0 at Pittodrie four

seasons previously in the Cup Winner's Cup, and went on to outplay Real Madrid in the final. I could not believe that they had improved enough to turn the tables on us, but I was wrong. I certainly did not wish to contemplate the alternative explanation: that out form had gone into reverse. We won 2-1 at home thanks to a penalty-kick struck by Jim Bett and an effort from Paul Wright, but in the return leg we were hammered 3-0. That European defeat proved a depressing point for me, as it came in the same month that Celtic beat us in the quarter-finals of the Scottish League Cup, sponsored by Skol, in a penalty shoot-out. John Hewitt and I were guilty of missing penalty-kicks. Out of contention in Europe and in the Scottish League Cup, our mid-table position in the Scottish Premier League confirmed our malaise. Fergie was furious and adamant that we must improve, but Manchester United were struggling at the time as well and had fallen into the relegation zone, and manager Ron Atkinson's head was on the block. The rumour-mill had been cranked up to overdrive, and we were waiting for the Old Trafford board to come calling for Fergie. I joked rather bleakly with team-mates that, because he was now on the Aberdeen board, he would have to decide whether to give Manchester United permission to speak to himself! We tried to stick to the task as if nothing was happening in the background, and we beat Dundee away from home by 2-0 with Davie Dodds and Ian Porteous making the scoresheet. On the Monday after that, rumours emanated from down south that Ron Atkinson was about to be sacked, and that Alex Ferguson was first choice to take over from him. The gaffer kept his counsel, but information in the media made it clear that it was only a matter of time before he left for Old Trafford.

On Thursday November 6 came the announcement that Ron Atkinson had been dismissed, and within hours the curtain finally came down on the Ferguson era at Aberdeen, when Manchester United Football Club made an official approach for his services. You might think that to a man we would have been openly emotional when Fergie told us he was leaving, but it did not turn out like that. Naturally, we were disappointed that such a splendid gaffer was riding off into the sunset, but when he came into the dressing-room to confirm the news, it was a bit of an anti-climax, and no terrible shock. I shook his hand and said goodbye. That was it.

Though club chairman Dick Donald had done his best to retain Alex Ferguson's unique services by appointing him to the Aberdeen board, he knew that nothing could stop him heading for Old Trafford. It was the end of an incredible era, a period of monumental success that Aberdeen Football Club might well not experience again. I felt isolated because, operating together, Fergie and I had been treated as hate-figures by myriad opposition fans. His departure meant that their bile would be aimed at me standing alone. I admit that I did come over with a certain arrogance that angered fans from other clubs, and I could understand why they were always keen to see me get my comeuppance. The day after Fergie left, a press conference was staged at Pittodrie to preview our league match away to St Mirren. I said what I thought were all the right things, and stressed to reporters that we had to work hard until the next manager was appointed.

FERGIE'S UNIQUE REIGN INSPIRED LAUGHTER TOO

In the remarkable eight-year Alex Ferguson era, Aberdeen Football Club had been elevated from the status of an average side to one that dominated Scottish football, and for a brief period the European scene. With Fergie in charge, we won the European Cup-Winners' Cup, the Super Cup, four Scottish Cups, a Scottish League Cup and three Scottish Premier League titles. He had started out at Pittodrie as a raw, young manager who rubbed a lot of people up the wrong way, but through time he developed into a gaffer that you could trust and rely upon. Totally.

He looked after the club and their players, and he gave me the belief as a footballer that I could take on the best in Europe, and beat them on a regular basis. Respect and understanding between us blossomed, mainly because we shared a positive outlook about football. Nothing was impossible when Fergie was manager, and I was his captain.

What many people don't know, or perhaps don't want to hear, is that laughter played a big part in Fergie's success as manager. With his great sense of humour, you could have a laugh and a joke with him when the time was right. Fergie taught me that the amount of laughter on tap was a good gauge of the club's health and welfare. The more successful a club, the bigger the laughs, and the bigger the wind-ups in the dressing-room. If you don't have laughter at a football club, you've had it.

Of course, there was a serious side to the boss, which has been noted at many points in this memoir, and he did explode with anger and with passion from time to time, but his funny side tends to be forgotten, or maybe ignored. He could make you laugh, and it was impossible to curb his enthusiasm. Not that you would wish to do that. In short, Alex Ferguson always had the best interests of Aberdeen Football Club at heart.

I have it on good authority that Alex Ferguson called Sandy Jardine at midnight on the day that Manchester United came calling, to ask if he would be interested in replacing him as Aberdeen manager. He had recommended Sandy to the rest of the Aberdeen board, for though he was leaving, he was still thinking about what would be best for the club. Sandy was doing a fine job alongside Alex MacDonald at Heart of Midlothian, and had just completed his playing days when he gained Fergie's vote. He thought long and hard about taking the job, but felt that he was at the start of something big at Hearts, and he decided to stay at Tynecastle. It meant that the Aberdeen board had to go back to square one in their quest for a new boss, which was a big blow. In our first game without Fergie, the team were in the charge of Archie Knox, who had returned to the club from Dundee, and had offered to remain as caretaker manager until an appointment was made. Willie Garner, who had taken over from Archie as Fergie's assistant had earlier left Aberdeen and moved to Edinburgh. Sections of the Love Street crowd actually booed Archie when he led the team out against St Mirren, though he could have gone to Manchester United at the same time as Fergie. Because he was such a stalwart figure, however, he stayed for a while to help the club out. Not surprisingly, the game had

the atmosphere of a wake, and a deadly-dull affair finished
without a goal being scored.

The Aberdeen board considered a number of possible replacements for Fergie, with Jim McLean and Tommy Craig being
mentioned as candidates, but no immediate appointment was
made. Archie Knox remained in charge for our next game against
Hearts at Tynecastle, which we lost 2-1, before he too took the
road for Old Trafford. By this stage I did not have a clue who the
new manager would be. My money had been on Jim McLean
moving up the road from Tannadice, but with him out of the
running, I was in the dark along with everyone else. On Saturday,
November 18, 1986, only a few hours before our home match
against Clydebank, news reached me that the board had appointed
Ian Porterfield as manager. I crossed the Pittodrie car park to be
greeted by the news from a woman who worked at the club. I was
stunned. I had heard of Ian Porterfield, but never in a million years
would I have thought that he was in the running for the job as
manager, and most people in football, including Fergie, were
surprised. Chairman Dick Donald clearly felt that Ian would
deliver the successes which had become an inspirational habit
during the Ferguson era, but lots of people were not so sure. As I
had worked under Jimmy Bonthrone, Ally MacLeod, Billy
McNeill and Alex Ferguson, I was confident that I could do
the same with Ian. His CV included spells playing for Raith
Rovers, Sunderland, Rotherham and Sheffield Wednesday, and
his time at Sunderland culminated in his scoring the winning goal
for them in the FA Cup final against Leeds United at Wembley in
1973. Football followers certainly remembered that one. He had
managed Rotherham first, then Sheffield United, elevating them
from the English League Division Four to Division Two. However, he had been sacked by Sheffield United in March 1986, and
been out of football until he was hired by Aberdeen the following
November to replace Fergie. The fact that he had been discon-
nected from football for a period worried me slightly, as did the
fact that he had not lived in Scotland for 17 years, and would be
out of touch with vital details of the game north of the Border.

Ian had a hard act to follow, but he impressed our supporters straight away when we beat Rangers in his first game in charge. Putting one over the men from Ibrox was the best possible way to endear himself to the followers of Aberdeen Football Club, and nothing has changed on that front. We then put together 15 Premier League victories before tasting defeat, which came with a 1-0 reversal at the hands of St Mirren at Love Street. Five fixtures later, they beat us again on a day that I would wish to forget, as I was sent off for the first time at Pittodrie. It was the third and final dismissal of my career, and two had come in matches involving Frank McGarvey. I blame him!

At this stage, harmony in the dressing-room was not much in evidence, as Ian had made some less-than-inspiring signings, which angered many of the more experienced Aberdeen professionals. John Hewitt demanded a transfer, as did Peter Weir, as they were not happy at the way Ian was running the team. Peter's request came after he had been left out of the side to play Rangers on May 2, 1987, which was my birthday, but that did mean much celebrating. Rangers needed to take a point from Pittodrie to win the league, and they took the lead through Terry Butcher. Brian Irvine scored for us just before half-time, and though we pushed them hard, we couldn't score again, despite Graeme Souness being ordered off. Their ten men hung on for the point needed to take the title, and Rangers celebrating their achievement at Pittodrie was difficult to bear. We finished fourth in the table, and on this occasion could not look forward to a Scottish Cup final, as we had been ejected by Celtic in the third round. A poor season, overall, but on the other hand, losing Fergie had been a telling body-blow, and Ian Porterfield took a while to settle in.

With the summer of 1987 came our first pre-season under our new manager, and I must say that the training was not as well organised or as entertaining as the Alex Ferguson Show. There was much movement in the transfer market, and though the club rejected a £500,000 bid from FA Cup-holders Coventry City for full-back David Robertson, that had to be tempered by the fact that Billy Stark went to Celtic for £75,000. Billy had scored 15 goals for Aberdeen in 1985-86 season and 14 the following season, and his skills would be missed. Three players were signed from down south, but for me they were mediocre and not of sufficient worth to replace those who had departed. Keith Edwards came from Leeds United for £65,000, and Tom Jones and Gary Hackett also arrived, but they did not add much to our cause. In fact, they made such limited impressions that I regret not being able to remember playing alongside Keith Edwards. On the plus side, the experienced Welsh internationalist, Peter Nicholas, arrived for £350,000, and he proved to be an excellent signing. Ian also had at his disposal the core of the side that had done so well under Fergie, including me, Alex McLeish, Neil Simpson, John Hewitt (still in harness despite his transfer request) and Jim Leighton. That experience in the ranks helped us to a superb start in the 1987-88 season. That was important, as many were expressing doubts about Ian Porterfield's ability to drive us on to further glory. It was important to him that he lifted a trophy or two early on, and his first bid came in the Scottish League Cup. We cruised past Brechin City and St. Johnstone, then overcame Celtic at Pittodrie by the only goal struck by Jim Bett. In the semi-final we beat Dundee 2-0, to set up a final against Rangers. That turned out to be the match that neutrals could enjoy, but it was not one of the finals that I recall with affection, simply because we lost, when the reverse should have been the case. We took an early lead through a Jim Bett penalty, which was cancelled out by an amazing Davie Cooper free-kick. I was in the wall as he prepared, and felt that I had positioned the defence pretty well, but he hit the ball so hard that it rocketed into the far corner of the net beyond Jim Leighton, who did not stand a chance.

Davie kept running us ragged, and helped his team to take the lead through Ian Durrant, though John Hewitt scored to make it 2-2. With nine minutes left, Willie Falconer scored for us and I thought we were home and dry, until Robert Fleck sneaked in to make it 3-3, so extra-time loomed.

I knew more than anyone at Aberdeen that we usually played well in extra-time, but were dreadful in penalty shoot-outs. Bearing that in mind, I tried to rally the troops to attack Rangers from the start, and thus inflict defeat within the additional 30 minutes. The battle-plan was a failure and Rangers missed lots of chances, and come the penalty shoot-out, I was again short of volunteers. I had failed to find five willing takers when we played Dynamo Berlin in the European Cup in 1984-85, and history was repeating itself. Everywhere I looked I saw the backs of players as they walked away. I finally rounded up four individuals, but could not persuade a fifth until Peter Nicholas offered his services. He did not really wish to take a spot-kick, but unlike some of my other colleagues, he had the guts to step forward. Ally McCoist scored for Rangers, Jim Bett levelled, Davie Cooper made it 2-1, and Peter Nicholas was next up, but unfortunately his effort grazed the bar on its way over the top. It was a crucial miss. Robert Fleck scored for Rangers, Peter Weir netted for us, then Trevor Francis and John Hewitt were successful, which left Ian Durrant to score with Rangers' decisive kick, which he did. The Scottish League Cup was heading for Ibrox once more.

○ ○ ○

THE GENIUS THAT WAS DAVIE COOPER

The contributions that Davie Cooper made to that final were outstanding, and I can say that the free-kick which allowed his team to draw level after our early goal was an absolute classic of its kind. I was a colleague at international level, and he was blessed with incredible skills and balance. He glided past opponents seemingly effortlessly, and was one of the most talented men that I played alongside. His death from a brain haemorrhage in 1995 at the age of 39 was a tragedy.

A true genius he was without doubts: he would run at defenders, show them a glimpse of the ball, pull it back, feint, and then with a shimmy he would be gone . . . He did it time and time again at training with Scotland, and I marvelled at his talent. I always thought he was like John

Robertson, the former Nottingham Forest and Scotland footballer, in that he was magnificent with the ball at his feet. On the other hand, Davy was obviously one opponent that I did not relish taking on, because he was such a fantastic performer, and it was difficult to work out what he would do next . . .

Aberdeen Football Club had come so close to winning the Scottish League Cup final that Skol, the competition sponsors, presented us with a special trophy to commemorate our part in what they deemed was an excellent match. Suffice to say, I did not show much appreciation when it was handed over. The defeat was an overwhelming disappointment for Ian Porterfield, who was inevitably desperate to succeed in a major competition, so that he could lay to rest the ghost of Alex Ferguson. Gaining a trophy early in his managerial career with Aberdeen would have gained him instant acceptance, and bought him time. He was at a club who were still expected to show off trophies in Union Street, not to head home as runners-up. In the event, other cup competitions in which we were involved that season brought disappointing conclusions, too. In the UEFA Cup, we sneaked past Bohemians of the Republic of Ireland after drawing 0-0 away, and winning 1-0 at home thanks to a Jim Bett penalty. That set us up for a second-round meeting with Feyenoord, and though we won 2-1 at Pittodrie, we went down by 1-0 in the Netherlands to go out again on an away-goals rule. It was not yet Christmas 1987, and yet we had failed in the Scottish League Cup final, and were out of the UEFA Cup. On top of that, our form was erratic in the Premier League, and only the arrival of Charlie Nicholas in January 1988 brought a sense of excitement to our followers. He turned out to be one of the most out-standing signings completed by Aberdeen Football Club, and joined us after five years plying his trade with Arsenal. He was an instant hit with the fans, and became one of my best friends at the club. More than 20,000 turned up to check out his 'home' debut against Dunfermline on January 16, 1988 – in contrast to 12,500 who had watched our previous match against the Pars at Pittodrie. He scored in his second game for Aberdeen against Motherwell, but even Charlie's presence in the side could not help our league form, and we again finished a disappointing fourth, 13 points behind champions Celtic.

Our best run of form came in the Scottish Cup, but as indicated above, that also ended in disappointment. We beat St. Johnstone, Hamilton and Clyde to set up a semi-final encounter with Dundee United. Or should I say that our win over Clyde set up a semi-final encounter between me and Jim McLean. Disquiet in the dressing-room under Ian reared its head at different times, and after David Robertson had criticised the club in a newspaper article, he was dropped for a few games leading up to the semi-final encounter with United. He was recalled by Ian, as we needed our strongest team to beat them. The first clash, which took place at Dens Park on April 9, 1988, was a dreadful affair. It finished 0-0, and Ian Porterfield and Jimmy Mullen, who had been appointed as his assistant, were sent to the stand after a confrontation with the linesman. It was in the replay, with Dens Park again the venue, that things became particularly heated. The first half had been as dismal as in the initial meeting, but things boiled over four minutes before half-time. Paul Hegarty brought down Charlie Nicholas, and I ran towards the scene of the incident near a corner-flag to check if Charlie was okay. There was no way as captain that I would stand back and let my best player be set upon by means of such a bad tackle. I ran some 20 yards towards Charlie, and as I passed referee Bill Crombie, I saw him making for his top pocket and knew that he intended to send Paul off the pitch. Paul protested, but was given his marching orders anyway, and thankfully Charlie was not seriously injured. With Paul Hegarty off the pitch, Charlie took full advantage of having fewer defenders to deal with, and he scored just before half-time. Not surprisingly, I had a spring in my step as I headed to the dressing-room, but as I jogged towards the tunnel, I spotted out of the corner of my eye that Alex McLeish and Maurice Malpas were trying to keep Jim McLean, the United manager, from heading in my direction. I

was a bit bewildered, and could not work out why Jim was so
wound up. I had done nothing to antagonise him personally in the
first half, so why was he trying to get to me and shouting and
pointing in my direction? He looked furious, and while Alex and
Maurice kept him away from me, Jimmy Mullen made sure that I
did not try to get near Jim. I remain adamant that Jim was the
aggressor, and with more than 17,000 spectators inside Dens Park,
I consider that his public display of anger could have provoked
crowd trouble. I have every respect for Jim's record as a manager,
but I thought that he was badly in the wrong this time. With all this
going on, I was fired up for the second half after the incident with
Jim, and I told my team-mates that I really wanted them to go out
and win the match, and win it well. For all our efforts, ten-man
Dundee United put up a great performance, and Mixu Paatelainen equalised to secure a draw for them.

In the aftermath, Jim McLean claimed that I was a disgrace
because I had run *70 yards* to tell the referee to send Paul Hegarty
off for his tackle on Charlie Nicholas. On the contrary, my habit
on a football pitch was to run only when I had to, and making a
70-yard dash was not my style at all. Jim's accusations were false
and stupid, in my opinion, especially when I knew that Mr
Crombie had made up his mind to order the Paul off the pitch.
Anything that I had said or done would have made no difference
to the official's decision. Jim's rant was not finished, and he
disrupted the presentation to man-of-the-match Charlie Nicholas, describing him in outrageous terms as he was receiving his
bottle of champagne. I can only assume that Jim McLean lost the
plot when Paul was sent off because he felt under pressure
because his side would be playing with ten men for the whole of
the second half, and no doubt would be up against it. But I found
it baffling that he was still having a go at Charlie even after they
had secured a 1-1 draw. In the event, the SFA fined him £4,000
fine and imposed a three-year dugout ban, which I felt was fully
justified. I watched the incident on television that evening, and
could not believe what I was seeing. I was amazed to see that Jim
had been in the stand alongside some bigwigs from the SFA, and

that he had to push past them on his way to remonstrate with me, so it was not surprising that they clobbered him with a substantial fine and a touchline ban. I could see no way in which he could defend his actions during this unsavoury episode, but in football these things happen from time to time, and Jim McLean was a manager who wore his heart on his sleeve. Because of the rumpus, the media hype was huge in advance of the second replay on April 20, 1988, also set down for Dens Park. Jim and his team had the last laugh, as we performed poorly, and they sneaked a 1-0 victory through a goal from Ian Ferguson.

Season 1987-88 was a downer for me, as I felt our best players were leaving, and that most of the replacements brought in by Ian Porterfield had made little or no impact. I was stunned when Jim Leighton told me that he planned to move on at the end of the season, but at least Aberdeen had turned down a bid from Manchester United for Alex McLeish, which came as a relief. To me Big Eck, Jim Leighton and I formed the backbone of the team, and Jim, despite being wound up by me outrageously on occasion, was one of the main reasons that we flourished under Alex Ferguson. Jim gave players such as me, Alex McLeish and Stuart Kennedy the confidence to attack the ball, and he kept us tight at the back. As a last line of defence, he was the best in the business, and the fact that in his final season with the club – a disappointing one at that – he established a record of 35 clean-sheets in 59 outings, spoke volumes for his talents as a goalkeeper. We had finished the season without a trophy to show for our efforts, and Ian Porterfield was under pressure. He had faced problems settling in the north-east of Scotland, and had appeared on the front of the tabloids as well as the back pages, and his troubled time in charge ended in the summer of 1988.

NICE GUY, WRONG MANAGER

The Porterfield period was not one that I enjoyed that much. He was a nice guy, but his working methods were different from any that I had experienced. Under Fergie, I was used to intensive coaching, tactical expertise and uplifting team talks, but I was used, above all, to having a football club where all aspects of the business were well organised. Completely and utterly.

In contrast, Ian was the type of manager who let you get on with it. Maybe that was his way, but I felt that we were not sufficiently organised during his stint at Pittodrie. I was used to high standards, and when I arrived for training in Fergie's time, for instance, the pitches would be ready, the goals up, the balls available, and the tempo of the preparation very high. If players turn up and there are no footballs to kick, the reaction must be: what the hell is going on here?

Tactically, Ian was satisfactory, but he was a man who brought in his own players and let them work on their own games at their own pace. Maybe that was something more common to the English leagues, for Graeme Souness and Kenny Dalglish revealed that all they did in training at Anfield was play five-a-side games. Whether the truth or not, it suggested that the Liverpool management thought that, if the players were good enough, they did not require to train them too hard.

I think also that Ian did not have sufficient insight into Scottish football before he took the job, and to make matters worse, most of his signings did not work out to the club's advantage, or to his. But then, whoever took over from Fergie was bound to struggle to emulate the great man. For me, Ian Porterfield was the wrong manager operating at the wrong club at the wrong time. Simple as that. It was good to see that we went on to success at other clubs and national teams all round the world after he left Aberdeen. As I said earlier, he was a likeable guy and I was greatly saddened to hear of his death in September 2007 at the age of just 61.

MY PAL CHARLIE

Some may consider Willie Miller and Charlie Nicholas to be as varied as chalk and cheese, with Charlie reflecting the more flamboyant character (not half), but we got on well, and with Craig Robertson, we forged friendships that continue to this day.

On the pitch Charlie called me 'Buffalo', as in Buffalo Bill, but more *often I was 'The Head Waiter', because I was there at the back observing, and letting the others do the dirty work, before stepping in to clear up the mess. By that, Charlie thought I was an organiser on the pitch, and I like to think that he was spot-on.*

I knew Charlie from my days with the Scotland team before he signed for Aberdeen, and I felt that he was subjected to unjustified flack. Some said that he should not have moved from Celtic to Arsenal, and should have chosen Liverpool, because Anfield had a better track record for nurturing Scots, such as Kenny Dalglish, Graeme Souness and Alan Hansen.

I accept that is a valid argument, but the bold Charlie was talented enough to star in any environment. He is an intelligent guy, and made up his own mind to attach himself to Arsenal, and is still remembered fondly by the Gunners' fan. So why bother questioning his decision to head for Highbury?

15

TROPHY OF RELIEF TOPS IT ALL OFF

*'I certainly felt the impact on my knee. It was horrendous,
and I felt physically sick'*

As a young player I had avoided serious injury, give or take the
odd scuffing from those dreadful red-blaes surfaces. At the age of
33, though, time was marching on, and I started to suffer from
thigh strains and knee problems, which was hardly surprising
considering that I had played for 16 years at the top level, and had
averaged 40 games a season. I was sure that I had a few good years
left in the locker, and I was intent on picking up at least one more
trophy with Aberdeen. Therefore, when the new management
team was revealed, I was convinced that my career would go
from strength to strength. Alex Smith and Jocky Scott were
named as co-managers, and were universally welcomed because
of their Aberdeen credentials. The board had been notorious for
keeping their cards close to their chests while they deliberated
over managerial choices, but made no attempt to do that this
time, as Alex and Jocky were always the front-runners. I
respected them, and knew that they would bring professionalism
and enthusiasm to the club, and we all certainly needed a lift after
Ian Porterfield's sudden departure.

Alex and Jocky had some rebuilding to attend to, as Peter
Nicholas, Willie Falconer and my respected, comrade Jim
Leighton had left in the summer of 1988. The new management team proved effective, and we put together a competent
run in the Scottish League Cup. We beat Arbroath, Morton,
Hibs and Dundee United on the way to a final against Rangers,
which provided a re-run of the previous season's scenario, when

we had lost out on those problematic penalties. My most notable appearance on the road to Hampden came against Arbroath, when I scored *twice* in a 4-0 result. Accumulating two goals was a rarity for me, and I did not let the strikers at the club forget it. So many teenagers were now involved in the squad that I felt like a father-figure, and I had to convince them that I had made my Aberdeen debut as a *striker*. They laughed. They didn't believe me. A bit disconcerting. The previous season, Ian Porterfield had been desperate to win the League Cup to endear himself to the fans after the departure of Alex Ferguson. Now Alex and Jocky were striving to do the same, for the same reason. I was just keen to win a trophy. Now neutrals tell me that the final against Rangers was a game to remember, but that comment I can do without. Two goals from Davie Dodds, and replies from Ally McCoist from the penalty-spot and from Ian Ferguson, had left the final poised at 2-2 with four minutes left, and the man who ruined my day was Ally McCoist, who ensured that Rangers sneaked it 3-2. I was gutted, and soon had to contend with the ignominy of being turfed out of the UEFA Cup in the first round by Dynamo Dresden. They defended deep at Pittodrie and manufactured a 0-0 draw, and in the return leg beat us 2-0, mainly thanks to the influential play of Matthias Sammer, who would progress to star in the German team that won Euro 96. In the Scottish Cup, Dundee United beat us in a fourth-round second replay, which had become a habit, but I missed out through injury, which meant that our cup campaigns under Alex and Jocky in their first season in charge had ended in anti-climax.

Our Scottish Premier League adventures were also a bit erratic, and indeed became embroiled in controversy. The tackle by Neil Simpson on Ian Durrant that put the Rangers player out of the game for a long period was an unfortunate incident that reverberated for years, and created even more bad feeling between the rival sets of supporters. Ian Durrant was an out-standing player, but the injury affected him severely in the long term. We won the match 2-1, but victory was overshadowed by the reaction to Neil's tackle, and the controversy centred on the decision by referee Louis Thow to book Neil rather than send him off.

O O O

BETTER IF HE HAD BEEN GIVEN MARCHING ORDERS

Neil Simpson's tackle on Ian Durrant was a bad one. There is no doubt on that score, and I'm sure that if he could have his time over again, he would not have made the challenge. In his defence, he was not the type of player who went over the top intentionally, or who set out to injure opponents. He was a hard player, but an honest one. The immediate criticism reached such a pitch that he asked for a transfer, but thankfully withdrew that request.

I would not wish to defend the challenge that he made on Ian Durrant, but I will defend Neil against the prolonged witch-hunt that went on against him. Every time we played Rangers, the incident was regurgitated in the media, and I can well understand why the Aberdeen fans got so fed up hearing about it.

Just when I thought the incident would be cast into history, it was thrust into the spotlight again when referee Louis Thow was taken to task by the SFA for not showing Neil a red card for the challenge. I had a lot of sympathy for Louis, for football in Scotland is played at an incredible pace, judgments must be issued in the heat of the moment, and refs do get it wrong sometimes. In retrospect, it would have been better if Neil had been ordered off, as the fact that he received a yellow card helped to keep the controversy raging on. Inevitably, Rangers fans continued to feel that the punishment did not fit the crime.

Despite the backlash over the challenge, Neil did his best to get on with his football career, and I hope that he will be remembered as a fine footballer rather than as a person who made an ill-advised tackle. Neil moved on to become accomplished coach working within the Aberdeen youth development department.

O O O

The next time that we played Rangers during season 1988-89, Neil Simpson was not included in the team, which was no bad thing considering the torrid time that he would have faced being taunted by opposition fans. But it would not have been a Rangers v Aberdeen match without some controversy to report, and I was thrust into the midst of the trouble. We lost the game 1-0, but the discussion, or argument, that I had conducted with referee Kenny Hope during play hit the headlines. I had been booked for a tackle on Kevin Drinkell, and I admit that I had fouled him, but I did not agree that my conduct was bad enough to merit a yellow card. At half-time, I walked towards the referee to protest about my booking, suggesting that he had been influenced by the 40,000 Rangers fans in the stadium, who had promoted me to Public Enemy Number One since the departure of Alex Ferguson. I was pleading my case, but not getting too far. Kenny Hope was from Glasgow, and could talk a bit himself, but he was an official that you could address with a few well-chosen words. He might not have agreed with your point of view, but you could talk to him. Our discussion was shown on television that evening, and the way that the recording was edited suggested that I had been gesticulating into the face of the referee, and that he was doing nothing about it. That was not the case. I was simply asking why I had been booked, and Kenny was explaining the yellow-card decision, but his face was not shown on the TV pictures, only his back. I had approached Kenny Hope again at full-time, and he told me to go away. I was still angry, partly over the booking, but mainly over the defeat, and it took Terry Butcher, the Rangers captain, who was a good friend, to cool me down and drag me away. In hindsight, perhaps I was mouthing-off too much to the referee, and did run the risk of being sent off, but I maintain that the SFA reaction was disgraceful. In a reprise of the Neil Simpson/Ian Durrant episode, because Kenny had not sent me off, he was called to a meeting of the SFA Disciplinary and Referee Committee to explain his actions. They found him guilty of not taking severe enough action against me, and banned him from officiating in any Scottish Cup ties during 1988-89. So much for referees being allowed to make their own judgments.

○ ○ ○

REACTING TO REFEREES AND THEIR DECISION-MAKING

Kenny Hope was the type of official who was quite happy to talk to players, and to explain his decisions during breaks in play. He always had something to say on the pitch, and I had great respect for him as a referee. We had both been involved in Scottish football a long time, and our exchanges on the pitch were nothing new.

Characters like George Smith or Bob Valentine were different, and you could not converse with them, as their style reflected a more officious type of referee. If the SFA had asked me, I would have explained all that to them. But I'm damned if I would have apologised. As I have said time and again, referees must be strong at Ibrox or Celtic Park. It's daft for anybody to suggest that if tens of thousands of fans are shouting at a referee and giving him a hard time, he isn't liable to react, and be influenced by that. If there is a 50-50 decision, the baying of the crowd might just have influenced them enough to award a penalty.

Is it any different these days? Answers on a postcard . . .

On that day at Ibrox, there was no way that I would not have stated my case to the referee. I was team captain, and felt that I had been unjustly treated. I thought that Aberdeen Football Club had been unjustly treated as well, and was certainly not willing to let that happen. If Kenny Hope had felt my protests were over the top, he had the power to take action, and he did not.

I didn't stand for any nonsense, regardless of where I played. I would contest every tackle, every decision, and I make no apology for it. That is what made Willie Miller, and that is what made Aberdeen so successful. If opposition fans did not like my style, that's tough.

○ ○ ○

Ironically, it would not have made much difference if Kenny Hope had sent me off, as a few weeks later I suffered a serious knee injury. It came in a match against St Mirren on December 10, 1988, and led to the longest lay-off of my career. I missed 14 games, and doom-and-gloom merchants suggested that I would not play again. But I concentrated on rehabilitation work, and spent what seemed like an eternity doing light training on the beach at Aberdeen. Running up and down the sand in winter wasn't much fun, especially for someone like me who did not even enjoy running about on the sand during the summer. I spent a lonely time trying to return to full fitness, and I really missed the buzz of match-days. Not until March 11, 1989, three long months after being injured, did I return to the first team. A rousing reception greeted me when I led the team on to the pitch against Dundee, and I felt relieved that my knee did not pose any problems during the game, which we won 2-0. I returned to the side just as they were hitting a purple patch. Much credit for the upsurge in form had to be directed at Theo Snelders, Jim Leighton's replacement as goalkeeper, who excelled throughout the season. Jim Bett had been a revelation, and I was concerned when I heard that Chelsea were interested in signing him. Charlie Nicholas was also banging in goals, and we pushed Rangers all the way, but they finally clinched the Premier League title with 56 points, three more than we had gathered. There were positives to be gleaned from the season, despite the fact that trophies had proved elusive. We had gone 16 league games unbeaten at the start of the season, and put together another eight successive victories from January 21.

And yet, after experiencing such personal woes, I was beginning to feel that if I received any more damage to the knee, I might be forced to hang up my boots. I was looking for a good start to the 1989-90 season, but my hopes were dashed in a pre-season friendly against Feyenoord in the Netherlands. A Polish international midfielder named Wodzimierz Smolarek caught me with a vicious tackle, the most severe that I had encountered in my career. He came in from the side, and caught me late. I had volleyed the ball away, but he followed through and smashed my right knee with his studs, taking a chunk out of my skin. I certainly felt the impact on my knee. It was horrendous, and I felt physically sick after he hit me. It was the most painful challenge that I had been forced to deal with. I was carried off, and that turned out to be the beginning of the end of my playing career, so no prizes for guessing the identity of the dirtiest player that I came up against on the football field. His challenge on me was disgraceful! The physiotherapist told me to rest the knee and to return to running up and down Aberdeen's breezy beach. I thought: 'Oh, joy, not again?' But to my surprise, I managed to get fit enough to play in our first league game of the season against Hibs, which we won 1-0 through a late goal from Paul Mason. Paul was setting out to play a major role for us, and he proved to be the star of our run in the Scottish League Cup. We easily beat Albion Rovers, Airdrie and St Mirren, and an Ian Cameron goal saw off Celtic in the semi-final of the tournament. The final was again versus Rangers, on October 22, 1989, and they were the red-hot favourites. They had won the four previous League Cup finals, and had beaten us in the two most recent battles for the Skol prize. Few outside the club and our supporters gave us a chance, but we took the lead through a Paul Mason header, but Rangers got back into the game by means of a controversial refereeing decision. Ally McCoist had got on the end of a Mark Walters chip, and was leaning back into me. I tried to stand my ground, but fell over, and Ally landed on top of me. George Smith awarded a penalty, and I just could not believe his decision. It was a howler, and completely wrong. I was so angry that I was rendered speechless, but my team-mates made up for that, and Robert Connor and Alex McLeish were booked for protesting, but to no avail. I just looked at the referee, and shook my head in disgust. Ally McCoist offered me a wee grin, and told me to watch the incident on television, claiming it was a definite penalty. Never! Ally fell over! Mark Walters duly scored from the penalty-spot after Ally's fall from grace, and we were up against it as Rangers started to exert control. Somehow we managed to take the game into extra-time, and during that 30 minutes our form was totally transformed. All thoughts of the

Rangers penalty left me as Paul Mason weaved some magic, and scored a fine goal to help us to victory. Lifting the Scottish League Cup that year was a moment to relish. I could not go on forever and winning any accolade in the twilight of my career was a bonus.

To me, that Scottish League Cup victory came as what I describe as *My Trophy of Relief*. The reason? I could not have lived with myself if we had been overcome by Rangers in three successive League Cup finals. That would have hurt . . . and I can recall standing in the Queen's Hotel, Aberdeen, at our post-match celebration party thinking back on the day. Staring into space I said to myself: 'Thank God we won that final.' The week after our latest triumph, I got the chance to parade *My Trophy of Relief* before the league match against Motherwell at Pittodrie, which we won 1-0. The trophy stimulated an outbreak of long-overdue smiles among our supporters, as by the time we lifted the Scottish League Cup, we had been cast out of the UEFA Cup at the first-round stage by Rapid Vienna.

Vanquishing Rangers in the Scottish League Cup final was to be the last great moment that I enjoyed during my playing career at Aberdeen. A few weeks later, I hurt the right knee that had been hacked into against Feyenoord, this time while representing Scotland against Norway, and I knew that I would be struggling to continue. I would give it my best shot, but the odds were stacked against me. I did return after missing five matches, but perhaps re-entered the fray too soon. What kept me going during the rehabilitation process was the fact that we were doing very well in the Scottish Cup in 1989-90. My aim was to be fit enough to play at Hampden again, as it would be my last final on the famous park. Two games before the end of the league season, I led the team out against St Mirren at Pittodrie in my first home game for six months. We fielded an under-strength side because co-managers Alex and Jocky wanted to rest their main men, such as Stewart McKimmie, David Robertson, Alex McLeish and Jim Bett, for the cup final. Among those making their debut was Scott Booth, who would go on to become another Aberdeen star. The challenge for me was to show the management team that I had recovered sufficiently from an operation carried out on my knee to merit consideration for the Scottish Cup final starting line-up, which would present an opportunity for me to collect a fifth medal from the competition. I felt that I cruised through my first test against St Mirren, though it proved to be a rather lifeless, end-of-season affair, which we won 2-0, I was hardly stretched. On my 35th birthday on Wednesday, May 2, 1990, I was presented with the positive news that Alex Smith wanted me to play in our final league game against Celtic at Parkhead. I was working on the assumption that he would not have picked me for such a high-profile game if he was not seriously considering me for the Scottish Cup final. I did pretty well, we won 3-1, and the press coverage centred on whether I would be selected for Hampden. The final decision rested with Alex and Jocky, which was a weird position for me to be in, because for most of my Aberdeen career I had been an automatic first pick. Not any more, and Brian Irvine might well be selected ahead of me.

The day before the final, I travelled with the team to our hotel near Glasgow, and my fate was sealed during the evening when Alex sat me down to tell me that I would *not* be playing. It was hard to take, but he revealed that he didn't think I was quite back to my best after injury. Now, what I did have going for me was my experience of the big occasion, and I had thought that might sway his thinking. It did not, and he decided to stick with the group of players who had taken us to the final, which meant that Brian Irvine, who had scored in the quarter- and semi-finals, kept his place. As I made clear much earlier in my career, I was not the sort of guy who liked to sit on the bench, but on this occasion I would have made an exception, as it could very well have presented my last chance to play in a major final. Even that was denied me, as Alex and Jocky did not select me as a substitute. I respected their decision, though they could have told me sooner, and not kept me hanging on so long. Their argument for keeping me in the dark was that they did not wish the news to leak out to Celtic. They wanted to keep our opponents guessing about whether I would play or not.

I attended the final as part of the squad, and it felt distinctly odd watching the action from a seat in the stand, and not being involved. I was never a good spectator, and being unable to influence events on the field was frustrating in the extreme. Aberdeen went on to beat Celtic in a penalty shoot-out by a margin of 9-8! The marathon session ended when Brian Irvine, my replacement, scored to win the Scottish Cup, and I had to laugh at the idea that *nine* Aberdeen players had to be drafted into the showdown. You will recall that when it came to penalty shoot-outs, as captain I had found it nigh-impossible to sign up even five volunteers. I was obviously pleased that the team had emerged with the silverware, but I was upset that I had not been part of the great experience. I did not feel that I had contributed anything to merit being part of the after-match celebrations, so that when we reached the outskirts of Aberdeen on the return north and were due to transfer to an open-top bus, I said that I did not wish to participate because I had not been part of the team. Instead, I was given a lift by one of my mates to Pittodrie to pick up my car. I still felt that I was a leader, not a follower, and I stress that I had done nothing to justify being part of the open-top bus parade. My stubbornness cost me dear, as Ian Donald, the club vice-chairman, fined me £1,000 for opting out of the bus parade. I still maintain that the players who had won the Scottish Cup were those who deserved the plaudits. Not Willie Miller.

In the summer of 1990, apart from following Scotland's progress in the World Cup, I made one last attempt to salvage my career by undertaking even more rehabilitation work on my knee. I got through some friendly matches without a problem, but things went badly wrong for me in the first competitive game of the new season, a Scottish League Cup-tie against Queen's Park at their home venue of Hampden. I had enjoyed some triumphs and tribulations over the years at the national stadium, but I had never experienced the barren slopes that greeted me as I led Aberdeen out. It was strange playing at Hampden in front of just 2,201 souls rather than 60,000, and I didn't feel at ease. My worst fears were realised when, within 10 minutes, I started to feel pain in my vulnerable right knee. An early goal from Eoin Jess did not settle me, and when Queen's Park equalised through Mike Hendry, I worried that we could be facing defeat. Thankfully, Jim Bett scored with 20 minutes left, and we held out. As I walked off at the end, I felt deep down that I might well have played my last competitive game for Aberdeen Football Club. My knee had swollen like a balloon, and I wasn't moving easily. No big announcement was made after the game about my fitness, as I had managed to last 90 minutes and to hide my discomfort pretty well. The next day's newspapers failed to mention the fact that I had struggled during parts of the game. The journalists assumed that I was okay, and would be fit to play for the rest of the season. I was struggling, but I made all the positive noises to the coaching staff that I would be back, and urged them not to worry about me. As the months passed and there was no sign of my return to the first team, they too concluded that my playing career was at an end.

I had played my first match for Aberdeen Football Club on April 28, 1973 against Morton at Cappielow, and my final appearance was made against Queen's Park at Hampden on August 21, 1990. I had packed lots and lots of adventures into my years with the club, and could retire satisfied that I had achieved all that I could for club and country. I suppose playing my final competitive game at Hampden was apt, as the ground had presented me with a host of stirring memories, but I had not had the chance to say goodbye properly to the Aberdeen fans. Nor, for that matter, to my beloved Pittodrie. I kept on training and combining that with coaching the reserve team with Teddy Scott as I had passed the SFA coaching badges, and was enjoying my new role. What made me smile more broadly was the board announcing that they would grant me a second testimonial, 10 years after my first and 20 years after I had signed for Aberdeen. Not until Thursday, November 29 1990 in the run-up to my testimonial game against a World XI did I announce officially that I was being forced to retire. I had not played since facing Queen's Park, and the club had long since realised that I must hang up my boots. When other clubs heard of my retirement, they grasped the wrong end of the stick, and assumed that I would wish to leave Aberdeen. Montrose went so far as to offer me the manager's job at Glebe Park, but not for a second did I consider leaving Pittodrie. I was enjoying my coaching role, and still had much to learn.

On Tuesday, December 4, 1990 I was granted my wish to say goodbye properly to the Aberdeen fans at Pittodrie, when I ran out for my second testimonial game. My testimonial committee, chaired by Bryan Keith and with Gordon Campbell as secretary, did a wonderful job, and everything had been organised superbly. My dodgy knee and diminishing stamina caused me concern, probably for the first time in my career, about how I would perform, especially against a World XI that contained so many famous names from the world of football that I felt humbled they were turning out for me. In saying that, Alex Ferguson had brought them together for me, and he was acting as their manager, so twisting a few arms would not have proved that difficult. Players of the calibre of Kenny Dalglish, Mark Hughes, David O'Leary and Bryan Robson turned out against an Aberdeen team sprinkled with former cult heroes such as Doug Rougvie. Eoin Jess, the star player at Pittodrie at that time, was in the Dons' line-up, and Charlie Nicholas took great delight in reminding me that, when I signed for Aberdeen in the 1970–71 season, Eoin Jess had not been born. A sobering thought. My big date would not have been complete without my mentor, Alex Ferguson, with whom I like to think I constructed the most formidable manager-captain relationship in the Scottish game during the 1980s. Fergie was not one to let sentiment get in the way of winning a football match, and was doing all in his power to stimulate the World XI to beat us. It may have been my testimonial match, but he didn't care, and I would not have had it any other way. Before the match, Doug Rougvie came up to me and jokingly said that my long career as a referee, which had proceeded in conjunction with my playing days, should ensure that I was not on the losing side. To the very end, friends and colleagues kept taunting me up about my supposed attempts to influence officialdom: I was merely trying to get them to balance things up, that's all!

For one night only, I restored my partnership with Alex McLeish in the Aberdeen defence. There was many a pub argument over whether we were the best centre-back partnership in Scotland, or if David Narey and Paul Hegarty of Dundee United were a superior duo. I know what my choice would be, and I also know who gained more Scottish caps. Before kick-off, I offered a special word of thanks in the tunnel to Bruce Grobbelaar, who took over in goals after Neville Southall of Everton had to call off, and Jim Leighton had suffered another finger dislocation. Typical Jim, missing out on my big night. It was also a shame that my pal Terry Butcher had to call off at the last minute because of club commitments with Coventry City. Our friendship had survived cup finals, tousy league matches and international confrontations, and we remain firm friends. For all that, my testimonial produced an entertaining encounter, and Kenny Dalglish, who was perhaps not quite so super-fit as of yore, was the pick of the outstanding bunch on duty, and was still able to display glimpses of genius. I was keen to play well, but things did not go to plan. With 20 minutes gone, Kenny Dalglish sent over a chip which landed at the feet of England internationalist Neil Webb, who tried to back-heel the ball over the line. Michael Watt in the Aberdeen goals saved it, but just pushed the ball out, and it hit me on the shin. All I could do was watch the football roll slowly over the line into my own net. Big Eck and Kenny Dalglish laughed heartily as I stood there with my face tripping me. Two minutes later, the World XI went two up when Mark Hughes scored, and their other goals came from Neil Webb, Hans Gilhaus and Steve Archibald. Aberdeen scored twice through David Robertson and Scott Booth. At the end, I said an emotional goodbye to Pittodrie, and thanked Fergie for putting the prestigious team together. 'We slaughtered you, and you were rubbish' he observed with all due sympathy while sporting a big smile. He always had to be the winner. A number of dinners were held in my honour over the next few weeks, and distinguished journalists, including BBC presenter James Naughtie and legendary writer Jack Webster, made some truly eloquent speeches. There were also golf days and meetings with old friends, as I closed for good the extended and inspiring chapter covering my time as captain of Aberdeen Football Club.

I now had to take stock and work out what I wanted to do with my life. There would be no more dressing-room banter or the buzz of playing big games; no more turning out for Scotland or lifting trophies, or victory parades through the streets of Aberdeen. Yes, I was still involved in coaching, but nothing could ever replace playing. I had been a lucky man for 20 glorious years, but now it was time for me to move on.

16

RISE AND FALL

'I donned my tracksuit and took the morning coaching session, but felt like a condemned man'

It took a few weeks for me to accept I would never again have the honour of serving as captain of Aberdeen Football Club. Granted, I had been winding down slowly as a player and had been involved more in coaching, but even so the harsh reality that I was finished was hard to take. I made a conscious decision not to keep nipping in to see my mates in the first-team squad, and to concentrate on my duties coaching the reserves. I became more and more detached from the first team, which was a curious feeling after spending so many years of my life at Pittodrie. I saw less and less of my former colleagues, and I quickly became a forgotten man. The fans had new heroes to cheer, and players forged new dressing-room friendships. That feeling of isolation is the reason that so many footballers struggle to cope with the real world when they retire. One minute they are having everything done for them, and the fans are singing their names in unison, the next they are sitting in the house wondering whether to head off for another round of golf. Because I had started to coach the reserves alongside Teddy Scott, when my playing career ended I did not have to make that difficult transition. I was more than happy to learn all I could about coaching from the bottom up. I helped to pick the reserve team and to arrange their training, and also undertook basic practical tasks, including making sure that the goals were set up, the balls were out and the pitch was marked. I got angry when that wasn't done properly in Ian Porterfield's spell as manager, and my approach was anything but sloppy. For me, preparation was everything, whether you were a player or a coach. The reserve side could field men such as Dennis Wyness, who went on to play for the first team and for Heart of Midlothian and Inverness Caledonian Thistle, and I very much enjoyed working with them. We did well in the reserve league, and I must have been doing something right, as offers to leave Aberdeen kept on coming. Ayr United and Arbroath asked me to become manager, but I turned them down. If I had been a bit of a nomad in my playing days, maybe things would have been different, but I was happy at Aberdeen, and my family were settled in the city.

I could follow the progression of the first team only from afar, and it was evident that Alex Smith and Jocky Scott, although they were doing a worthwhile job, carried an incredible weight of expectation on their shoulders. In season 1990-91, my first as reserve team coach, Alex and Jocky helped Aberdeen to push Rangers all the way in the Scottish Premier League, and with one match left the clubs were equal on points, which meant a winner-takes-all encounter at Ibrox. Theo Snelders was unfit to play in the vital match, and young Michael Watt was pitched in. He was a dependable goalkeeper, albeit a bit inexperienced, and he was clattered by big Mark Hateley in the first few minutes. That was a signal of intent from Mark, who scored twice to secure the title for Rangers. Aberdeen finishing second in the league was not considered good enough by some people, but if coming just behind a very good team from Ibrox was looked upon as failure, it was obvious that Alex and Jocky were fighting a losing battle. Despite their undoubted qualities, when Aberdeen experienced a poor start to the 1991-92 season, they were under real pressure. I could feel the bad vibes around Pittodrie at that time, and though I was not involved with the first team, I could see that we had problems. Matters came to a head on Thursday, September 19, 1991 when some 700 supporters gathered outside Pittodrie after our 1-0 first-round, first-leg defeat by Copenhagen side BK1903 in the UEFA Cup. Vice-chairman Ian Donald told the fans to blame the players, not the

managers, and reminded them that Alex and Jocky had lifted the
Scottish Cup and Scottish League Cup in their second season.
Despite Ian's comments, changes were afoot, and two days after
the fans' protest, Dunfermline persuaded Jocky Scott to move
into the manager's office at East End Park, leaving Alex in overall
charge on his own. Alex moved Drew Jarvie up the coaching
ladder to serve as his assistant, and he asked me to take over as
first-team coach. I was delighted at the offer which, to be honest,
wasn't a big surprise. That was because Alex had said, when
making me reserve-team coach, that he felt I would be his
successor as manager at some stage. I joked with him that, for his
sake, I hoped that would not be for a while.

Despite me enjoying working on the training field with the
first-team players, business was going from bad to worse on the
field of play. Heading into the home game against Hibernian
on Saturday, February 8, 1992, we had won just three of our
previous 17 games, and the knives were out for Alex. The match
was drifting towards a 0-0 draw when Mickey Weir scored the
winner for Hibs two minutes from time. That was the signal for
the crowd to start booing, and at the final whistle they gathered
outside the main doors at Pittodrie to demonstrate. The writing
was on the wall for Alex Smith. I felt he should have been given
more time, but 48 hours after the defeat by Hibs, Alex met the
Aberdeen board of directors, and was sacked. He was more upset
than anyone by the team's slump, and it pained him that many
had forgotten that, apart from Alex Ferguson and Dave Halliday,
he was the only other post-war Aberdeen manager who had
brought the club two trophies. Feverish speculation broke out
that the board would approach me to become manager, and it
was clear that if they did, I would say yes. Ian Donald, who was
now Aberdeen chairman, offered me the job, and it was a great
honour to be asked, but obviously I felt uncomfortable taking
over from Alex. I owed him a lot, as he had given me the job of
reserve-team coach when my playing days were over. He was a
very popular figure, and on the day that he left many people shed
tears. When I went to say my own goodbyes, a cleaner was

giving him a big hug and was crying too. Alex offered me his best wishes, and said that he had tried to pass on as much about management as he could in the period that we had worked together. He was honest and said he felt that I needed a bit more time to learn about being a manager – and that I had been thrown in at the deep end a bit too soon. Alex informed me that the Aberdeen board had asked him to resign, as they did not wish to be seen to be sacking him. But he was adamant that he would not do so, as he had not quit anything in his life, and did not intend to start now. There was no doubt that he felt bitterness towards some people at the club, but he kept that to himself and did not make derogatory remarks as he left. A telling quote emanated from Ian Donald as he tried to explain the decision to dismiss Alex. 'What was acceptable in the past is not acceptable now,' he said, by which he meant that finishing second was not good enough for Aberdeen Football Club. His comments showed the pressure that I would be under to deliver trophies.

Though the club gave an assurance that I would have money to spend on players, the new Richard Donald Stand at the Beach End of Pittodrie, incorporating executive suites and restaurants, cost around £4.5m. Some of that money might have been earmarked for me, but building work took priority. It pointed up the idea that it is unwise to work as manager of a club redeveloping their ground, as money tends to be tight, though they did their best to release some finance to me. Though around 50 per cent of the money for the stand came from the Football Trust, we needed average gates of 15,000 at home games to break even that season. To reach such figures, I had to make Aberdeen successful once more. On the day that I was appointed to the hot seat, a radio reporter pointed out that I was the club's 13th manager. I wondered whether I would be unlucky. I had inherited Drew Jarvie as first-team coach, and was happy to go along with that set-up until I found my feet, and had time to work out who I wanted as my full-time assistant. Moving into the manager's office was a strange experience, as I had been on the other side of the desk on many occasions while talking to

Fergie. Now I was sitting in the very chair that he had occupied for, among other things, checking the horse-racing form first thing in the morning. On my second day in office, I called the first-team squad together and told them I was wiping the slate clean, and would give everybody a chance to prove themselves. Even players who had languished in the reserves for years, like Andy Gibson, who had been signed from Stirling Albion for £50,000 three years previously, was to be given an opportunity to break into the squad. My first week as was an intensive learning experience. I wanted to do things my way, and had real doubts about whether to select Hans Gilhaus for my first game in charge against Rangers, because I felt that he had lost form badly and also a bit of his desire under Alex Smith. He was supposed to be one of our top strikers, but I called him aside after training on the Friday before the game, and informed him that he would not be playing. He wasn't happy, but there was no serious bust-up, and he accepted my decision.

Such was the interest in my managerial appointment that my first game in charge was broadcast live on television, and newspapers, radio and TV were after me for interviews. I did not take readily to the never-ending demands from the media, and I was pleased to put such matters aside and to concentrate on the Rangers game. I received a rousing reception from our fans when I walked down the tunnel, and overall I thought we played reasonably well in a match which offered no goals. Observing the team through my early weeks in charge made me realise that I needed an out-and-out goal-scorer. I had restored Hans Gilhaus to the side, but I was not confident that we had enough quality strikers at the club. The team had shown determination and commitment, but also an inability to turn chances into goals. I lacked the positive feeling that, when we got the ball into the penalty-box, someone would score. With that in mind, I scoured England and Scotland seeking a big striker who would put that right, and the first that I approached was the man that I signed, though in retrospect I had obviously benefited from beginner's luck in the transfer market. Attracting Finnish international Mixu

Paatelainen from Dundee United for £300,000 proved to be an excellent piece of business. Mixu could play through the middle, he could play wide, was good in the air and most skillful, and he could score goals. His experience and physical presence took the pressure off young stars like Scott Booth and Eoin Jess, and I also managed to persuade three of my best and most-experienced professionals to agree to new two-year contracts. Alex McLeish, Jim Bett, and Brian Grant agreed to stay, which was a great boost, as it suggested they had faith in me as manager. I decided to offer Alex a new contract as he was a leader on the park, as I had been, and my only concern was over his fitness, as he had been plagued with injuries. Alex may have been 33 and in his 16th season with the club, but he was a VIP at Pittodrie. I had been Fergie's eyes and ears on the pitch, and I wanted Big Eck to fulfil a similar role for me as manager. I wanted to put Bett on an extended deal, as he was one of the most gifted midfielders in the land, and his decision to retire from the national team meant that he would be all the fresher for Aberdeen Football Club. I also needed strong midfielders, and Brian Grant, who had been at Pittodrie for almost eight years, fitted that bill.

I tried to ensure that we played attacking football, and got close to the perfection I desired in a game against Motherwell at home on April 11, 1992, a game that we won 2-0. I decided I would play Hans Gilhaus, Mixu Paatelainen and Eoin Jess upfront, and they were a revelation. We finished 1991-92 in sixth place in the Scottish Premier League, and I was confident that we could improve on that in the following season. To do that, though, I needed more players, including a couple of new strikers, as well as a bit of help on the coaching side. Drew Jarvie had done a great job as first-team coach and temporary assistant, but I required extra expertise. I had to ensure that I got the right man, and thought long and hard about who to go for. I was seeking a leader, a distinctive individual who could drive the team forward, and after surveying the Scottish football scene and talking to a few senior figures in the game, I came up with a name that surprised the Aberdeen following. Scotland manager

Andy Roxburgh was first to recommend that I take a look at former Celtic captain Roy Aitken, who had impressed him at the SFA coaching school at Largs. The more I thought about it, the more it made sense to approach Roy. My decision to try to attract him to Pittodrie was not universally applauded by fans, who recalled that he had been a thorn in the side of our team down the years. I had experienced a few tough encounters with Roy on the pitch, and remember vividly putting him up in the air with a late tackle at Parkhead. When he got up, I thought he was about to tear my head off. The fact that he was still playing for St Mirren when I approached him was a distinct bonus, as I could bring him to Pittodrie as player/coach. Roy was keen to come, and when St Mirren accepted a £100,000 bid for his services, I was delighted. Though we were deadly rivals on the field, we held each other in great respect. I knew him from my time with the Scotland national squad, and we were very much alike. Bringing Roy in was a significant help, as he was an effective sounding-board and someone to whom I could turn to when the going got tough.

My other top pre-season target proved elusive. A verbal offer of £650,000 for John Robertson of Hearts was rejected, as the Tynecastle club wanted £1m. I returned with an improved bid of around £750,000, but manager Joe Jordan refused to sell, so I didn't hang around waiting for them to change their minds. Instead, I turned my attention to Duncan Shearer, who had been playing for nine years in England. The Fort William-born striker cost me £550,000 from Blackburn Rovers, and though he had never worked within the Scottish Premier League, his record in the south with Chelsea, Huddersfield, Swindon, and Blackburn suggested that he could be a genuine asset. During his years in England, Duncan had averaged a goal in every two matches, and I had a hunch that he could keep scoring goals north of the Border. I now had a superior player/coach in Roy Aitken and a top new striker in Duncan Shearer, so it was no surprise that I couldn't wait for the dawn of 1992-93, my first full season as manager.

We won our first league game 3-0 against Hibs, a victory that gave me deep satisfaction, as we played superbly. We were persistent, patient, uncompromising, and unwilling to settle for anything less than a comprehensive victory. Duncan Shearer scored twice, and Roy Aitken displayed the skills of a veteran and the energy of a teenager. I knew instinctively that we were heading into a decent season, as did Ian Donald and the rest of the Aberdeen board, who had made it abundantly clear to me that they wanted the team to win trophies. My team were playing with a more positive approach than Aberdeen had done for several seasons, and I really did think that we could challenge the Old Firm, as we had done in the Alex Ferguson years. The first competition was the Scottish League Cup, which still carried the Skol brand name, and we breezed past Arbroath, squeezed past Dunfermline and disposed of Falkirk to set up a semi-final against Celtic at Hampden. Liam Brady was manager at Parkhead, and the fact that his team had lost nine goals in their three matches going into the final suggested to me that we could score a few against them. I wasn't nervous when I took my seat in the dugout at Hampden, partly because I knew Roy Aitken and Alex McLeish would keep the team right out on the pitch. We dealt impressively with anything that Celtic threw at us early on, and a goal from Eoin Jess won the match for us. We were now set to face Rangers in the Scottish League Cup final, just seven months after I had taken over as manager. We had played them three times in the final in recent years, and each time the game had been worthy of its place in the history books, though I would have much preferred a full sweep of Aberdeen successes. Rangers had won in a penalty decider in 1987-88 and by 3-2 the following season. Our 2-1 win against them after extra-time in '89-90 proved to be another close and exciting match. In my first final as manager, I had my game plan set out, but it was disrupted early on when Roy Aitken had to leave the field injured, and I had to change tactics. We also lost a stupid goal when Brian Grant played the ball back to Theo Snelders, who was still getting used to the back-pass rule, and made a real hash of trying to bring the ball under control on his chest before clearing it. He let the ball bounce away from him straight to Stuart McCall, who scored. To say I was furious was an under-statement. We did get back into the game when Duncan Shearer equalised in 62 minutes, and yet another final moved into extra-time. We were doing fine until Gary Smith headed the ball into his own net. With such incidents games are won and lost, and Gary's mistake handed the cup to Rangers. I felt a bit sorry for Gary, who was inconsolable afterwards, as he had played brilliantly until his momentary lapse of concentration. I really felt that we had missed a great opportunity to lift the trophy, and though angry that we had lost two stupid goals, I was pleased at the way we had performed overall. Winning the Scottish League Cup would have eased the professional pressure on me, but at least I felt that I had a group of players who could take Aberdeen into more cup finals. We would return to Hampden!

An example of the fighting spirit that I had instilled in the team was indicated by the fact that time and time again we fought back to secure late wins. A case in point came against Dundee at Dens Park on November 7, 1992 when we were drawing 1-1. Lee Richardson, who had moved north for £150,000 from Blackburn Rovers, scored in injury-time to give us victory.

A DISCONCERTING PHONE-CALL

While the important business of Aberdeen Football Club was proceeding apace on the field, I was shocked to take a personal phone-call during my first season in charge from my wife, Claire, informing me that she had been beaten up. I immediately assumed that some idiot who didn't like me or the club had discovered that she was my wife, and had attacked her. There was no such ulterior motive, as it turned out as Claire was simply in the wrong place at the wrong time.

An unemployed man had been on a drinking binge, and when he walked out of a pub the first person he saw was my wife, and he set upon her for no reason, pulling her hair and hitting her on the legs with a wooden fence post. She suffered cuts and bruises and was badly shaken up, but thankfully there was no lasting damage.

The man pleaded guilty at Aberdeen Sheriff Court to causing a breach of the peace by shouting and swearing, striking a car with the post, and assaulting a policeman by kicking him on the legs, and admitted 19 previous convictions A defence agent said that the accused accepted that it must have been a terrifying experience for my wife. He had been drinking, and remembered little of his attack on Claire. It was disturbing incident, but she is a strong woman and managed to put the attack behind her.

I must say that I was pleased with the progress we were making in footballing terms. By December 1992 we remained in with a shout for the championship, but I was under no illusions that Rangers had a much stronger and experienced squad. We enjoyed a reputation for developing young talent and players that I had on the books – Eoin Jess, Scott Booth, Gary Smith and Stephen Wright – were as talented as any of their age in the country. During my first full season in charge I talked a lot to Alex Ferguson, and he revealed that the vibes he was getting back from his friends in Aberdeen were that I was doing a great job. He agreed that my appointment of Roy Aitken as player/coach was a good one, and the physical approach of Duncan Shearer was perfectly suited for the rough and tumble of Scottish football. But overall, the balance of power had been slowly but surely switching back to Rangers, who had the financial clout to strengthen their squad. My spending on players was mere loose change compared to that, but that cut no ice with the Aberdeen board, who assumed our success would continue, come what may. What they seemed to have forgotten was that our achievements under Alex Ferguson had been a massive blip, and had been the work of an exceptional manager who had put together a remarkable group of players. Before Fergie came along, the Old Firm had dominated Scottish football, and now Rangers were starting to pull away again, and were buying top British and European players to strengthen their squad. Regardless of the money that they spent, I still believed that Aberdeen played the more attacking and exciting football. By the end of December 1992 we had hit 50 league goals, just five short of our entire haul of the previous season. Our star marksman was Duncan Shearer, who had amassed 21 goals in 20 games until he was sidelined by a knee injury. The downside of our outstanding form was that some teams who visited Pittodrie simply shut up shop. It was a negative approach and most frustrating for fans, but it was a phenomenon we had to live with.

The only significant problem posed by supporters during my first full season as manager involved a small section who kept getting on the back of Jim Bett. He had continued to play despite carrying a groin injury, and though he was not at the top of his game, he still merited selection. A few fans disagreed that he should take his place in the starting line-up, and gave him a hard time, which I thought most unfair. The lesson I learned from that passage of play was to be entirely open with fans, and to tell them when a player was suffering a bit. It might have alerted the opposition to his problem, but at least it would stop that player from becoming a target of derision.

Our ability to score goals meant that we kept ourselves in the hunt for the league title until February, when we met Rangers in a midweek fixture at Pittodrie, and were on the wrong end of some dreadful refereeing decisions. Only 15,600 fans could be accommodated because of improvement work at Pittodrie, and they saw Mark Hateley score in 59 minutes. Though we had opportunities to equalise, Andy Goram was in sparkling form in goals for Rangers, and their win meant that they stretched their lead over us to seven points, and any hopes we had of finishing top of the Scottish Premier League were dashed. The encounter left me deeply frustrated, especially as I felt that we had got no change from referee Hugh Williamson. He had rejected two stonewall penalty claims, and after I watched the incidents on television, I was even more certain we had been robbed. After that game I went public in calling for a change in the system of choosing referees for particular fixtures, because it was my belief that they should be drawn from a neutral area of Scotland or perhaps, for big games, another country. I believed it to be a valid suggestion, but it made no difference to the SFA who ignored my point of view – and fined me for speaking my mind, into the bargain. As the season drew to a close, I had the honour of being the manager who faced Jim McLean in his last Scottish league game in charge of Dundee United. I had lots of respect for Jim, which may seem strange considering he had faced up to me and had to be restrained at half-time in a game during my playing career. He had spent 21 years in charge of Dundee United, and to last so long at the top was an incredible achievement. He had done much for Dundee United and Scottish football, but I wanted to beat his team, badly. I'm sure the feeling was mutual, but it certainly rained on Jim's parade that day as we won the match 4-1.

WHICH TEAM WERE FRONT-RUNNERS WITHIN THE NEW FIRM?

I have been asked about the rise of the so-called New Firm, the idea that Aberdeen and Dundee United emerged from the shadows to challenge the might of Celtic and Rangers, but I believe that it was simply a coincidence that two teams from outwith Glasgow were challenging for honours at about the same time. I think it was simply down to two highly-committed managers in Alex Ferguson and Jim McLean assembling two fine sets of players which led to a tale of two cities.

I emphasise that I had the greatest respect for Jim and his club, and they did beat us at some crucial points in competition, but I always felt that they did not have the finishing touch when it came to winning trophies. During my playing days, Aberdeen lifted trophies on 13 occasions to Dundee United's three. I felt that we could handle the big occasion better than they could, and though they recorded some fantastic results, they fell just short on several occasions.

They had the inherent ability to beat Celtic, Rangers and teams such as Barcelona, PSV Eindhoven and Borussia Moenchengladbach, but they were defeated in the UEFA Cup final by Gothenburg, and they did not lift the Scottish Cup during my extensive career as an Aberdeen player. They won the cup eventually in 1993-94, when Ivan Golac was in charge, and I was filling the manager's chair at Pittodrie. They had won the league in 1983 and gained two Scottish League Cups, on one occasion after beating Aberdeen, but they did not carry home a European trophy to Tayside, which allows me to conclude that we were the senior partners in what some described as the New Firm.

Don't get me wrong in this summation. Dundee United built up a fine team, though perhaps they could not call upon the individuals of brilliance that Aberdeen had stacked within their ranks over many seasons. United blended superbly well, of that there is no doubt, and much of that was down to the tactical nous of that man Jim McLean. The key to their success apart from that was the strong backbone provided by Hamish McAlpine, Paul Hegarty and David Narey, with Paul Sturrock operating upfront.

But I am adamant, and the statistics back me up in this assertion, that over the piece Aberdeen were much the better side in the so-called New Firm.

O O O

In the Scottish Cup competition of season 1992-93, we had beaten Hamilton, then Dundee United, but had struggled against Clydebank, and finally moved forward by 4-3 after a quarter-final replay which followed a 1-1 result at Pittodrie. We came up against Hibernian in the semi-final, to be played at Tynecastle of all places, but I was not happy with the fixture pile-up with which we had to contend with in approaching such an important meeting. We had to travel to Glasgow for a midweek league match against Rangers, head back home to Aberdeen, then travel to Edinburgh again on the Friday for the cup match on the following day. That added up to a few hundred miles. It was diabolical scheduling by the SFA, and we should not have been thrust into such a logistical logjam, but despite our travelling nightmare, we managed to beat Hibs thanks to a goal from Scott Booth to set up another Scottish Cup final against Rangers. I must say that, by the eve of the Hampden showdown, I was growing weary of journalists questioning me about whether my team were as good as the Fergie version. Of course not, but the sports-hounds kept asking. My philosophy was to look forward, not back, and I was not interested in comparing my team with those assembled by Alex Ferguson. All that mattered was beating Rangers in *this* Scottish Cup Final.

I was faced with a tough tactical decision. Eoin Jess was one of my most effective strikers, but he had recovered from a broken leg only recently. Because of his lack of match-fitness, I decided to leave him on the bench, and I informed him a couple of days beforehand. I had taken to heart what Alex Ferguson had preached relentlessly, that preparation for the big occasion was vital, and I had everything the way I wanted it to be on the day of the game. Or so I thought. I had walked on to the pitch with the players when an Aberdeen official summoned me back into the tunnel. I had no idea what was wrong, but he wore a worried look, and informed me that Rangers fans had attacked the car in which my wife Claire and children Victoria and Mark had travelled to Celtic Park, a temporary cup-final venue as Hampden was being developed. Supporters had noticed the official Aberdeen club badge on the vehicle as Claire attempted to enter the car park, and had started to bang on the window, rock the car and shout and swear at Claire and the kids. What heroes! Police officers eventually managed to pull the supporters away, and to clear a safe passage for my wife and children. Not surprisingly, Claire and the kids were distraught and broke down in tears when I met them in a back room at Parkhead. It all happened about half-an-hour before kick-off, and I had to rush from the essential task of comforting my family after their ordeal to presenting my vital team-talk. I was obviously flustered over the outrageous incident involving my wife and children, but I hid my feelings from the players. I urged them not to let themselves down. I wanted them to come off the pitch at the end of the game feeling they had given 100 per cent and I did not want them to have any regrets.

We started well and dominated for the first 20 minutes, but

luck did not run our way. A shot from Neil Murray was going nowhere until it was deflected over Theo Snelders by Brian Irvine to give Rangers a lucky lead. Mark Hateley got another just before half-time, and to go into the break two goals down was a dreadful position for Aberdeen. I reminded my men at half-time of how well they had played in the first 20 minutes, and told them that I wanted them to start like that in the second half. I was duly proud of their efforts in the second 45 minutes, and when Lee Richardson scored with 13 minutes left, I felt we had a chance. We took the game to them, but Andy Goram put in another outstanding performance as our final obstacle before the finishing line, and they held on to win. Bloody Goram! When I looked back on the '92-93 season, though, I do so with a sense of quiet satisfaction. We may not have brought home any trophies to parade down Union Street, but we had finished runners-up to Rangers in all three domestic tournaments, and had qualified for the UEFA Cup by finishing second in the Scottish Premier League, albeit nine points adrift. But our end-of-season report card was greeted with little enthusiasm, and our achievement in finishing just behind Rangers in each of the challenges was described in one newspaper as 'a low point'. In the atmosphere of the time, and in a mantra that I must repeat, second was simply not good enough for Aberdeen Football Club.

In season 1993-94 I was looking forward most to taking Aberdeen into the UEFA Cup, for involvement would bring prestige, and offer the fans more interesting options. Our first opponents were Valur of Iceland, and we beat them 3-0 in the far north and by 4-0 at Pittodrie to ensure a pleasant European baptism for me as manager. Next came Torino of Italy, who provided the type of high-profile European match that I had relished as captain. During my research, I found that they had been the leading team in Italy in the late 1940s, and had won four national championships, but city rivals Juventus soon usurped their standing in the city and in Italy. They were underpinned by a rich football history and attracted some outstanding performers, among them Enzo Francescoli, who had played for Uruguay against me in the World Cup game in Mexico in 1986, and Italian international defender Robert Mussi. Venue for the first leg was the Stadio della Alpi, and because I knew they would come at us from the start, I decided to keep strikers Duncan Shearer and Scott Booth on the bench, and to slot Robert Connor in as an extra man in midfield. I had hoped to come away from Italy with a low-scoring draw, but Mixu Paatelainen and Eoin Jess were on the ball, and my team were two goals in credit after 24 minutes. Just as I thought that we would retain that advantage until half-time, full-back Sergio scored deep into stoppage time to make it 2-1. The second half turned into a rearguard action, and when Fortunato scored and then Alguilera's free-kick was deflected past Theo Snelders, we had allowed a 2-0 advantage to turn into a 3-2 defeat. And yet it wasn't the end of the world, as a one-goal victory at Pittodrie would see us through. I told the team to keep it tight early on in the second leg and to try to claim the first goal, and things went according to plan when Lee Richardson gave us a lead after just 12 minutes. When Carbone equalised five minutes before half-time, I knew that we must take the game to them and risk leaving gaps in defence. It was a high-risk strategy that did not work, as Silenzi, who was top goal-scorer in Serie A, made it 2-1 on the night and 5-3 on aggregate.

In other competitions we blew hot and cold. We hammered Motherwell by 5-2 in the third round of the Scottish League Cup, then lost 2-1 to Rangers to make our exit. Our Scottish Cup run was full of promise, and we proceeded past East Stirling, Raith Rovers and St. Johnstone to set up a semi-final encounter against Dundee United. In the match at Hampden we took the lead through Duncan Shearer, and we were two minutes away from the final when Brian Welsh equalised. It was hard to take, as I felt we had dominated the game and that United did not deserve the extra chance. The replay was scrappy, and Dundee United scored the winner from one of the few cohesive moves that ended with Jim McInally knocking the ball into the goal. Ivan Golac took United to Scottish Cup success that season, and

the City of Discovery celebrated in style while I was left
wondering what might have been. During that season I lost
Jim Bett, who returned to Iceland, and old comrade Alex
McLeish, who was promoted to managing Motherwell. This
was a significant blow as Alex was a mate and a huge influence in
the dressing-room: he possessed a presence which would stand
him in good stead in the sphere of management.

MILLER AND MCLEISH A DREAM TEAM?

*Football followers have asked me if I ever thought of making Alex
McLeish my assistant manager when I took over the reins at Aberdeen
Football Club as he was club captain at the time. Offering Big Eck the
assistant's job didn't even cross my mind. Can you imagine what the
burden of expectation would have been if Miller and McLeish had been
the management team at Pittodrie! It doesn't bear thinking about, for the
pressure on us would have been unbearable.*

*I wanted Alex to keep playing for Aberdeen for as long as he could,
because he was hugely influential. He undertook a bit of coaching for me,
and when the offer of the manager's job at Motherwell came along, I knew
he would jump at the chance.*

*Alex was always a prime candidate to make a smooth transition from
player to manager. He has proved his skills in man-management, and at
Aberdeen he also proved that he could gain the respect of players before
even a ball was kicked.*

I decided in the summer of 1994 to blood new young players and
to revitalise the youth system at the club. Some observers
considered that I was being rather foolhardy, as I had lost two
of my most experienced players, yet here was I trying to bring on
the young players rather than replacing like with like. I was
determined to make fundamental changes, but with hindsight
perhaps I should not have acted so forcefully. I felt the way
forward was to produce my own players rather than buying them

in. Time has proved me right, but at that juncture it proved to be my undoing. Fergie's teams blended youth and experience to great advantage, and I was seeking such a mix. Like the fans, I wanted Aberdeen to finish first, not second or third, and I was obsessed about making the club the best in Scotland. The 1994-95 season was to be my third full season as manager, and I wanted to take Aberdeen to the next level.

Despite all my excitement over the side that I had put together, I came back down to earth with a bump in the first game of the season. It proved to be the lowest point of my managerial career, and ultimately contributed a great deal to me losing my job as Aberdeen manager. We had drawn Skonto Riga, a relatively-unknown team from Latvia, in the preliminary round of the UEFA Cup, and we were awful. On August 9, 1994 we drew 0-0 away, and two weeks later the result at Pittodrie was 1-1, and we were pitched out on the away-goals rule. I was now experiencing what it was like to be a manager under pressure. All sorts of stupid stories emerged about Skonto Riga following the defeat, some of which have been wildly exaggerated. They were a *full-time* side, not part-time as many people had made out. They included nine Latvian internationals in their team, and going into the tie their goalkeeper had conceded just five goals in two years. That's not an excuse for our dismal performance, but it suggests they were not as bad as everyone seemed to think. Our early-season domestic form did not help my fortunes, as we were beaten by Celtic in the semi-final of the Scottish League Cup, which was now sponsored by Coca-Cola, and in the league we struggled to find consistent performances. Duncan Shearer missed nine games with a knee injury, Eoin Jess was absent from eight because of a broken foot, and Theo Snelders was not available for goalkeeping duties for six matches after injuring himself in training. By Christmas 1994, I felt that I was not receiving the support that I needed from the board, and that their confidence in me was ebbing away. A rift opened between myself and chairman Ian Donald, and it got wider. Now Ian was the man who had told me at the start of my managerial career that finishing second wasn't good enough, and when we started to fall out we were lying eighth in a ten-team league. I did not need a crystal ball to predict that his patience was wearing thin. In the New Year of 1995 we started with draws against Dundee United and Falkirk, and followed that up with a win over Partick Thistle. I thought our fortunes were improving, but a 4-2 away defeat against Hibs was followed by a dreadful Scottish Cup performance against lowly Stranraer. We won 1-0 thanks to a goal from Eoin Jess, but we missed at least six easy chances. I was under pressure as it was, and I was becoming more wound up over the way my strikers had gone from scoring goals at will to missing everything that came their way. After the match I was utterly furious. I flung open the dressing-room door and began shouting at my team straight away, but what I had not reckoned on was confronting an old door that swung back against the wall, and parted from its hinges after I gave it that almighty shove. I heard a crash, and turned round to see men fleeing from the path of the falling door. Nobody was laughing, but I would have understood had anyone enjoyed the funny side of my dramatic entrance. I had no alternative but to continue as Mr Angry. I tried to forget the collapsed door and laid into the players, but it was difficult for us to concentrate given the slapstick interlude.

Though storm-clouds were gathering, I continued as normal and pushed ahead with plans to improve the youth system at the club from the grass-roots up. Craig Brown, who was Scotland manager at the time, praised me on television for pioneering a Dutch-style youth programme to improve standards. Craig declared that the initiative by Aberdeen was an example that other clubs must follow. I had set up a network of 113 coaches throughout the north-east of Scotland to operate the seven-a-side football programme, and 1400 youngsters were involved. The concept had emanated from the Netherlands, where some truly-magnificent players had been produced, and I was a devoted advocate of the need for kids to develop their close control, and the way that they could do that was by practising on small pitches and by being encouraged to evolve a passing game. Watching the enjoyment on the youngsters' faces cheered me up a lot in what was a trying time for me professionally. The following game against Kilmarnock could make or break my managerial career, as we were now second-bottom in the Scottish Premier League and languishing in the relegation play-off spot. When we lost 3-1 to Kilmarnock at Rugby Park, I knew that I could be facing the sack forthwith, and no-one was more frustrated than I was at our lack of form. But I was trying to put the foundations in place to guarantee Aberdeen a supply of young talent for the future while creating a winning side. Maybe I had promoted too many youngsters to the first team, and too soon. Either way, I was left with my own thoughts on the coach journey back to Aberdeen after our defeat against Kilmarnock, as chairman Ian Donald didn't say a word to me all the way home. He may not have been speaking to me, but clearly someone had been briefing the Sunday newspapers. It is galling to read that you are about to be sacked, before you are informed yourself, and it was the first time that it had happened to me. I read that the Aberdeen board would meet on Monday morning, and my future was the only item on their agenda. I chatted to family and friends on Sunday evening, and decided to continue as if nothing had happened.

I turned up for work as usual on Monday, but ominously a posse of press photographers were waiting for me outside Pittodrie. I provided them with a wee smile, and proceeded into work. I donned my tracksuit and took the morning coaching session, but felt like a condemned man. I had lunch with the players, and was just about to have a shower when a club official told me that Ian Donald wanted to see me for a chat. 'Aye right', I thought. A chat would mean that he was going to sack me. The atmosphere was decidedly frosty when I entered the room, but the knife was stuck in quickly. He said that the board had been disappointed with the results, and they wanted me to leave the club. I must say that I felt very disappointed with Ian Donald and his role in my dismissal. Although his family had done a lot for Aberdeen Football Club and his dad Dick had been a great servant, I felt that I was being removed from my post without much thought being devoted to my priorities. Given more time, I was confident that the team I had put together could take the club away from the bottom reaches of the league and to success in years to come, but I was not given that chance. I went to see Roy Aitken to inform him that I had been officially sacked, and to tell him also that he could take over as caretaker manager if he wished. I gathered my personal possessions and headed for the door. I vowed that, as I had walked in the front door of Pittodrie more than 20 years previously with my head held high, I would leave in the same way. I was devastated, but managed to stay calm and collected as I made my way through the hordes of journalists who had been stationed outside Pittodrie to catch, in close-up, me being sacked.

17

THE FALL GUY SPEAKS HIS MIND

*'The pressure of being the manager at times became
intolerable'*

Being ordered to leave your job is a huge blow, whoever you are
and whatever you do for a living. I am a confident bloke, but I
did have moments of self-doubt after being dismissed. It was the
worst moment in my football career. Ever. Managers will tell
you that being shown the door is the only certainty when you
take the job. That may be true, but nothing prepares you
properly for the emotional turmoil when it happens. I felt I
had to speak out about the way I had been treated by the board. I
accused Ian Donald of making my position untenable by under-
mining my authority, and pointed to lack of finance as a factor in
my failure to win trophies. The expectation of the fans was to
challenge the Old Firm, but Aberdeen did not have the monetary resources to do that. The board knew that I would have
sweated blood to bring about success, but as Celtic had sorted
themselves out financially, they were about to spend as much as
Rangers on new players. The whole game in Scotland had
changed, and Aberdeen had to change to compete, but we
had failed to do so. I had been isolated by the Aberdeen board
when the going got tough. I was willing to slog it out, to battle to
achieve a respectable position for the club. Unfortunately, I was
left stranded in the trenches myself. I may have been a formidable
leader of footballing men in my days at the heart of Aberdeen's
defence, but I was a man alone when I was sacked. I had tried
reason, I had tried insult, but no matter what approach I used in
management, the response from my players was never emphatic

enough. Failure ate deeply into my psyche, and though I was much too proud an individual to allow any public demonstrations of my pain, it would be some time before I came to terms with what had happened to me. I was used to winning; it had become a way of life. Now I was the fall guy. As the gaffer of a major force in the Scottish game, I carried the can. I knew that came with the territory, but I felt I deserved more time to prove myself as manager.

I must stress that I learned a lot from my time as manager, and came to realise that what were deemed positives during my playing career might have turned to negatives by the time I was in charge. For instance, I did not suffer fools gladly as a player, but that became a handicap when I was manager, as not every professional that I worked with was of the best quality. One of my mistakes was in not appointing a more experienced man to work alongside Roy Aitken and me. Roy was an excellent assistant manager, but he started out as a player/coach, and we could have done with an older, more experienced man helping us. Hindsight in a wonderful thing, but if the directors had retained Alex Smith as director of football, say, I might have lasted longer in the manager's chair. I learned that some of my players were not mentally strong enough to take on responsibility when the going got tough. I assumed, as I had been a proud part of an Aberdeen team bursting with strong characters, that I would be able to fill my dressing-room with similar-minded men. I was wrong, and not having enough players who would lead from the front when we were performing badly was my biggest disappointment as a manager. I did make some signings that worked out well, and Duncan Shearer, Lee Richardson and Mixu Paatelainen fell into that category. Some, such as Colin Woodthorpe, did not. What surprised me more than anything was how some players could not handle the *pressure* of playing for Aberdeen Football Club. When I asked for a bit more, I just didn't get it. Okay, part of that must have been my fault because they did not respond to my methods, but there is such a quality as *personal pride*. I don't necessarily think that teams reflect a manager's personality, but they do reflect the manager's values. I always wanted my team to be super-fit and able to battle to the final whistle, a doctrine that was drummed into me by Alex Ferguson. He wanted nothing less than 100-per-cent commitment from all his players, whatever their standing in the game, superstars or not, and you had better not shirk a tackle! I learned from my mentor that your players must have that attitude of never-say-die.

On the positive side, I remained pretty cool during my time as a manager, and not once was I sent to the stand for confronting a referee. That fact surprised some people who had criticised me as a player for incessantly moaning at officialdom. I was very happy fulfilling the coaching side of the manager's role, but what got to me, and affected my health, was dealing with all the other hassles. As I did not have a director of football, there was no cushion between me and the board. It was up to me to run the club from top to bottom, and that was tough indeed. One of the biggest stress-makers was dealing with the press on a daily basis. I had been brought up under Alex Ferguson to look on the press as enemies, and I could not shake off that feeling. They obviously had a job to do, but I should have treated their questions with less seriousness and got less wound up by their probing. The reason the press bothered me was that they acted as a barometer of how fans were feeling, and I wanted to do well for our supporters. When the press got negative, I knew things were not going well, and some things written about you can hurt . . .

I cared so much about Aberdeen Football Club that the pressure of being the manager at times became intolerable. I can understand what Paul Sturrock went through during his time as manager of Dundee United, likewise Tommy Burns and Billy McNeill at Celtic, Kenny Dalglish at Liverpool, John Robertson at Hearts and John Greig at Rangers. I think that you crave success more if you have enjoyed a successful playing career at the club you proceed to manage. I certainly put myself under more pressure than anyone should have to bear, and my mental health suffered accordingly. Make no mistake, it was an honour to manage the club I had played for, but it did bring its own pressures. I certainly was very hard on myself when we did not win, and fell into black moods. The standards I set for myself were so high that when we finished second in all domestic competitions to Rangers in the 1992–93 season, I was furious that we had not won anything, though satisfied in some ways with progress made. Nowadays, any Premier League manager would be delighted to have split the Old Firm, but back then it was looked upon as failure by me, the fans and the Aberdeen board.

I realise in retrospect that I was chasing an impossible dream. I wanted Aberdeen to beat the Old Firm and to be transformed into the dominant team in Scottish football. But if I had been frank with myself, I would have admitted that these days vanished the minute that Alex Ferguson left for Manchester United and Rangers started to spend big under Graeme Souness. I simply cared too much, and managing Aberdeen engulfed me. It took over my life, and again if I am frank with myself, to be sacked might well have been a blessing in disguise. I needed a break from the game, and having the burden of responsibility lifted from my shoulders was a huge relief. When I was a football manager, I was cocooned in my own little world, and nothing else mattered, which was an unhealthy state of affairs.

The most dedicated footballers put everything else on the back-burner during their careers. Sadly, to a degree that includes family life, and organising summer holidays with the kids proved a problem for me, as they had to be taken out of school in early June, which was hardly fair on them, to fit in with footballing commitments, such as pre-season tours or international duties. As a player I was pretty relaxed at home, but as a manager football took over my life. Entirely. Being a manager changed my personality, and I am not particularly proud of the person that I became. For three years I felt that I was carrying all the cares of the world on my shoulders, and I took the ball home with me, and that was not smart at all. You must draw the line somewhere, because if you fail to do so, you turn into this argumentative, stress-ridden person; that was me for a difficult period of my career. Many years later, in the summer of 2007, I read about Paul Jewell when he stepped down as manager of Wigan. He revealed that the stress of managing a club, the 24-hour pressure, had changed him as a person, and he was arguing with his family and on a permanent short-fuse. As the reader will have concluded by now, I could relate to that in view of my experiences. The fundamental problem I had was being a young manager, who did not have the experience of dealing with constant demands from players, press and public

That said, I felt no bitterness towards Aberdeen Football Club as an institution when I was forced out, but I did harbour simmering resentment towards certain board members, who had let me down when the going got tough. Indeed, the divide between me and these individuals was so wide that I was forced to lodge a claim for unfair dismissal. The last thing that I wanted to do was to take the legal route, but the board, though they denied it, dragged their feet on the important issue of compensation. It was not until August 1995, six months after I had been sacked, that I agreed a settlement with the club. The deal had been worked out on the eve of the Aberdeen annual general meeting, at which the directors were seeking approval to launch a share issue. That was to be the next big plan for the revitalisation of Aberdeen Football Club. Unfortunately, it was set to take place without me on board.

18

INTERNATIONAL AFFAIRS

'The news was even worse . . . Big Jock Stein was dead'

I played 65 times for Scotland, captaining my country on 11 occasions. I appeared in two World Cup finals, and was part of the Scotland team that beat England at Wembley in 1981. I was inducted into the Scottish Football Association Hall of Fame, as were Kenny Dalglish, Denis Law and other greats of the game. I served my country well, and of all the wonderful international moments in my career, which one do the fans tend to mention when they speak to me? Sadly, it's the time that Alan Hansen and I collided in the 1982 World Cup match versus USSR. It is a moment everyone in football seems to remember, and one that Alan and I will not be allowed to forget. Our *Laurel and Hardy* impression was probably all the more funny because neither Alan nor I was renowned for doing anything too daft on the pitch. Till then, at least. I still get taxi-drivers, those born comedians, asking if I have bumped into Alan Hansen recently. Alan gets the same treatment. It will never stop.

Just in case you were on another plantet at the time or your dad or granpaw hasn't chuckled his way through the story, Alan and I got tangled up in a World Cup game played in Malaga, Spain. We were drawing 1–1 in the final match of the group stage, and needed to win, when Alan went to meet a high ball near the touchline. I thought he was going to miss it, so I went behind him to cover. Alan back-pedalled and got a slight touch on the ball, which took it away from me. His momentum kept him falling backwards, and he clattered into me. I went down, and as I fell head over heels, but not in love, the Soviet striker Shengalia sneaked in to divert the ball past Alan Rough. A Graeme Souness goal made it 2-2, but it was but a parting shot, and we were no longer in the tournament. What made the mistake even more annoying was the fact that I had performed well before the turning point. I had put in worthwhile tackles, broken up play and linked well with the midfield, but I'm probably the only human being who remembers that I had done well. Well, I think my mum thought that too!

The reasons that the incident has remained so long in people's minds are two-fold, at least. One is because it was in a vital World Cup match, the other is because Alan and I remain in the public eye. In addition, football followers probably enjoy a laugh at our expense, which is fair enough. Joking aside, I learned from bumping into Alan that we were not suited to playing together, and we seldom did so again. I had the feeling that we were too similar in approach, and that we did not form a partnership that was made in heaven. Thus a choice had to be made: Willie Miller or Alan Hansen, and Scotland managers chose me on the majority of occasions. As the record books show, Alan gained 26 caps to my 65. I can look back and smile over Alan and me making plonkers of ourselves, but that is because I secured a lot more caps. If it had been the other way round, I doubt that I would allow myself the odd grin. I accept that the collision might well have cost Scotland victory, but a draw was not a bad result against the might of the USSR.

That said, I maintain that the reason Scotland went out of the World Cup in 1982 was mainly because we lost two goals to New Zealand in the first match of the tournament. I didn't play in that game, and was very angry that I was not picked. The reason I was furious was because I had played in most of the qualification and build-up matches. Indeed, Jock Stein's decision to select Alan Evans instead of me in the opening game still riles me. I could not understand the logic of such a choice. Alan had been in the Aston Villa side that had lifted the European Cup, but he had occupied a peripheral position in the Scotland set-up, and was awarded only four caps. I had helped Scotland to reach the finals and had played out of position, against my better judgment, against Sweden, and also looked on when an unfit Kenny Burns took my place in a game against Israel during qualification. In Stockholm, it was originally meant to be Alex McLeish and me playing at the back, with Alan Hansen in midfield. When Jock Stein went to Alan and suggested that he operate in midfield, he told the manager that he did not wish to do that. Jock came back to me, and asked me to play in midfield to accommodate Alan. Seeing it was for my country I decided to make the change, and did okay as we won 1-0. When we played Israel in Tel Aviv, I was overlooked, and an unfit Kenny Burns took my place. He was well overweight, but he got the nod, and I was forced to watch from the bench as there ensued the worst 45 minutes of defending I had witnessed from a professional footballer. It was a great puzzle how we managed to reach half-time without the opposition scoring, as Kenny was well off the pace. I came on in the second half, and Kenny was pushed into a sitting midfield role. How he lasted the 90 minutes I still don't know, but we managed to win the game 1-0. I felt that I deserved a place in the first game of the finals against New Zealand, but I was dumped at the last minute in favour of the said Alan Evans. I was not a happy chappy when Big Jock told me that I was not playing. I sat in frustration watching the game, which we won 5-2, when the score should have been 5-0. We lost two goals in inept fashion, and I felt that if we had been set up to play with a sweeper such as me, we would not have surrendered even one goal. I don't wish to appear big-headed, but I am calling it as I saw the action unfold on the night. I felt that Alan Evans and Alan Hansen were set too square when the New Zealand goals went in, and if I had been playing I would have been sitting deeper, and would have occupied a better position to close down their striker. Don't forget that Scotland went out of the 1982 tournament on *goal difference*, and losing those goals to the Kiwis plus the Miller-Hansen mishap versus USSR proved to be Scotland's undoing.

HOW JOCK STEIN WAS INFLUENCED

I believe the Jock Stein's decision to play Alan Evans instead of me in the World Cup finals encounter with New Zealand in 1982 was influenced by the press, and the fact that Alan had been thrust into the limelight thanks to Aston Villa's European Cup victory. In my opinion, Jock took heed of football journalists much more than the Tartan Army would have believed of him. He did so for what he believed were the right reasons, for he was a clever man who realised that it was vital to get the press and the supporters on his side. He thought that if he picked form players, those that the press and public wished to be involved, no-one could complain about his team selection.

I asked Alex Ferguson to speak to Jock in 1979 to ask why I was not being picked more often for Scotland. His response to Fergie was that I had to be part of a team who were winning trophies, to ensure that I was considered on a regular basis. That was like a red rag to a bull so far as Alex Ferguson and I were concerned, and we both set out to show Jock that we could certainly be part of a team that won trophies.

As his words spurred me on, they also indicated how it was easier for those men involved with the Old Firm to gain international honours, as it was for players plying their trade in England. I was competing for a Scotland jersey against candidates from successful English clubs of the time, including Leeds United, Nottingham Forest and Liverpool.

I think that to this day Old Firm players are given preference when it comes to international duty. How often have we seen those from beyond the big Glasgow concerns making their mark, but being ignored by their country, then lo and behold they sign for an Old Firm team, and receive a Scotland call-up? It is clear to me that Scottish players who are not sporting the colours of Celtic or Rangers have to work harder to make the Scotland squad. That was certainly the case with me.

○ ○ ○

Our other match of the 1982 World Cup finals was against the mighty Brazil in Seville, and we were well beaten. I dared to dream that we could pull of a surprise when David Narey put us ahead with what the English commentator Jimmy Hill described as 'a toe-poke'. Dave's shot was no toe-poke. It was a fine strike against a world-class team, and should be remembered thus. Alan Rough in goal did not have many saves to make, but the Brazilian finishing was clinical, and the heat got to us as it hit 48 degrees centigrade before kick-off. I was gasping for breath while the Brazilians were casually wandering all over the park. It was like a cauldron, conditions suited them and the run of play was so one-sided at times that all I can say is: I enjoyed watching them play in the second half, and did not see much of the ball. Zico among the Brazilians was the most intelligent player that I ever came up against, and was difficult to mark as he pulled opponents all over the pitch and made optimum use of the space available. Indeed, all the Brazilians that I encountered in the World Cup were tactically clever, and also most adept at working for each other, a quality that is sometimes overlooked because their individual skills are so outstanding. I was singled out to take the after-match drugs test with Socrates, the Brazilian captain, and after playing in searing heat for 90 minutes, it took a while for me to get enough fluid in my system to pass water. To help me along I asked for a Diet Coke, and Socrates requested a couple of bottles of beer, and 20 cigarettes. I sat with my soft drink while one of the greatest Brazilian stars lit up his fag and guzzled a bottle of beer. As we chatted, he told me that he was qualified as a medical doctor, which I found astonishing considering his post-match routine. Smoking and drinking clearly did not affect his football. I wish I knew his secret.

In the run-up to qualification games for the 1986 World Cup, Jim McLean had resigned as Jock Stein's assistant and Alex Ferguson had taken over, combining these duties with his responsibilities towards Aberdeen, and his first match beside Big Jock was a 6-1 romp in a friendly against Yugoslavia. Fergie was not picking the team Jock made sure that he did that – but it was good to have his expertise on board. I played my part in helping Scotland to the 1986 World Cup finals, but the run-up was shrouded in tragedy. I played in qualification games against Iceland, Spain and Wales, then captained the side on the fateful night that Jock Stein collapsed and died. Wales fielded a talented side with the likes of Ian Rush, Mark Hughes and Neville Southall in their ranks, and had beaten us 1-0 at Hampden earlier in our World Cup campaign, so I knew it would be tough. Our task wasn't helped by the fact that on the eve of the game at Ninian Park, Alan Hansen told Jock and Fergie that he had picked up an injury, and couldn't play. It meant that we had to make last-minute changes to the defence. Because Hughes and Rush were so lethal, Richard Gough was given the job of man-marking Rush, and Alex McLeish would shadow Hughes. I would play behind them, picking up the scraps. In the first half we played badly, and Hughes put Wales ahead deservedly. At half-time Jock had a go at Gordon Strachan, claiming that he had not been playing well. Midway through his rant, physio Hugh Allan whispered in his ear and he shot off into the area near the bathroom. I had no idea what was going on, but the upshot was that Alan Rough was coming on to play in goals in place of Jim Leighton, who had lost one of his contact lenses! Now I do not know what proved the bigger shock: the fact that Jim had lost a contact lens, or that he wore them in the first place. I had spent years with him at Aberdeen, and not once had heard him talk about his contact lenses, or watched him put them into his eyes. Now, at half-time during a vital World Cup qualifying match, he was being replaced because he could not focus on the ball. Many a time I had joked with Jim about his eyesight being deficient, but this was the first time that I had been proved right. Even Fergie did not know Jim wore contact lenses, and he reflected a mixture of embarrassment and fury when he was told. As assistant manager of Scotland and the man in charge of Aberdeen, Big Jock assumed that Fergie would know his goalie required lenses. He didn't, I didn't and Alex McLeish didn't, and this was not the best time to find out. As it turned out, Alan Rough showed no sign of nerves, and pulled off a couple of fine saves. We had a stroke of luck with 10 minutes to go when David Speedie was chasing a loose ball, and it bounced up and hit Welsh defender David Phillips on the arm. It was a soft penalty award, but strictly speaking the correct decision. *Cool Hand Luke*, alias Davie Cooper, stepped up and slotted the ball into the net, and with that I knew that most probably we would be a step closer to Mexico.

At the final whistle, as captain for the night I was leading the celebrations, and I was delighted to have led my country a step closer towards the world's biggest football tournament. Fergie came on to the pitch and urged me to keep the players out there, and to milk the applause. I was wondering where Big Jock was, for this was his achievement, and eventually as I walked up the tunnel I started to sense that something was wrong. By the time I got to the dressing-room all talking had stopped, and a general sense of foreboding pervaded the atmosphere. Fergie came in to tell us that Big Jock had collapsed at the end of the game, and had been taken to hospital. Ernie Walker, who headed the SFA, then came in and informed us that the news was even worse . . . Big Jock Stein was dead. I sat in the dressing-room head down in a world of my own. I had gone from a high of captaining Scotland to the World Cup finals to the low of hearing about the sudden death of one of the most significant figures in Scottish football. I could hear the fans outside chanting Jock's name, but as news of his death was spread, the noise died down. Fans were still inside the stadium in Cardiff, but they were totally stunned, as were the Scotland players. The Tartan Army fell silent.

Jock's sudden death took the edge off Scotland's campaign, and it was hard to concentrate on the fact that we faced a play-off against Australia, who had won the Oceania Group, for a place at the finals in Mexico. It was obvious that Fergie would be approached to take Scotland into the play-off games, and to the finals if we managed to beat the Aussies. Fergie had enough on his plate at the time, but I knew that his love for his country was overpowering, and he would take on the task of being manager of Scotland as well as Aberdeen. From my point of view, I did not feel that I had to justify my selection in any way within the Scotland set-up, as Alex Ferguson would pick men only on merit, and never let sentiment interfere with his judgment. Whatever, I knew that I was good enough to be a member of the Scotland team, regardless of who was acting as manager.

Our first Scotland game under Fergie's sole control was a friendly against East Germany that we drew 0-0. He tried out some ideas of his own, and Andy Goram came on at half-time to gain his first cap, replacing Jim Leighton in goals. Australia made for Hampden and our vital World Cup qualifying game in November 1985 as unknown quantities. They played it very tight and were a big, physical side, as with most Australian sporting units, but we managed to come away with a 2-0 victory, thanks to goals from Davie Cooper and Frank McAvennie. We would have our work cut out to do well in the return leg in Melbourne, and Fergie made sure that we arrived in Australia six days before the fixture, so that we could get used to the hot weather. Good thinking, for it was extremely humid, and it took a while for me to acclimatise. We had a few days to get to know Melbourne, and it proved to be an outstanding city. Fergie had ensured that the younger element in the squad would be catered for by hiring a room in a pub owned by his mate, Hugh Murney, where they could let their hair down. I didn't participate in the high jinks, and met up with George Murray, a former coach at Aberdeen, who introduced me to the delights of the capital of the state of Victoria, of which there were many. We managed to come away from Australia with a 0-0 draw, and the clean sheet was mainly down to the exceptional form of Jim Leighton. He may have lost a contact lens in the match against Wales, but he certainly had his eye in for the match against the Aussies. I roomed with Jim on that trip, and I was like a kangaroo with a sore head in the mornings. I was not a morning person at the best of times, and jet-lag made it difficult to work out when dawn broke. Indeed, I got so grumpy that there was no point in Jim attempting a conversation with me until lunch-time. I felt sorry for Jim, as he had to tip-toe out of bed in the morning and did not have the option of watching television. If he had switched on, then Mr Grumpy, alias Willie Miller, would just have moaned and groaned.

O O O

SLEEP AS A PROFESSIONAL REGIME

While I'm on the subject, if I appear on the TV show Mastermind my speciality, while being questioned in the big black chair, will be Sleeping for Scotland. I did much of that on international duty, and while others were striding out on golf courses, I preferred a quiet round in the Land of Nod.

I must say that sleep was a main part of my training regime. I trained, slept and played football. I slipped into that routine early in my career, and stuck to it. I tend to be a laid-back person who did not worry about things too much, when playing at any rate, and I found it easy to switch off before games. I could nap virtually anywhere: trains and boats and planes.

My routine, apart from sleeping for an extended period each night, of course, was to nap for three hours in the afternoon three days a week, and to be in bed by 9pm on the evening before a football match. Even the night before the European Cup-Winners' final in our hotel outside Gothenburg, I slept like a baby.

The concentration on rest was all part of my professional approach; I did not sleep because I wanted to, but because I felt it to be important. Guess what? Afternoon snoozes ended when I was appointed as manager of Aberdeen. Time was not my own, and I was on the go for 14 hours a day, six days a week. I had little time for sleep at that time in my life.

○ ○ ○

Before the World Cup in Mexico in 1986, we went to Santa Fe in New Mexico for ten days, then to Los Angeles for fitness work before moving to high-altitude training in Mexico. Fergie had taken me, Alex McLeish, David Narey and Richard Gough as the centre-backs, and left Alan Hansen at home. We were beaten by Denmark in our first match in Mexico, and were due to play West Germany in the second. When I phoned home on the eve of the game, my wife Claire told me that Ally MacLeod, my former manager at Aberdeen, had said on television that I shouldn't be playing, and that he preferred David Narey. I obviously disagreed, and was hurt that my former manager did not believe I merited a starting place against the Germans. What made me even more determined to do well was that it would be my 50th cap. Nowadays, they make a big deal of milestones, but I received a pat on the back and some words of congratulation from the boys, and that was it. Although Gordon Strachan opened the scoring against West Germany, we lost 2-1, which meant that we had to beat Uruguay in our final match. Fergie dropped Graeme Souness and made me captain, because he felt he had been tiring in the previous games. To captain your country in a World Cup final is one of the top honours, and our cause was aided after just 40 seconds when Uruguay had Jose Batista sent off. We were playing against ten men for the rest of the proceedings, and qualification for the next round was beckoning. Sadly, in the Scottish tradition, we snatched failure from the jaws of success, and the 0-0 score-line put us out of the tournament.

Playing in two World Cup finals was the pinnacle of my international career, and other highlights and madcap moments occurred along the way. My problem was that I could never say no to Scotland. Even if I was carrying an injury or felt weary after a long, hard season, there was no way I could turn down the chance to play. Something in my blood drove me on. As a boy growing up in Glasgow, I did not venture to Hampden as a spectator, and I was on the ground staff at Aberdeen when I attended a first international match. I did not have to travel far, for Scotland v Belgium in 1971 was staged at Pittodrie, and I was one of the ballboys on duty. That evening I watched and dreamed about playing for Scotland. I took note that Kenny Dalglish made his debut as a second-half substitute in the 1-0 win, and I wanted to follow his lead. I was selected six times for the national youth team, 10 times for the under-23s and made two over-age appearances for the under-21 side, so I had served my apprenticeship for Scotland. These matches taught me a lot: for instance, I featured against Holland in a European Championship under-23 quarter-final in 1976, which was a real physical encounter. I went up for a challenge and was hit with an elbow in the throat, and that nearly put me out cold. Tackles were flying in, and despite the Dutch team being in the lead by 2-0, their fans started to throw bottles at us. So much for silky Dutch football, and supporters who recognised the finer points of the game! In the return leg, which was staged at Easter Road, we played brilliantly and won 2-0 to take the tie into extra-time. It came down to a penalty shoot-out, the first of many that I faced during my career. I volunteered to take a spot-kick and scored, along with John Brownlee and Frank Gray. Unfortunately, Tommy Craig and Joe Jordan both missed to give the Dutch victory. I loved matches where I represented my country under genuine pressure, and wanted more.

My breakthrough to full international honours was against Romania in 1975, and it came as a shock, as I was fielded in place of the great Billy Bremner. The manager was Willie Ormond, who had not picked me for the full squad, but Jock Stein had selected me for Scotland's under-23s, and I anticipated playing for them. However, the week before the game, the contingent from Leeds United, including Billy, pulled out because they had been playing a European tie. When we got to Bucharest, Willie Ormond decided that he needed more players in the main squad, and called me up. It wasn't as big a step as it sounds – it just meant that I travelled on a different bus to training. Now representing Scotland in Billy Bremner's position was an exceptional honour, but somewhat daunting. He was one of my favourite players, and I followed his lead to the extent that I put in a couple of crunching tackles, and chased and harried for 90 minutes. I was pleased with my performance, and we drew 1-1. I had developed from a schoolboy goalkeeper in Glasgow, who had signed as a striker at Aberdeen, where I had been turned into a defender, and had now made a senior Scotland debut as a midfielder. Flexible or what? I was realistic enough to realise that would be a one-off experience, and that I would struggle for a place after the Leeds boys returned to the fold. I played against Bulgaria in a friendly at Hampden in February 1978 just as World Cup fever was starting to build up. I was on stand-by for the finals in

Argentina that year, but Ally MacLeod decided to take Gordon McQueen in my place. It was known that Gordon was injured and would not play, but Ally took him anyway, but then some people commented that I was lucky to miss the debacle. I didn't buy that. Representing my country, regardless of the circumstances, is something that I would never miss. And imagine what it would have been like to have been present on the field when Archie Gemmill scored that great goal against the Dutch!

I played in a European Championship qualifier against Belgium in 1979, but I had to wait until the Home International Championships in 1980 to become a regular. I scored the goal that beat Wales 1-0, my only strike for Scotland as it happened, and kept my place in the side who were beaten 2-0 by England at Hampden. I enjoyed a few days off, then gathered with the Scotland squad to play friendlies against Poland and Hungary in what turned out to be an eventful trip. We took on Poland in Poznan, and the day before I was out for a walk with a few teammates. We were a bit bored, and when our interpreter said she knew a cinema that screened movies in English, we thought we could pass a few hours being entertained. The film was titled *The Stranger*, which was unfamiliar to even the intense film buffs among us. We all trooped into the cinema wearing Scotland tracksuits, and drew curious stares from the Polish audience, but before the film started an image of Soviet President Leonid Brezhnev was flashed up on the screen. Cue for bedlam. The Poles started booing and slow-hand-clapping, and I thought that they would storm the screen when newsreel depicted dignitaries from the USSR visiting a road project in Warsaw was shown. The reason for the spontaneous outburst, of course, was the growing gulf between the Poles and Soviet-inspired Communists, who controlled their nation. We were visiting Poland at a time of growing civil unrest, and three months on Lech Walesa led the Gdansk shipyard strike, which gave rise to a wave of similar industrial action throughout the country. Walesa demanded more workers' rights, and the authorities were forced to capitulate. And what of the main feature, *The Stranger*? The subtlety of the title in English had been lost in translation, and what we watched was the original *Alien* movie: I had seen it before.

Moving on to Hungary, we were beaten 3-1, and after the game I passed up the chance to be transformed into a movie star in my own right. Hollywood had come to Hungary, and scenes for *Escape to Victory*, starring Sylvester Stallone and Michael Caine, were being filmed at a nearby football stadium. All the Scotland players were offered the opportunity to stay behind for an expenses-paid holiday, so that they could feature in the football scenes. Pele and Bobby Moore were already signed up, but I was having none of it, as I had weathered a long, hard season and wanted to get home. The only Scot who did not feel like that was John Wark of Ipswich Town. When *Escape to Victory* was released, Warky was limited to one line of diction, and I swear that they dubbed his voice even for that.

My Scotland career continued to flourish, and in the 1981 season I like to think that I proved that I had developed into an international-class defender. The game that did it was the Home International Championship match against England at Wembley. The home side included Peter Withe, Tony Woodcock and Trevor Francis upfront, but the Scotland defence did not give them a kick. Indeed, the whole team played superbly well, and a John Robertson penalty-kick gave us victory. It was only after I had performed so well against England that people south of the Border noticed me. That game at Wembley gained me credibility, and allowed me to become well established in the Scotland team.

I was promoted to captain of Scotland on our tour of Canada in the summer of 1983, when we played the national side three times in eight days at venues in Toronto, Edmonton and Vancouver. I was skipper in the first game, which we won 2-0, and we went on to make a clean sweep of the Canadians by 3-0 and 2-0. Being Scotland captain did not win the instant respect that I had taken for granted. In 1984, for example, I was captaining my country in a friendly against France, a match I had looked forward to as my opposing captain was Michel Platini, who was a magnificent player. How he progressed to his election as president of UEFA is beyond me, as back in his playing days he certainly lacked diplomacy. After the toss-up he walked towards me, and I thought this was the cue to exchange pennants, but Michel was clearly full of himself, and did not wish to exchange anything. Instead, he asked whether I wished to be photographed with him! He was patronising the wrong guy. At the end of the game, which France won 2-0, he walked towards me, and this time I thought he was about to shake my hand and exchange shirts, captain to captain. However, he strode past me and handed his shirt to Neil Simpson, who had come on at half-time.

My only regret is that I did not play in a Scotland team that made the European Championships, though taking part in two World Cups more than compensated for that omission. I did help Scotland to reach the World Cup finals in 1990, but that contribution brought the curtain down on the role of performing for my country. I had played in our 3-1 defeat to Yugoslavia in Zagreb in September 1989, but manager Andy Roxburgh wanted to proceed with a younger squad because he felt that at 35 I would be too old to play in the finals the following year. He changed his tune when he realised that we needed to take a point from our final qualifying game, at home to Norway, when he needed all the help he could get. I can say that it was the first time that I had contemplated saying no to a call to arms by my country. It took a lot of thought on my part, because Andy Roxburgh had squeezed me out and brought in younger players. In the end, I just could not say no. I was reinstated, and we achieved a 1-1 draw against the Norwegians that took Scotland to the World Cup finals in Italy. Unfortunately, in the second half I was hit by a late tackle that caught me on my bad knee, and it again swelled up like the proverbial balloon. It was an accident, as the Norwegian striker did not hear the whistle, nor did I, and he followed through with a challenge. The damage was done, it was a career-threatening injury, and while the Scotland players were celebrating qualifying for Italia 90, I went to the dressing-room for immediate treatment. I felt really down, and a few days later had to undergo a cartilage operation. I soldiered on for a few league games, but the match against Norway was my Scotland swan-song. Despite exacerbating my knee injury, helping Scotland to make the World Cup finals was a high at my point of departure. Playing for Scotland had been a lasting honour and a fantastic experience, and every sportsman and woman should feel the same.

As it turned out, Andy Roxburgh *did* take me to the 1990 finals, as a member of his backroom staff, and I compiled reports on our opponents, worked with the defenders on the training ground and took a few coaching sessions. I enjoyed the experience to the full, though when the Scots ran on to the field for their World Cup games, I felt twinges of regret, quite naturally, as I would have loved to have been out there in the thick of the action. After I retired, I kept in close contact with the Scotland team through media work, and travelled across Europe watching them play. There were highs and lows, but the lowest of the lows came when Berti Vogts was in charge of the national team.

WHY, OH WHY WAS BERTI VOGTS GIVEN THE JOB?

Thinking about the Berti Vogts debacle still makes my blood boil. Where was the passion from the players? Where were the tactics from the manager? And why were caps handed out like sweeties to wee boys? It was the worst time ever in the history of the Scottish national side, in my opinion, and I couldn't understand why he was appointed in the first place. If you are going for a foreign coach, make sure he is a good one, and superior to anybody in the Scottish game.

I did give Berti the benefit of the doubt, and didn't jump in after he had a couple of bad results, but after a while I could not help myself. At times it would have taken a mathematical genius to work out what tactics he was employing. And few footballers are experts in geometry and algebra.

To make matters worse, guys I had not heard of were awarded caps, then disappeared after one or two performances. I had no personal axe to grind with Berti Vogts, but this is my country, and he was messing about with our national game. It was an awful time, and I breathed a huge sigh of relief when he departed.

Walter Smith was an excellent appointment as his replacement, and my old mate Alex McLeish was another man who cared for his country, who wanted the best for it, and who deserved the honour of being Scotland manager thereafter.

As a former captain of Scotland, I call on the Scottish Football Association not to appoint another foreign coach again, until they have exhausted all hope of attracting a Scottish candidate of the right calibre. You cannot buy that Scottish passion. Berti Vogts reflected the biggest mistake made in the history of Scottish football. Let's not repeat that mistake ever again.

19

GETTING LIFE BACK ON TRACK

'I ambled in and got behind the microphone with a few seconds to spare'

When I was forced out of Aberdeen Football Club, I wanted a break from the game, and I needed one badly. Battling away as manager had taken a lot out of me mentally and physically, and adequate time was required to recharge my batteries. The intense managerial experience had left me drained, especially emotionally. Being sacked as coach of the club that I loved was the worst feeling I had endured in my life, and I admit that I hit an all-time low when I departed from Pittodrie. I have always been positive in my outlook on life, but I struggled to cope with the fact that my career had come crashing down around me because of one bad season as a manager. To be fired by the club to which I had been devoted since I was a schoolboy was a huge blow. I did the things that people tend to do after they have lost a job: played lots of golf, took holidays, even tended the garden. But throughout that period, a dark cloud was hanging over me. Constantly. I felt depressed and very low. It was a tough time for me, and it took three months before I was ready to bounce back, and to start rebuilding my life.

Did I doubt myself around this time? You bet, I did. Anybody would have. That fear of failure drives lots of people, even the likes of Alex Ferguson. I learned, though, that some things that happen in life are outwith your control, and do not arise because you have acted unprofessionally. When I was manager, I gave my life to Aberdeen Football Club, for 24 hours a day, seven days a week. I lived and breathed the job. Such devotion did not protect me from what some people would call fate. Yes, I made some bad decisions along the way in terms of signings and tactics, but sometimes circumstances simply act against you. I always felt that an individual could shape his destiny by means of hard work. I still believe that to a degree, but I now accept that hard graft and dedication sometimes may not be enough, whether in business or in your personal life. Once that fact had been taken in, I became a far more relaxed person.

No human being can stay confident for every hour of every day, but at times of adversity it is important to have faith in yourself. I lost confidence for a period after my dismissal, but I just had to bounce back, or I would have run the risk of disappearing for ever. Everyone must deal with the hard knocks that life hands out, but it may be that being forced to cope with disappointment was harder for me, as I had enjoyed a relatively-successful career up to that point. Trophies had been won, league titles secured. It had been the best of times, but had been transformed dramatically into the worst of times.

That said, the only failure in life is when you give up finally and fundamentally, and there was no way that I would throw in the towel. I felt I still had a lot to give, though I had to endure solitary moments when negative thoughts were nagging away at me. I could not think straight, everything was getting on top of me, and in a curious way it was similar to the time, near the end of my spell as Aberdeen manager, when I would sit on the edge of the bed in the morning, and think: 'Here I go again . . . 24 hours of God knows what.' Back then, I had been obliged to psyche myself up and get back into the firing line, particularly when things were going badly. Put it this way: there were times in those final days in the managerial chair when I felt that *everybody* out there was wielding a long-range rifle with the telescopic lens directed straight at my head. It takes a strong person to get up and do battle day after day, particularly if you are a big name in the public eye, and the odds are stacked against you. Every manager has felt that way at some stage, and it can be a tough, lonely world. To sum up, I had to shake off the

emotional scars of dealing with feelings of rejection and isolation
at being dumped as manager. Those feelings had to be laid to rest
in a box, and the lid screwed down tight. I had to get on with my
life.

It took a while, but it did get better. I obviously did not
become a changed man overnight, but not having so much
pressure bearing down on my shoulders did act as a relief. I began
to feel genuinely relaxed, and enjoyed a few good night-outs
with old friends at my pub, The Parkway in the Bridge of Don.
And I knew that I was getting better and busier, because my golf
was getting worse! When I left the football club, I found a kind
of solace on the golf course, but some months on I was struggling
to find time to play, as my life was getting back together again. I
have always felt that the worse my golf becomes, the harder I
must be working.

Just as I was becoming a bit bored merely concentrating on
my business interests, I received a call from Dougie Wernham,
then head of BBC Radio Sport, who asked if I fancied doing
some work for them. An interesting proposition! I had been
indoctrinated by Fergie into believing that the press were the
enemy, and now I was being asked to join their ranks as a
pundit. Dougie said all I had to do was to turn up and give my
honest opinion on the game I was watching. I thought about it
long and hard – I could easily combine my business interests
with radio broadcasts, as I would cover matches mostly in the
evenings or on Saturdays – and I started to like the sound of
what Dougie had suggested. I had a chat with BBC sports
presenter Richard Gordon, who is a big Aberdeen fan and a
friend, and I resolved to give it a go.

EMBRACED BY AUNTIE BEEB

*I knew that I was leaving myself open to criticism by getting involved with
the media, and that some people would call me a hypocrite. I could
understand that point of view. After all, I had openly despised some of the*

newspapermen who had written dreadful things about me during my time as Aberdeen manager. I was a big enough man to put that behind me, and to work alongside them. I had never been small-minded, and that is exactly what I would have been if I had turned down the chance to undertake radio work, simply because I did not care for a small section of those working in the profession.

Becoming involved in radio broadcasts meant remaining connected with football, but without the pressure being exerted by directors, fans and the rest. All I had to do was talk about the game, and I would always give an honest opinion, irrespective of who was involved: Aberdeen, Rangers, Celtic or Scotland. I understood the game, and what was going on out there on the pitch. If things were not going right, I would voice that opinion. There was no way that I would fudge football issues.

I did have plenty of experience of being interviewed throughout my years in the game, so I harboured no fears about sitting behind a radio microphone or in front of a television camera. Dougie Wernham was delighted when I agreed to give it a shot, and he threw me in at the deep end . . .

O O O

I had not been back to Pittodrie since being sacked in early February of 1995, and three months later I was being asked to return and to commentate on Aberdeen's first-leg relegation play-off match against Dunfermline. Not the easiest of games with which to launch a new career, as I still felt club chairman Ian Donald had let me down when I was manager, and because it was such an important fixture, the team were bound to be feeling loads of tension. I rationalised that I would have wanted to be present anyway to cheer on Aberdeen, so why not go and do a bit of commentary into the bargain? It did feel strange to be at Pittodrie and not to enter via the door for players and officials. Instead, I made my way to the press entrance, and I received a warm enough welcome from the fans as I made my way up to the radio gantry. I sat with Richard Gordon for the 90 minutes, and lapped up the experience, which was helped by the fact that Aberdeen won 3-1. Maybe if we had been beaten, the reaction to my return would have been different, but being back at the stadium was most enjoyable. And Aberdeen winning the return leg by 3-1 to stay in the Scottish Premier League cheered me up no end.

A few weeks later, I was asked to be part of the BBC Scotland television commentary team for an international match between Scotland and San Marino. I found that role to be even more straightforward than radio, in that we sat in the studio watching the match and could contemplate our responses, rather than having to present snap judgments. Because I was not inhibited by suspicion of the question or questioner, and not worried about protecting my players or my club, I was relishing my new role. I tried to give informed tactical expertise when it was needed, and highlighted the good when there was any to be seen. I received positive feedback on my introduction to broadcasting, but did not give future appearances much thought. However, in the summer of 1995 I received another call from Dougie Wernham, this time asking whether I would consider becoming a permanent TV and radio pundit for the BBC. Now never in a million years had I anticipated my career going in such a direction, but I had to admit that I found giving my opinions to be most stimulating, and I agreed to join their team. I refused to sign a contract, though, and said that I would take part only when I was available. Former Rangers player Gordon Smith and presenters Alistair Alexander, Richard Gordon and Chick Young made up the BBC crew, and I much enjoyed working with them. The fact that Richard was part of the team was a bonus, as being interviewed by him was akin to having a chat down the pub with a mate.

I had engineered a good balance in my life between media and business, which is something that I could not say about my high-pressure period as manager of Aberdeen. I continued to expand my business interests, and in March 1998 gained approval, with my business partner Stan McEwan, to open a 160-seat Harry Ramsden's fish-and-chip restaurant at the Beach Esplanade, Aberdeen. I had taken on a franchise with Harry Ramsden's, and I made a few trips to the firm's main restaurant in Guiseley, West Yorkshire, to watch how it was run, and eventually learned to batter fish with the best of them. When I wasn't helping to put together finance for the restaurant or buying up properties in Aberdeen, Glasgow and Edinburgh, I was travelling to matches to commentate, and I was revelling in life once more. The old Willie Miller was back in action.

One of the bonuses of being part of the BBC commentary team was that I travelled to the World Cup finals in France in 1998 to cover Scotland's campaign. That team included Dougie Donnelly, Rob MacLean, Richard Gordon, Alastair Alexander and Gordon Smith, and two days before Scotland opened the tournament with a game against Brazil, I was presented to a special visitor. You may recall that as a kid watching the 1966 World Cup, one of my heroes was Eusebio, and I got a chance to meet the Portuguese wizard more than 30 years on when he turned up for an interview with BBC Scotland. We went for lunch afterwards, and though we had to converse through an interpreter, it was a great honour to meet the great man. I visited the Scotland training camp, and talked to manager Craig Brown and some of the players about the honour of taking on Brazil in the opening match, and also enjoyed a chat with my old mate, Jim Leighton, who was still in fine physical and mental shape despite approaching his 40th birthday. The day before the match, I met television celebrity Ulrika Johnsson, who was a guest on the *Ally McCoist and Fred MacAulay Show,* which was being beamed live from France. I told my friends that I had accompanied Ulrika up the Eiffel Tower, and though the story made them laugh, that is exactly what I did. Ulrika and I were guests on Fred and Ally's TV show, and we got on very well. She invited me to the Auld Alliance bar in Paris where she was going that evening with Fred, Ally and her then boyfriend, Stan Collymore. I couldn't make it, which was just as well, as I would have been furious at what happened there. Unbelievably, Collymore *beat up* Ulrika in the bar, which was packed with Scottish fans, and they went to her aid. Scottish Television reporter Martin Geissler was on duty in the pub, and his cameraman captured evidence of the whole, shocking incident, which was broadcast back in the UK. Not nice.

During my time in the broadcasting media, I infuriated some of the anxious BBC radio bosses by turning up a few minutes before each broadcast. They liked you to be in the stadium at least half-an-hour beforehand, but I was no fan of such demanding time-keeping, and though I cut it fine a few times, I was never too late for going on air. For example, on the day that Scotland played Sweden in the World Cup in 1998, I ambled in and got behind the microphone with a few seconds to spare. Richard Gordon asked me what had happened, and I told him that my taxi had been late in arriving. I also remarked that I was more used to turning up at a big game in the team bus with a police escort, rather than in the back of a cab, which raised a laugh among the BBC radio crew. Though Scotland went out of the World Cup at the group stages, just being at the finals was a superb experience. I returned relaxed and very happy over the hand that I had been dealt, eventually, since leaving direct involvement football. I carried on with media work, and my businesses continued to grow.

Then, come January 1999, I was delighted to be given the chance to help to honour Teddy Scott, who had been one of the biggest influences on my football career. Alex Ferguson brought up a Manchester United team full of top stars including David Beckham to play a game for Teddy, in what was perhaps the most deserved testimonial in the history of Aberdeen Football Club. The stadium was packed to capacity and it was an honour for me to even be in the stadium to honour such a great man who had been associated with Aberdeen for an amazing 44 years.

Before kick-off, the 1983 European Cup Winners' Cup winning side, including me, were reunited with Alex Ferguson and Teddy in parading the trophy. I took my seat in the stand to watch what was a decent, pretty competitive game for a friendly.

After a lively but goalless opening-half, the introduction of £12 million striker Dwight Yorke galvanised United who moved ahead after 51 minutes. Another substitute, Jesper Blomqvist made ground on the left flank, Yorke striking the cross against the underside of the bar from close range before Ronny Johnsen volleyed in the rebound. Aberdeen equalised after a Michael Hart cross picked out Mike Newell to level.

Ultimately it all came down to penalties, and when fringe Manchester United player John Curtis had a penalty saved by Derek Stillie, Aberdeen won 7-6 on penalties. The real winner, though, was Teddy Scott, and quite right too. Just for the record, Aberdeen were the only team to beat Manchester United in the six months of 1999, the year they won the treble which culminated in their Champions League victory over Bayern Munich.

In the past, Fergie had inadvertently given Gordon Strachan the unexpected opportunity to sum up Teddy's worth. On arrival in Switzerland for a vital European tie, Fergie had discovered that the stripes on the socks that Teddy had packed were not of the colour that he had expected. Tongue in cheek, he threatened to sack Teddy when we got home, which prompted Wee Gordon to inquire: 'And where will you get the *six people* to replace him?' In the place that we called Teddy's Aladdin's Cave, set in the bowels of Pittodrie, he had guided, comforted, chastised and prepared players such as me at various times during their football careers. His special abode was near the changing-rooms, and was our equivalent of the Liverpool boot room. The respect in which he was held by everyone that he had influenced was abundantly clear from the collection of football shirts and memorabilia received as gifts from past and present Aberdeen players, who had helped him to create a virtual football museum. Acquisitions included a Newcastle jersey from Stephen Glass, Manchester United shirts and, reflecting his other passion, an England cricket jersey and a bat signed by Sir Ian Botham which enthusiast Mike Newell had acquired for him. He kept diaries of his time at Aberdeen, and records of every reserve team match. An incredible man to whom I owed a lot, I could never repay him totally for all the help that came my way during his years at Aberdeen, but I wanted to display my gratitude in distinctive fashion. Because of that, I decided to give him my 65th and last Scotland cap, the one that I won against Norway. It is the only Scottish cap that I have given away, and it could not have gone to a more deserving recipient. (One thing that Teddy achieved, which I did not, was to gain total control over referees. He trained them for many years, and was made an honorary president of their Aberdeen association).

I also enjoyed a great night-out with Teddy and the Aberdeen staff when Alex Ferguson was given the freedom of the Granite City. It was an accolade reserved for special people, and the list also included Mikhail Gorbachev, Nelson Mandela and the Queen Mother. The City Fathers closed off Union Street, set up giant video screens and released a multitude of balloons as thousands turned out to welcome their returning hero. Through a sea of red and white, Fergie was borne to the Music Hall for a ceremony with roots dating back to the 12th century. The Beach Ballroom was the venue for a civic dinner, and a video presentation featured the golden years of the Ferguson era, watched by the latest freeman and several of his exceptional squad, including me as proud captain, Alex McLeish, Neil Simpson, Doug Rougvie, Stuart Kennedy, Dougie Bell and John Hewitt. It was a night of heady nostalgia, emphasising how soon great moments can be dispersed into the sands of time. Yet to me, on that special night, it all seemed no longer than yesterday.

Sad to relate, and in contrast to the stream of accomplishments that had been inspired by Alex Ferguson, contemporary success seemed a long way off. As the end of the 1998-99 season approached, rumours grew that Alex McLeish, who was by now the coach to Hibernian, would be approached to take over from Paul Hegarty as manager of Aberdeen Football Club. I spoke to Big Eck and told him that, based on my experience, he would need to receive certain assurances about having money to spend on players, if he ever decided to return to the north-east as manager. As it turned out, no official approach was made to him, but he went on to become a hugely-successful manager at club and international level, which was certainly Aberdeen's loss.

At this point, the discontent among Aberdeen fans over the club's lack of success had reached such an extent that a pressure group, Aberdeen 2000, called for my appointment as chief executive at Pittodrie. They issued a press release which stated that I should be appointed to the role, as I had the necessary business skills, knew football and the media, and loved Aberdeen Football Club. They described me as the perfect candidate, and I felt humbled by their comments and support. What a difference a few years can make to the way folk feel about you! Still, I did not mind that much if I was offered the job or not, but I did welcome any attempts to restructure the managerial and administrative set-up at the club, because the manager required all the backing he could get. What was important was to allow the coach to coach, and for the chief executive and director of football to take the pressure off him in all other matters. Keith Burkinshaw was in place as director of football at the time, which meant that the club had various layers of management, but for some reason the system wasn't working properly. As Aberdeen floundered on the pitch, I was delighted to sit at home and watch Fergie's finest hour with Manchester United thus far, when they beat Bayern Munich in the final of the European Champions League in 1999. Once again he demonstrated that he was prepared to make tough decisions, such as bringing on Teddy Sheringham and Ole-Gunner Solskjaer to clinch victory. Having the guts to take risks is what set him apart.

Now I had been surprised by various Aberdeen managerial appointments when I was cast in the role of player, and I felt like that once more when the club took on Ebbe Skovdahl as coach, in place of Paul Hegarty, on May 31, 1999. I watched from a seat in the stand with my head in my hands as we lost 5-0 at home to Celtic in the opening game of the Scottish Premier League campaign for 1999–2000. It was another reminder of how far we had fallen since the heady days of the early 1980s. Barely 16,000, including a huge travelling contingent from Celtic, turned up for one of the season's most attractive fixtures, which saddened me and confirmed that we had to provide fans with some excitement to bring them back to Pittodrie in adequate numbers. But for me, there was nothing to set pulses racing in anticipation at Aberdeen under Ebbe. I met him a couple of times, and we got on all right, and he was the type of personality who, rightly or wrongly, created a strong bond with the supporters. Don't ask me how he managed to do it, though. It's still a mystery. When I was a player, the intention was always to beat Rangers and Celtic, and we held that ambition. We were in receipt of a few hidings along the way, but it didn't take away any of our self-belief. I felt that Ebbe did not hold that belief, and not once did I hear him declare that his team were capable of beating the Old Firm. I could not accept that attitude. I thought Aberdeen were better than that, or should be better than that, and it's hardly worth getting out of bed in the morning if you lack a positive attitude. That's where my big problem lay in those three years of Ebbe as manager. A nice guy, but I don't think that he matched up to that mysterious bond with the fans. I mean, his team were getting beaten heavily at Celtic Park, and the fans were chanting his name! No Aberdeen manager deserves such praise if his team are being taken to the cleaners on a regular basis.

Off the park, the club were going through a period of losing chief executive officers, and I was most concerned about what was going on, as were supporters who expressed their points of view eloquently through the Aberdeen Football Trust. Firstly, chief executive Gordon Bennett was found to have taken too close an interest in members of the city's Red Light Army, and successor Dave Cormack left citing family reasons. Keith Wyness was brought in as the third chief executive in less than two years, and my initial dealings with him were far from cordial. I was one of those people putting together events to celebrate the club's centenary in 2003, and we had planned a few high-profile events, and organisation was under way. Along came Keith to announce that he wanted what seemed to me like hundreds of events spread throughout the centenary year. Indeed, his bull–in–a–china–shop approach made a mockery of all the hard work that had been put in to arrange some significant events, so I felt I had no alternative but to resign from the organising committee in protest. In the event, only 4,407 spectators turned out for Aberdeen's centenary match against Hamburg, then Keith had to apologise for the club not officially inviting to the game John Hewitt, who had scored the winning goal in the 1983 European Cup-Winners' Cup final against Real Madrid. Embarrassing! Some Aberdeen fans did warm to Keith for his outspoken views on the Old Firm, and delighted in his describing them as 'being like painted ladies standing on Sauchiehall Street, hitching up their skirts at every division that passes by', which was his response to their attempts to be accepted into the English Premiership. I felt uncomfortable with his attitude. It was fine to wind up the Old Firm when Aberdeen were capable of beating them on a regular basis. To criticise them when we were falling behind, on and off the park, did not strike me as clever. I became more involved in the Aberdeen Trust, which tried to raise funds for the club, as I realised that some major changes were needed at Pittodrie. It was no surprise to me when Ebbe Skovdahl was removed as manager in 2002, and though Steve Paterson and Duncan Shearer replaced him, no great improvement was evident.

Personally, 2003 was a bad year for me. In September, fire destroyed my restaurant, Cafe Continental, on the Aberdeen seafront. The restaurant and adjacent Harry Ramsden's outlet had to close for a year for refurbishment, and when we re-opened, turnover was down by £150,000 as we struggled to attract diners back through the doors. Ultimately, I was left with little option but to call in a liquidator as losses continued to mount. My firm, Fishlike, was placed in administration by the Court of Session in Edinburgh, as we had debts of around £632,000, and having spent years developing the business, it was an extremely sad way for it to end. It also put intolerable strain on my personal life and marriage to Claire. It was a sad period in my life, and like many in my position, I threw myself into my work.

In April of 2004 a surprise call on my mobile phone from Aberdeen's chairman, Stewart Milne, asked if I was available for a meeting. Newspaper stories had suggested that he would ask me to become a director, so I didn't even query what the meeting was about. Stewart had been on the Aberdeen board at the time of my sacking as manager, so I was a bit wary about trusting him straight away. It was up to him to convince me to return to Pittodrie, and if he had done his homework, he would have realised that certain conditions would have to be met. As reiterated previously, I had felt let down by Ian Donald, who was chairman when I was manager, and I would not return until he had relinquished all power at the club. He was still a director when Stewart approached me, and his continued role was an obvious barrier to me going back to Pittodrie. The first meeting with Stewart was held at my house, and he suggested that changes were afoot which might smooth my path. I told him that, if I did come back as a director, I wanted to wield some power and not be a simple figurehead. I certainly did not wish to be one of those former players who turned up on match-days to talk to the fans, and did little else. I wanted to get my hands dirty, and to have responsibility for football matters. In other words, I would not return to Pittodrie just to wear a blazer and tie, and to fulfil a ceremonial role. I wanted to help the manager, and I had been banging on for some time about the need for a proper director of football and I felt that such an appointment was vital. I told Stewart that I wanted to take a few weeks to look at what was happening at Pittodrie from the outside, before deciding what to do. He understood my reticence, and said that he would call me again in a few weeks' time.

On May 4, 2004 Ian Donald decided to retire as a director of Aberdeen Football Club. Although he stepped into the new honorary role of club president, he no longer filled a decision-making role at the club. Ian had joined the board as a non-executive director in 1980, and he became chairman after the death of his father, Dick, in 1993. He stepped down in 1998 to allow Stewart Milne to take over as chairman, and his decision to leave the board removed the biggest obstacle in the path of me returning to Pittodrie. Stewart Milne built up his attempts to convince me to return to the club as an executive director, with the hands-on role of director of football. He visited my house again, and I listened as he mapped out what he had on offer. My job would include overseeing youth development, scouting, transfers and the coaching staff. I would also help the manager to improve the on-field product, which a series of candidates had failed to achieve in recent years. Steve Paterson was in charge when I was first approached to join the board, and suggestions were made in some quarters that I could return as manager, as things were not going smoothly for him. Becoming manager again was *never* mentioned by Stewart Milne, and if such an offer had been made, I would have turned it down, without a doubt. What could not be overlooked was that Aberdeen were £7m in debt when I was thinking about returning, and money to buy new players was tight. It would be no easy ride if I decided to go back, in whatever capacity.

After much thought, and one further meeting with Stewart Milne, this time at his home, I felt that I could make a difference at Pittodrie, and I was genuinely excited at the thought of a return. I felt that nine years out of football had refreshed my ideas, and I was ready for the challenge. Before I re-entered the fray, Stewart Milne axed Steve Paterson and Duncan Shearer, which he said he had done to present me with a clean slate. Stewart told the press that Steve had been given as much time as possible to revive the club's fortunes, but radical action was now required. He announced that I would be joining the board, and he was convinced that the most effective way forward would be to allow me the opportunity to bring in my own management team. It was now up to me to choose a new manager for Aberdeen Football Club. It would be the most important decision of my life, and if I got it wrong, my time as director of football would prove to be woefully short. Luckily, I knew exactly who I wanted. It was a chap that I had played football with when we were at school, and I was sure that he would not let me down.

20

WILLIAM FERGUSON MILLER,
DIRECTOR OF FOOTBALL

*'No-one at Pittodrie had remembered to earmark an office for
me, or even a desk. Embarrassing!'*

I returned to Aberdeen Football Club as director of football with
my soul intact, and a lot healthier and happier than I had been
when I had departed all those years before. I spoke to Gordon
Smith, who was one of Scotland's leading media pundits before he
became chief executive of the SFA, about going back, and what I
had learned during my time away. I told him that as manager I had
struggled to cope with the demands of the media and their
constant sniping, but my time on the other side of the fence,
working for the BBC, had given me an insight into their role, and
because of that I was prepared to deal with whatever was thrown at
me as director of football. As manager, I had taken the media's
criticism much too personally, but I had emerged stronger, and
would not let it get to me. In saying that, I wholeheartedly agree
with Gordon Strachan when he says that, if someone attacks a
journalist for what he has written, he gets all defensive, yet press
men and women can't understand why managers fight their
corner when something negative is written about them. Put it
this way: if a journalist has done lots of research and written a piece
of which he is proud, when someone criticises his words, he is
likely to react with anger. But when a manager picks a team after a
lot of thought, and he is subjected to criticism, he's not supposed
to get angry. Double-standards or what? It has always struck me as
amazing that writers are surprised when *you* get angry, and want to

get *your* own point of view across to them. Gordon Strachan tends to do that with his sharp tongue, and you would think that journalists would welcome his candour, but they don't. They get resentful because as a football manager some journalists don't expect you to fight your corner.

○ ○ ○

SLINGS, ARROWS, REPORTS AND OPINIONS

It is wrong to think that football people simply shrug off any criticism that is aimed at them. It hurts, and that is why a lot of managers and players don't read the papers or listen to football phone-ins on the radio. As manager of Aberdeen Football Club, naively as it turned out, I didn't think it was important to build a rapport with the media. Fergie did not have such a rapport, and was successful, so why should I bother? I thought it was more important to achieve decent results and to work out tactics than to run to press conferences or answer a succession of press calls.

My time away from Pittodrie made me realise that I had under-estimated the role of the press, and whether I liked it or not, I would have to feel comfortable dealing with their constant questioning again if I wanted to be a successful director of football. I felt that if I took the press calls, it would divert pressure from the manager.

*Part of the problem was that I came from a generation in which the sportswriter's role was **reporting**. Not any more, it ain't. Nowadays, match reports are full of opinion. The great Alastair Macdonald, who was one of the best sportswriters of his generation, was fair and accurate, and was someone I hugely respected. Now the coverage is all about opinions. For instance, after the 2006-07 Scottish Cup final, one tabloid journalist spent the first three paragraphs of his story criticising Gordon Strachan for substituting Neil Lennon. Any football person who watched the game would have realised that Gordon was spot-on in his decision-making. Indeed, I said at half-time on BBC Radio that I thought Lennon had to go. Gordon's decision to take Neil off was the turning point in the game and, in my humble opinion, it led to Celtic going on to lift the trophy.*

○ ○ ○

I knew that the press corps had grown in numbers since I had served as manager, but I had not expected the barrage of column inches and television and radio time that would be devoted to speculation over whether Jimmy Calderwood would be my first choice as manager of Aberdeen. I had not kept in close contact with Jimmy since we had played for the Glasgow primary schools' select team that toured in the United States. That had been more than 40 years previously, and since then our career paths had taken us in completely opposite directions. Jimmy had moved south to sign for Birmingham City, and had spent most of his career in the Netherlands. I had gone straight to Aberdeen, and we had lost contact. We did not meet again until he returned to Scotland in 1999, but even then it was only when we bumped into each other at matches. We certainly weren't bosom buddies. Acquaintances, maybe, but nothing more than that, and it was a popular misconception that he was my big pal, and that this was part of the reason why he landed the job at Pittodrie. *Absolute rubbish!* Jimmy will confirm that. We had a mutual respect, but were not best buddies.

After Steve Paterson and Duncan Shearer left Aberdeen, I knew that I wanted Jimmy and his assistant, Jimmy Nicholl, to be our management team because of their coaching abilities. Jimmy was the type of big personality and enthusiast that I wanted at the club. He was a man who liked to keep things upbeat, and I knew that he could lift the dressing-room, which had been stuck in the doldrums. He had all the European coaching badges, the result of spending his own cash to study while playing in the Netherlands. He had learned a lot there, which isn't surprising considering he had worked under the likes of Louis van Gaal, Johan Cruyff, Arrigo Sacchi and Rinus Michels. And the Dunfermline team that he had put together inevitably played attractive, open football, which was what I wanted at Aberdeen. Attracting Jimmy to Pittodrie was my main priority, but as a club director and director of football, I was in charge of restoring the club's fortunes at every level, from the first team down to the youth levels. I would also work on negotiating players' contracts, and be wheeled out to give positive statements to the media when required. If a tough decision was needed, such as firing a manager or disciplining a player, I would be involved. I would be content doing all of that, but I certainly did not wish to re-visit the coal-face as a manager, operating on a short-term plan running from Saturday to Saturday, and suffering frayed nerves and fraught temper every day. I did not want to live a life like that again.

On the Sunday before my first day back at work at Pittodrie, I was slightly nervous, but it was a positive energy of a type that I had not felt for a long time. As I have explained previously, I was not the excitable type, and even before big games could easily fall asleep in a bus travelling to the stadium. This time things were different. The feeling I had was one of anticipation. Come Sunday evening, I studied in detail the administrative set-up at the club. Remember that I had been away from Pittodrie for almost a decade, and though I still had friends there, things had changed a lot since then. I calculated that when I started as a player at Aberdeen in 1971, we had 50 players on the books at the very most. Now we had more than 120, including the youth development squads, and I would be taking on overall respon-sibility for the lot in one way or another. The club was broken down into the football department and the financial and com-mercial department. I would look after the football department, and let others look after the rest. I was now an executive at Aberdeen Football Club, not a coach or manager. I would employ the manager, and would give him as much support as I could, but that was it. I was aware that, at clubs throughout the world, a manager working alongside a director of football who meddled too much in team affairs, led to nothing but confusion. I would not create confusion.

A blaze of publicity greeted my arrival at Pittodrie for my first official day at work as director of football on Monday, May 24, 2004. In interviews I stressed how much I was looking forward to the job, pictures were taken of me walking in the front door, and I did so offering a big, cheesy smile. Inside I was given a warm welcome by staff, and with the introductions completed, I asked where my office was. Deadly silence. I hadn't anticipated anything fancy, but I had expected a desk and chair, at least. No-one at Pittodrie had remembered to earmark an office for me, or even a desk. Embarrassing! I was eventually found a place to sit, but it was little more than a broom cupboard: very small with no windows, but a skylight which threw out a little light. But it was from that broom cupboard that I helped to work out the deal to bring Jimmy Calderwood to Aberdeen.

I was sure that Jimmy's unseasonal (and at times rather unusual) suntan would bring the glow back to Pittodrie, and on May 26, two days after I had started, my chairman Stewart Milne stepped up our bid to get him. It was a bit weird to begin with working alongside Stewart, though I did not bear him any grudges for being on the board that had sacked me. At least he was man enough to invite me back to Pittodrie as club director and director of football. It takes a big man to do that. He also helped to bring players such as Steve Lovell and Barry Nicholson to Aberdeen, and has the welfare of the football club at heart. I know that he is one of Scotland's richest men, but I have always believed that his money is his to spend how he likes. He has invested substantially in Aberdeen Football Club, but some people still look at the size of his personal wealth, and expect him to plough in even more. What people might forget is that Stewart is Aberdeen's financial safety net, in similar fashion to Sir Tom Farmer with Hibernian. Because Stewart's name and wealth are associated with Aberdeen, it means that we won't run into any substantial difficulties with the banks. That is something that should never be taken for granted. Of course, I would be delighted to take lots and lots of Stewart's money, and put it to good use by bringing in great players to Aberdeen, but simply having him associated with the club is vitally important.

His business acumen came into its own when talks about employing Jimmy were started with John Yorkston, the Dunfermline chairman, and I was confident that a deal could be reached because of Stewart's involvement. By the same token, I

needed a safety net just in case the talks did break down
unexpectedly, so I drew up a long list of other candidates that
I gave to Stewart and the rest of the Aberdeen board, just in case.
Compensation was obviously an issue, and it took two days of
negotiations to thrash out a deal with Dunfermline, but I was
delighted when Stewart told me that we had got our man. When
the deal was finally done, Jimmy phoned to ask me a few general
questions, and he also wished to know a bit more about the
club's training facilities. I said simply: 'The training facilities are a
bit of an embarrassment. You could say we train on the beach.
When the tide is out.' Jimmy saw the funny side, but there was a
nervous laugh at the end of the phone that suggested he expected
better.

Despite his concerns, I was delighted that on Friday, May 28,
2004, at the end of my first week at the club, Jimmy Calderwood
was introduced as the new manager. He had been in Majorca on
an end-of-season break with Dunfermline, and when he walked
through the Pittodrie door for his press conference, he was even
more sun-tanned than usual. I informed the press conference
that, since Alex Ferguson had left for Manchester United,
Aberdeen had lived in a world of make-believe created by
the astonishing success that he had provided. For many years
thereafter, Aberdeen fans had genuinely considered their team to
be on a level footing with the Old Firm, but for me they had
been living in cloud-cuckoo-land on that one. I stressed that
Aberdeen were badly in need of a dose of reality. It may not have
been the message that our supporters wanted to hear, but I felt it
was long overdue. Jimmy told the assembled scribes that my
presence at Aberdeen had been one of the main reasons that he
had taken over at Pittodrie, and he revealed that he would not
have moved north so readily but for my involvement and
enthusiasm. That was gratifying to hear. He signed a two-
and-a-half year contract, and observed that the potential of
managing Aberdeen excited him greatly, and quite rightly so.
The fan base was huge, and we would attract bigger crowds,
provided we were successful.

I like to think that Jimmy thought I had spoken with measured optimism about the future. It was important to get the tone just right from the start, because I did not want the public to think that success would be automatic. Jimmy had left Dunfermline, who had finished fourth and reached the Tennent's Scottish Cup final, for an Aberdeen team who had finished second-bottom of the table. He was not taking over a club that had been doing well. I had grown weary of the ridicule directed towards Aberdeen while travelling around SPL grounds in my role as a BBC radio summariser. I got the butt-end of the jokes about the club, and it was frustrating. I might have been away from Pittodrie for several years, but people asked me what was happening to 'my club'. I was adamant that I would help to restore the club's respectability and credibility, and to make it an organisation where people felt things were being done properly. I was keen to improve the scouting system, and flew to Portugal for talks with football people that I wanted on board from Slovakia and Hungary. I had not given up on British talent, but was keen to explore all avenues for new players. Yuri Venglos, son of Josef, the former manager of Celtic, turned out to be my contact in Slovakia, and he proved to be a sound adviser.

Going into the 2004-05 season, we had a new manager, new kit, a new pitch, and refurbishment had made the dressing-rooms feel new, too. Season-ticket sales were up by 1,000 compared to the previous year, and we had signed Scotland internationalist Scott Severin, from Heart of Midlothian. I felt we had developed from a club that seemed somewhat down-trodden into one with a spring in the step. I was keen to get Jimmy out to meet the supporters, as I knew his personality would win them over, and he took part in a number of roadshows for fans where he talked a great game. Now it was up to him to show that he could produce the goods on the park. We had budgeted for a squad of 21 players, and had 19 plus Paul Sheerin, Leigh Hinds, Fergus Tiernan and Markus Heikkinen, who were all available for transfer. Derek Adams and Steven Craig had signed, and Darren

Mackie had returned from being on loan to Inverness Caledonian Thistle, but the release of Scott Booth and David Zdrilic
meant that the need for a proven goal-scorer was obvious.

DRESSING-ROOM DECLARED OUT OF BOUNDS

*Before the season started, I made it clear to the new manager that I had
decided that I would **not** interfere in team matters. I had already informed
Stewart Milne, but wanted to tell Jimmy Calderwood in person. I also
reiterated my pledge never to enter the dressing-room before or after games,
or to try to influence his team selection, and I have remained true to that
promise. I did talk to Jimmy once, but only once, about tactics and I will
explain why later.*

*I would watch matches on my own from the stand, and would keep my
counsel on any football matters. Yes, I would chat to him about possible
signing targets and anything that was particularly bothering me, but
Jimmy was the man in charge. My door would always be open to Jimmy,
and the players knew where I was. I would have lunch with them in the
canteen, have a natter to them in the hallway, but never, ever in the
dressing-room.*

*I cannot stress the point enough: the dressing-room is no place for a
director, not even one who is also fulfilling the role of director of football.*

Jimmy started his first season in charge with a draw against
Rangers at Pittodrie, which was a reasonable result, but the 3–2
win over Celtic at Parkhead on October 27, 2004 was an early
highlight for me. That victory sent expectations soaring, but I
went on radio to stress that my job was to marry expectations to
realism. I didn't want anybody to get too carried away, too soon.
It was good to be fully involved in football again, and before we
played Rangers again in our next game, I jested via a text message
to their manager, Alex McLeish, and urged him to tell his players
to go easy on us, reminding him of his links with Aberdeen. It
was an exciting time for me, and the club. We had a manager

who knew how to prepare and organise a team, and who could ensure the players were mentally strong whenever they played the Old Firm. My only slight concern was the fact that Jimmy had come to Aberdeen with a gung-ho reputation, and was looked upon as a manager who would rather push eight players forward and get beaten by four goals, rather than lose by just one. That approach was welcomed by many neutrals, but I did not favour that plan of attack at Aberdeen. I went to talk to Jimmy about tactics on one occasion, and that was after the five-goal defeat against Rangers at Ibrox, which came despite me texting Big Eck, and followed the 3-2 victory over Celtic at Parkhead, that had got everybody so excited. I told Jimmy that Aberdeen did not get beaten by five goals; that we couldn't afford to take hidings from any club; that it might have been acceptable with other teams that he had managed, but not by Aberdeen; not when I was involved. Other clubs might be two goals behind, and throw caution to the wind and end up losing by five or six, but Aberdeen had a reputation to uphold. I had watched in horror our big defeats against the Old Firm when Ebbe Skovdahl had been in charge, and there was no way that I would allow Aberdeen to revert to the bad old days. I was trying to repair the club's reputation, and stressed to Jimmy that Aberdeen was not the sort of team that should be beaten by a barrowload of goals. He took the point, and eight-man Aberdeen attacks were placed on the back-burner. For a while at least!

Jimmy Calderwood's first season in charge saw us finish in fourth place in the SPL, just out of the race for a UEFA Cup spot, but it was still a big improvement on the previous season when, under Steve Paterson, we had finished second-bottom. One of the problems was enticing players to the club. The allure of playing for Aberdeen had faded in line with the club's fortunes, and we could not trade on past glories. To make matters worse, many clubs in the lower leagues in England could offer better money to recruit key players. Despite average crowds growing by around 2,800 to an average of 13,189, the transfer budget for the following season would remain tight. Despite knowing that,

Jimmy displayed his loyalty by turning down an approach by Derby County to become their manager. He wanted to build a team at Aberdeen, and when times get rough, which they always do for football managers, some fans would do well to remember that. In the summer of 2005, he asked me if he could bring in Sandy Clark, with whom he had worked with at Dunfermline, as the reserves' coach. Such was Sandy's striking prowess as a player, it made sense to have him working with the first-team strikers, as well as handing him a key role in the development of the club's emerging talent. Although we released significant funds to sign established names, such as Stevie Crawford, Barry Nicholson, Jamie Smith and Steve Lovell, in the expectation of a second solid league campaign, it turned out to be all rather disappointing. We finished within the top six for the second season in a row, but did not set the heather on fire. I still wanted to improve the infrastructure at the club, and appointed Peter Weir, my former team-mate, to head the scouting system in Glasgow and to branch out into Edinburgh, a city that had produced Gordon Strachan, but which had been badly neglected by us through the years.

The club visited South Africa on a pre-season tour before the start of the 2006-2007 season and the trip took me back to the mayhem that I had encountered when travelling with the Aberdeen first team on my first foreign tour as a player back in 1974, and the changes that had taken place since then. Back then we ended up in places as diverse as Australia, Iran and New Zealand and the trip was crazy, as I mentioned earlier. This time around, as I sat in the lounge of my plush hotel in South Africa, I reflected how far more professional things had become. The team were on strict diets, had training programmes and could even have beaten me when it came to sleeping in the afternoons!

We played four games on the tour, beating Jomo Cosmos 2-0, Benoni United 3-2 and Bloemfontein Celtic 2-1. It was a very good tour and I felt confident that the appointment of Jimmy as manager had been a good one.

Over dinner one evening I told Jimmy that I wanted us to win a trophy, sooner rather than later. I automatically assumed that we would do well in the league, but felt the fans deserved a bit of excitement from a stirring cup run as well. What happened? We were put out of the CIS Insurance Cup, the brand now attached to the Scottish League Cup, and the Scottish Cup in our first matches in each competition. I shall not mention cup competitions to Jimmy again, because of that. The CIS defeat came in August 2006, a few weeks into the season, and I was as shocked as any Aberdeen fan that we were beaten in a penalty shoot-out by Queen's Park, against whom I had brought the curtain down on my playing career. I was wheeled out by the club, as I had expected, to calm people down after the defeat, and insisted there was no panic despite the dreadful result. This was not the time for knee-jerk reactions, and I had seen many good managers being shown the door, unfairly, on the back of one bad result. That was not going to happen with Jimmy, and my judgement proved to be right, as by late November we were up to joint second place in the Bank of Scotland Premier League after a six-match unbeaten run. A gradual rise in the quality of players came with the emergence of recruits from the club's youth system, such as Michael Hart, Ricky Foster, Andrew Considine and Chris Clark, who could perform alongside men such as the captain, Russell Anderson, who had been a stalwart in central defence for many years and who sadly left to join Sunderland. In the Scottish Cup, a competition in which I had fancied we might do well, we lost to Hibs in the third round, which left us with just the league left to play for.

For a while, we chased Rangers pretty closely for second place, but fell away, which meant that we had to ensure we finished third to bring UEFA Cup football to Pittodrie for the first time in five years. As the season drew to a close, it was neck-and-neck between Aberdeen and Hearts for third place. The key game was the third-last of the season, when we took on Hearts away from home. Travelling to Tynecastle is always difficult, and this time we had to head for Edinburgh without the services of Russell Anderson, who was serving a suspension. Scott Severin moved into defence alongside Zander Diamond and Andrew Considine, as Jimmy changed our formation. I travelled down on my own and enjoyed Sunday lunch in Bonham's Hotel, which is not too far from the stadium. Aberdeen fans had turned out in numbers, and they were not disappointed. We put in a fine show, and were unlucky to be trailing to a Andrius Velicka goal with a few minutes remaining. Jimmy had instilled a never-say-die attitude in his team, and Barry Nicholson's last-minute goal had me out of my seat celebrating. The 1-1 draw meant that Hearts had to beat Hibs and Kilmarnock in their final games, and pray that we slipped up against Celtic and Rangers. As it turned out, Hearts beat Hibs 2-0 in the Edinburgh derby, and we were unfortunate to lose 2-1 to Celtic at Parkhead: we missed loads of chances, and deserved to take at least a point. That defeat, on top of the win by Hearts, meant that Aberdeen were one point ahead of them with one match left for each club, both of them tough fixtures. Hearts were due to play Kilmarnock at Rugby Park, while we had to take on Rangers at Pittodrie.

I had always relished matches against Rangers, and I knew that they would not be coming to Pittodrie to do us any favours. They had suffered only one defeat in 15 matches since Walter Smith had taken over as manager from Paul Le Guen, and would be difficult opponents. In the week before the match, I made it clear to the press and everybody at the club that, regardless of the result to come, I felt that Jimmy Calderwood and his management team had done a great job. He had put together a team that had challenged near the top of the league, and though some supporters who were stuck in the past might not have considered that to be success, it certainly was. I could not alter people's perceptions about what constituted success. All I could do was to give Jimmy my full backing, and issue reminders that he had taken the team into a position where they were challenging for a UEFA Cup spot. Privately, I realised that the match against Rangers was the biggest that Aberdeen had faced for years, but publicly I tried to play it down to take the pressure off Jimmy and the team. This was a game in which I felt the team had to stand up and show what they were made of, an encounter in which players had to reflect cast-iron character. They had to prove that they could handle the big occasion, and deal with the pressure of playing Rangers in front of a full house at Pittodrie. We had lost our three previous games against the Ibrox side, and did not want that to happen again.

At home on the morning of the Rangers match, over a cup of coffee, I looked through our squad and concluded that Russell Anderson and Scott Severin could be big players for us on the day, and that the team could beat Rangers. I do not usually become uptight before a match, but I was a bit on edge, as I knew how much was riding on the outcome. Before kick-off, I joined some of the sponsors in a lounge named Miller's, which is dedicated to me and displays on its walls a series of pictures of me at various stages of my career. Pittodrie was caught up in a tremendous atmosphere with a capacity crowd of 20,000, and such was the importance of the fixture, former player Theo Snelders had flown in from the Netherlands to join the throng. From the moment the match kicked off, I just knew the Aberdeen team were about to come of age. Scott Severin set the tone with a ferocious opening goal from 30 yards: it was one of the best, and most important, strikes that I had witnessed at Pittodrie. Steve Lovell got a second, and from then on we controlled the action, and I knew that we were on our way into the UEFA Cup. Great stuff! The fact that Kilmarnock had beaten Hearts meant that our win over Rangers did not matter mathematically, but the players were not aware of that during the 90 minutes. The team, quite rightly, celebrated wildly at the end, and Jimmy Calderwood admitted to me afterwards that he had felt the weight of expectation on his shoulders as he prepared for the clash. He told me that he realised he would never match Alex Ferguson's record, but he wanted to bring regular success to Pittodrie, and making the UEFA Cup was a step in the right direction. Striding back into Europe was a huge lift for the club. The fact that we had done it the hard way, by means of league performances and by winning the last game of the season, made it even more gratifying. To finish 'the best of the rest' behind the Old Firm was a great achievement, and should not be under-estimated. It was my best moment since my return, and gave me a great sense of satisfaction. My decision to renew my connection with Pittodrie had been right.

A big celebration after the Rangers game left me with a bit of a sore head on Sunday morning, and I decided to take a walk, only to be greeted by lots of Aberdeen fans shaking my hand in celebration. As I walked through the Queen's Cross area of the city, I thought how lucky I had been to be associated with such a great club. As I looked back on my career on that crisp Sunday morning, I found it hard to believe that I had been at Pittodrie for more than a quarter of a century. Time had flown, and it seemed only yesterday that I was stepping off the bus for the first time at Aberdeen station as a wide-eyed youngster wondering what lay ahead. It still amazes me that I stayed at Aberdeen for so long, and that I am still involved with the club. How many footballers have spent an entire career at one club, as a player, then manager, then director of football? I don't regret not moving on, though I saw many great players, Gordon Strachan, Mark McGhee and Jim Leighton among them, departing during our most successful period. I had my chances to go, most notably to Rangers and Sunderland, and the successes marked up by Aberdeen meant that there was always a lot of interest in me as a potential employee, but the best decision I made was to stay at Pittodrie. It was a second home to me, and I felt like I was in with the bricks.

The obvious career highlight was winning the European Cup-Winners' Cup, and the events of that final on May 11, 1983 in Gothenburg will remain with me forever. The celebrations that followed, the warmth of the Aberdeen fans towards me, the huge excitement throughout the city and indeed Scotland, are recalled vividly. The greatest match at Pittodrie in which I was involved was earlier in that successful European Cup-Winners' Cup campaign, when we beat Bayern Munich. I still get a tingle up my spine remembering the tumultuous roar of the crowd that night, and the huge celebrations that followed the 3-2 win. League titles were won, Scottish Cups and League Cups brought back to Pittodrie, and great laughs were had by all. Inspiring characters, such as Alex Ferguson, Archie Knox and Teddy Scott, made it a privilege to be fully involved at Pittodrie.

To sum up, I have been blessed with a football career that brought great success, and just a bit of failure. I have experienced more highs than lows, and I have learned much about myself along the way. May Aberdeen Football Club continue to flourish, and go from strength to strength. As long as I am involved, I shall be doing my utmost to ensure that comes to fruition. *Bon Accord!*

Postscript

WILLIE MILLER'S DREAM TEAMS

'My goodness, they would be great to watch'

As I was putting the finishing touches to this book, my thoughts turned to all the wonderfully-talented players that I had encountered during my 18 years as a professional. Some I played alongside, others I came up against in World Cup encounters and in European club matches with Aberdeen. When I sat down and thought it through, I realised that I had shared a pitch with some of the greatest players of my generation. So I grabbed a bit of paper, thinking it would be fun to share my very own dream teams with readers, though trying to put them together, and in formation, was never going to be easy. I came across some of the best in the business during my playing career, so whittling numbers down to two starting XIs and substitutes was always bound to be difficult. I cheated a bit, and allowed myself the luxury of picking six substitutes for each squad. I could say that I spent ages pulling my hair out in frustration trying to work out my two teams, but you will have noted my hairstyle nowadays, and will realise that I don't have that many tufts left to pull out. Let's just say that many cups of coffee were consumed and formations scrapped before I settled on my teams of world-beaters. It was a daunting task, and you might not agree with my choices. Indeed, some stars I have left on the bench may not be at all happy. Sorry, Kenny Dalglish, then! But he is in good company as a substitute, alongside Socrates, George Best and Michel Platini. I shall explain all . . .

Many Aberdeen fans would suggest that our best team-ever

won the European Cup-Winners' Cup back in 1983, and I'm not of a mind to disagree with that. The side from that era did form the best collection of players assembled by Aberdeen Football Club, and they were certainly the best team that I played in. We worked for one another, covered each other's backs, and were a side packed with men possessed of great character and, of course, we had the benefit of the services of Alex Ferguson, the best manager in the business, to keep us right. Picking the best two teams, though, is not the point of this exercise: I have tried to put together sides made up of the *best 11 individual talented players* that I played with, and against. Indeed, they may well not knit together well on the pitch, because too many showmen are placed in the line-ups, but my goodness they would be great to watch. I decided to play both sides in an attacking 4-3-3 formation, as we would want lots of goals, and that would be guaranteed with the bunch that I have chosen. There is some cross-over, in that some of the players with whom I took the field are included in Willie Miller's Scottish Dream Team, while others are selected for Willie Miller's Opposition Dream Team. For instance, Kenny Dalglish is placed on the Opposition bench because I played against him when Liverpool beat Aberdeen in the European Cup. I wanted to include what I considered to be the best players and mixing and matching them was the only way that I could get them all in.

○ ○ ○

Starting with the Scottish Dream Team, who else could I choose in goals but **Jim Leighton**? He was the best shot-stopper in the business, and he would never let you down. He worked hard on his game, and formed the rock on which the Aberdeen and Scotland defences were built. I recall that late, great managerial figure, Brian Clough, describing Jim as a rare bird, a Scottish goalkeeper who could be relied on. Jim was more than that and was, in my opinion, the best Scottish goalkeeper of his generation. Choosing my right-back was probably the easiest job. **Stuart Kennedy** was the finest right-sided defender that I played with on a regular basis. He was a reliable and intelligent team-mate, who knew exactly what he was doing. He also displayed a moustache like mine, so he's in, no problem. Seriously, Stuart was the man who made my job much easier. As I stressed earlier, I never had to worry about him. I knew instinctively that, if the left-winger had made a late run and the ball had been played in behind, Stuart would have the pace and anticipation to get back and clear the danger. **Alex McLeish** would be my main central defender, and captain of my Scottish Dream Team. Big Eck took all the broken noses and kicks on the shins for me, and by the time that an opponent had struggled to get past Alex, which did not happen often, that man would be bruised and demoralised. All I had to do was take the ball off the would-be attacker, and find one of my midfield players. Alex made me look good, for which I give thanks.

I have decided not to include myself in my Scottish line-up, as I would rather watch the team in action. In my place would go **David Narey**, a sweeper who impressed me when he played for Scotland, albeit most of the time at right-back or as a sitting midfielder. Big Eck and I kept David Narey and Paul Hegarty out of the Scotland team on many occasions, but when David was drafted in, he was magnificent. I'm picking him partly because he was a man who read the game superbly well, and also to thank him for scoring that memorable goal against Brazil in the 1982 World Cup. I'll never forget his strike . . . Graeme Souness found John Wark, who headed the ball on to David. Taking the pass in his stride, and despite the presence of three Brazilians, he beat goalkeeper Peres with a sensational right-foot shot. We were 1-0 up against Brazil after just 17 minutes. Dreamland, and it was certainly not a toe-poke, as commentator Jimmy Hill claimed. It was a fantastic strike. Unfortunately, dreams of beating Brazil dissolved when they came back at us to win 4-1, but I shall not forget David's expression when he scored the goal of his career. I had to think long and hard over who to place on the left side of my Scottish Dream Team defence, as Aberdeen experienced a bit of a problem in that position. Big Doug Rougvie put in a good run for us there, but it was not his natural place in the team. I felt John McMaster was the best left-back that I played with at club level, but because he was so versatile he was also employed at right-back and left midfield, and because of that I can't consider him for the left-back berth. I would choose for that position another Dundee United stalwart, **Maurice Malpas**, who was capped 55 times for Scotland and who played alongside me in vital matches for my country. He was, like Stuart Kennedy, Mr Dependable. You need players that you can count on around you when you are a defender, and Maurice fitted the bill.

Gordon Strachan is my choice on the right side of midfield. Looking for someone to get up the noses of the opposition by producing some great runs and killer passes? Look no further than wee Gordon: he was an absolutely brilliant player, who had the vision to match. He took crap from nobody, and what he lacked in height, he made up for in attitude. **Graeme Souness** would be cast alongside him, and that pair together in midfield would create a formidable partnership. Graeme is a born winner and yes, he was a bit arrogant and had a certain swagger, but I would rather play with him than against him. Some Anglos maybe did not have the dedication to the Scotland cause that Graeme demonstrated, and what can't be forgotten is that he turned out for his country 54 times, which is a proud record. On the left side of midfield, with orders to get up the pitch and take on the right-back and become an extra forward, would be **Peter Weir**. I always felt that Peter was the unsung hero in the Aberdeen team, but he was a real team player, a man who would track back and defend, and who could also get to the byline and put in some killer crosses.

Up front I would have three men of differing personalities, but all with the ability to score goals at will. **Charlie Nicholas**, as I confirmed earlier, was one of my best mates at Aberdeen. Charlie always had an eye for goal, and he could ghost past the best defenders. He was a flamboyant player and a regular goal-scorer, who would always be guaranteed to make the most of the chances that came his way. My main striker is a man who could be the bane of my life! To the public, **Ally McCoist** is a real cheeky chappie, who likes a bit of fun; to me he was anything but that. He was a pain in the bum, because he was a great striker who gave me all sorts of problems on the pitch. He would pop up when you least expected him to score vital goals, but in picking my Dream Team, I concluded that I would much rather have Ally in my side, performing as he did for Scotland, than against me, as when he was with Rangers facing Aberdeen. I would also play **Mark McGhee** up front, and he would noise defenders up and make the space for Ally to score. Mark showed that he could do it at the top level with Aberdeen and Hamburg among others, and I did not believe that he received the full praise he deserved. He was a fantastic striker, and a big personality in the Aberdeen dressing-room. A few growls from Mark would have the opposition quaking in their boots.

Bobby Clark, chosen as my reserve goalkeeper, was the figure who taught me a lot when I arrived at Aberdeen Football Club as a raw teenager. A genuine gentleman, he gave great service to the club. Other Aberdeen players making my Scottish bench would be two great strikers, wee **Joe Harper** and **Steve Archibald**. Joe was coming to the end of his career at Aberdeen when Fergie took over, but his importance cannot be over-looked. He was a huge favourite with the fans, and quite right, too. He had great personality and was a real penalty-box player, and he deserves to be classed as an all-time Aberdeen great. Steve Archibald was another top striker who scored vital goals for Aberdeen and Scotland. The fact that he also did well at Barcelona stresses that he was a world-class striker. The other striker on the Scottish bench would be **Andy Gray**. I came up against Andy when he was a youngster at Dundee United, and I also played with him in Scotland colours. He was one of the bravest players around, and he got on the end of every cross that came his way. Also on the bench would be **John Robertson**, the Nottingham Forest winger who was impossible to dispossess at times, and **Paul McStay**, the Celtic midfielder. I played with them at international level, and clearing the ball to either was a great out for defenders. If you gave it to Paul, he could calm things down in the middle of the park, and he would hardly ever lose possession. And if you managed to get the ball wide to John, off he would go on one of his mazy runs, leaving a trail of defenders in his wake.

○ ○ ○

I am well satisfied with my Scottish selection, but I must admit that, on paper, the Opposition Dream Team I have chosen to play them might be even better. In fact, it must be said that when I first had a look at the Opposition, I thought they could win the World Cup final. In goals I would have **Andy Goram**, who was a superb shot-stopper. I played against him near the end of my career, and was impressed by his all-round ability, which was demonstrated to the full at Rangers. At right-back would be that legend of the Scottish game, Celtic's **Danny McGrain**, who had a tranquility about him and a certain elegance. He never looked flustered, even when the opposition left-winger was heading his way. The centre-back partnership is one that enthusiasts would pay good money to watch in action. Imagine **Terry Butcher** and **Franz Beckenbauer** playing together! A defensive partnership made in football dream-team heaven. The description Captain Fantastic was made for Terry Butcher, who was great in the air, strong in the tackle and an inspiring leader of men. He is one of the greatest players of his generation. I came up against him when he played for Rangers and England, and though we tried to get one over on each other out on the pitch, we became good mates. Beckenbauer was one of my boyhood heroes, and I would give him the honour of captaining the Opposition Dream Team. I came up against the German legend when he represented Hamburg near the end of his playing career, but he still had class written all over him. He was never in a hurry, and calm as you like. An absolute superstar. On the left side of defence would be **Mick Mills**, the former England captain, who was never flashy, but was dependable, and never put a foot wrong.

My midfield three would get the pulses racing. On the right side of midfield, I would nominate **Paul Gascoigne**. I came up against Paul in a friendly match against Newcastle United, when he was starting out, and nobody could get the ball off him. Initially, I thought it was because it was a friendly and no-one was trying to tackle him properly, but I had a go, and I was struggling! Paul possessed poise and wonderful balance, and I would love to think he could straighten his life out, because he was one of the greats of the British game. In the middle of the park, I would select **Lothaur Matthaus**. I faced him in the 1986 World Cup, and he was a world superstar with honours to match. In 1990, he was named European Footballer of the Year and World Soccer Player of the Year after captaining West Germany to victory in the World Cup. One year later, he was also named the first-ever FIFA World Player of the Year. He played in five World Cups – 1982, 1986, 1990, 1994 and 1998 – which was more than any outfield player, and he holds the record for the most World Cup matches played: 25. He is the most-capped German player of all time, and retired with a total of 150 appearances, 83 of them for West Germany, and 23 goals for his country. What about that for a career record! It would be a distinct honour to have Matthaus, who moved back to sweeper as his career progressed, in my side. The only major honour which eluded him was winning the UEFA Champions League. He came within two minutes of picking up a winner's medal in 1999, only to have his hopes dashed by Fergie's Manchester United, who scored two goals in injury-time in the final. Shame that. On the left, I would play **Zico** of Brazil, and give him the freedom to get forward as often as he could. Who could forget his great free-kick, which left Alan Rough with no chance when Brazil beat us 4-1 in the 1986 World Cup? Sheer class from a class act.

Up front I would employ another German, **Rudi Völler**, who was an annoying sod to play against. His sheer physical strength made him a difficult man to pin down, and he was also good in the air. Völler earned himself the German nickname of *Tante Käthe* (Auntie Cathy) thanks to his curly grey hair-do, but there was nothing lady-like about him, I can assure you. Alongside Voller would be **Karl-Heinz Rummenigge**, against whom I had an almighty battle in the famous Cup-Winners' Cup quarter-final match between Aberdeen and Bayern Munich. He was at the top of his game when I faced him. He was quick and difficult to mark, with a great eye for goal, and in 1980–81 he was named European Footballer of the Year. For the next two or three years he was, in my opinion, also a serious rival for Diego Maradona for the unofficial honour of best player in the world. He really was that good. The final member of my Opposition Dream Team has to be the late **Davie Cooper**. I have placed him among the opponents despite the fact that I played with him for Scotland, because I know he would have loved to appear alongside the likes of Zico and Matthaus, and to have a target man like Voller to get on the end of his crosses. Davy would definitely be as good as, if not better, than any of them. He was the best striker of a dead ball that I encountered. Better than the Brazilians. Better than the Italians. He was sheer class.

The bench I have chosen shows how hard it was for me to name a starting line-up. **Neville Southall**, of Everton and Wales, was a bulky fellow, not unlike Andy Goram, and was an equally good shot-stopper. He would provide ample cover for Andy. **George Best** would be an automatic first pick in most dream teams, but I played against him when he was at Hibs, and he was miles past his peak. For that reason, and that reason alone, he would be on the bench. **Michel Platini** would also feature on the bench because he was a patronising prat when I captained Scotland against France. As I revealed earlier in my adventures, before kick-off he asked if I wanted my picture taken with him, as if it was an honour for me to be on the same pitch as such a famous Frenchman. Aye right. **Socrates** nearly put Paul Gascoigne out of my dream team starting line-up, but the Geordie got the nod because he had more flair. Putting the Brazilian captain on the bench was a hard choice to make, as he was a fantastic player. Everybody knew he smoked and drank, but it seemed not to affect his football. He was a big bloke, and you will recall that when the two of us were asked to take drugs tests after the Scotland v Brazil World Cup match, I asked for a soft drink, and he requested booze and fags. Also on the bench, which is rather full I know, would be **Uli Stielike**, who was supposed to be the man who would stop Aberdeen playing in the Cup-Winners' Cup final against Real Madrid. Wrong there, then. Stielike was a hard man, but proved no match for the likes of Mark McGhee. He was a class act, nonetheless, and the sort of guy you would want in your squad. My final substitute would be **Kenny Dalglish**, it must be stressed only because of the 4-3-3 formations both teams would play. King Kenny was a figure who dominated club and Scottish international football. He had it all: balance, poise, elegance and an ability to score wonderful goals. Kenny would be my first substitute, and I would bring him on at half-time. So there you have it: two teams who would play a match that football fans throughout the world would wish to see.

I would have Sir Alex Ferguson as manager of the Scottish select, and Jock Stein would be in charge of the Opposition.

The referee would be Kenny Hope, who was the best official that I came across during my career. Fergie and Jock were greats of the Scottish game, who took even friendlies seriously, and they would want to win, even in a dream-team encounter. I would follow the proceedings from a perch in the stand, and would reminisce about how fortunate I had been to share a pitch with some of the greatest players ever to grace our wonderful game.

And the score? I would predict a 7-7 draw, with the referee abandoning the penalty shoot-out because no player would come close to missing the target. I can dream, can't I?

For the record, the teams are (4-3-3 formation):

WILLIE MILLER'S SCOTTISH DREAM TEAM
Leighton; Kennedy, Narey, McLeish, Malpas; Strachan, Souness, Weir; McCoist, McGhee, Nicholas.

Substitutes: Clark, Archibald, McStay, Robertson, Gray, Harper.

WILLIE MILLER'S OPPOSITION DREAM TEAM
Goram; McGrain, Butcher, Beckenbauer, Mills; Matthaus, Gascoigne, Zico; Voller, Rummenigge, Cooper.

Substitutes: Southall, Dalglish, Best, Platini, Socrates, Stielike.

Referee: Mr Kenny Hope.
Venue: The Stadium of Dreams.

INDEX